SKY AS FRONTIER

NUMBER ELEVEN
Centennial of Flight Series

Roger D. Launius, General Editor

SKY AS FRONTIER

ADVENTURE, AVIATION, AND EMPIRE

David T. Courtwright

Texas A&M University Press \ *College Station*

First edition

The paper used in this book meets the minimum requirements
of the American National Standard for Permanence
of Paper for Printed Library Materials, z39.48-1984.
Binding materials have been chosen for durability.

Library of Congress Cataloging-in-Publication Data

Courtwright, David T., 1952–
Sky as frontier : adventure, aviation, and empire /
David T. Courtwright.—1st ed.
p. cm.—(Centennial of flight series ; no. 11)
Includes bibliographical references and index.
ISBN 1-58544-384-0 (cloth : alk. paper)
ISBN 1-58544-419-7 (pbk. : alk. paper)
1. Aeronautics—History. I. Title. II. Series.
TL515.C69 2004
629.13'009—dc22 2004007731

Title page image: *Spirit of St. Louis.* Painting by William J. Reynolds.
Courtesy National Air and Space Administration History Office

For Pat Toomey and Ashley Godeaux

Gone West too soon

Contents

Preface

When the Wright brothers invented their flying machine, Americans lived in a nation of two dimensions, bounded by lines drawn on an ordinary map. A century later their nation existed—in fact, reigned—in three dimensions. Two million Americans slipped the surly bonds of earth every day; American civilian and military aircraft operated in every part of the world. The airplane had turned the sky into a new domain of human activity, a fast-developing frontier. The first to venture onto that frontier had been mostly adventurous young men. Then came the rich and the hurried. Then just about everybody.

The idea that the airplane enabled America and that America, in turn, enabled the world to develop an aviation frontier dates to the 1920s and 1930s. The odd thing is that no one has tried to tell the story of aviation as one of frontier expansion or has even thought carefully about what aerial frontier expansion might mean. As an American historian interested in frontiers and flying, I found the invitation too tempting to pass up.

Frontier development is a social process that cuts across space and time. When a frontier disappears, a distinctive social world disappears with it, evolving into a more conventional order or moving elsewhere. Aviation's frontier stage lasted a scant three decades, then vanished as flying became a settled experience. This book recreates that pioneer world and shows how commercial and military imperatives destroyed it by routinizing flight. At bottom, it is the story of a tradeoff. Rationalization killed adventure in flying but made possible fast aerial expansion. With it came commercial growth and global military reach. America's path to empire ran through the sky.

Flight's rapid maturation affected all nations, not just the United States. I have concentrated on the American experience partly for reasons of size—as late as 1965 the country's airlines accounted for two-thirds of the world's air commerce—and partly for reasons of aeronautical leadership, which the country has maintained since the late 1920s. Alexis de Tocqueville's motivation for studying American democracy—his belief that it offered the purest case study of a momentous historical development—applies equally to American aviation. Nowhere else did social life, productivity, and military operations become so intertwined with aerospace advances or have such large consequences for national power and prestige. A thousand years hence people may remember two things about the United States, that it was history's first mass democracy and its first air and space nation.

Even when limited to the American experience, a century of aerospace development requires a large canvas. Rather than load it with the impasto of thick detail, I have sketched my theme, illustrated it in pointillist fashion, and trusted the reader to connect the dots. The biggest dot belongs to Charles Lindbergh. As an aviator, he epitomized the aviation frontier and its passing. As a memoirist, he wrote the one indispensable source. The chapter I have devoted to his life barely begins to repay my debt.

I am indebted also to the American Historical Association, the National Aeronautics and Space Administration, the University of North Florida, and Duke University's Hartman Center for research funding. Carol Clark, Andrew Courtwright, Kent Dickinson, W. G. Dickinson, Mary Futch, Ashley Godeaux, Joseph Grubbs, Jay Huebner, Harold Hyman, Charles Malone, Shelby Miller, Dennis Montagna, Christopher Parrish, Ira Peck, Dominick Pisano, and Jack Rogers commented on manuscript drafts, as did the students in my aviation history seminar.

My search for unusual sources and illustrations would have been impossible without assistance from librarians, archivists, and other researchers. I particularly want to thank Barbara Tuck, Alisa Craddock, and Bruce Latimer at the University of North Florida; Jane Odom, Stephen Garber, Colin Fries, and Nadine Andreassen at the NASA History Office; Elizabeth Dunn, Ellen Gartrell, and Jacqueline Reid at Duke University; Craig Likness, Ruthanne Vogel, and Marcia Evanson at the University of Miami; DeVonde Clemence, Larry Wilson, Marilyn Graskowiak, and Colleen Horin at the National Air and Space Museum; Michael Basanta at National Archives II; Aaron Schmidt at the Boston Public Library; and John Waggener and Leslie Shores at the University of Wyoming's American Heritage Center. Janet Bednarek, Roger Bilstein, Stephen Marshall, and Michael Neufeld provided timely research leads. Teresa St. John, John Morrell, Debra K. Abbott, David W. Wilson, and Deborah F. Miller assisted with graphs and illustrations. Jenny Bent, my agent, and Noel Parsons and the staff of the Texas A&M University Press advanced the project from proposal to book. I owe a special debt to series editor Roger Launius, who knows almost as much about frontier history as he does about aerospace history. Blessed be the coincidence.

SKY AS FRONTIER

PART I

The Age of the Pioneers

All journeys are toward the West.

—BERNARD DE VOTO, "TRANSCONTINENTAL FLIGHT"

CHAPTER 1

Sky as Frontier

Captain Eddie Rickenbacker, a man of sharp features and sharper opinions, waited his turn at the big NBC microphone. He had come to Rockefeller Center's sunken plaza, beneath the gilded statue of Prometheus, to join a marine color guard for a retirement ceremony. The retiree was a Pitcairn Mailwing, the last open-cockpit airplane to fly the U.S. Mail. The leaden November sky suited the occasion. The early mail pilots had often run into this sort of overcast weather. They had not always come out on the other side.

Charles Graddick, superintendent of the U.S. Air Mail Service, spoke first. He told the national radio audience that the plane had made its last scheduled trip only six weeks before, climbing into the night sky above Chicago on October 14, 1935. That flight, he said, was like the last ride of the Pony Express. It marked the end of a pioneering era. The Mailwing pilots had been true trailblazers, daring men who had prepared the way for fast, safe, and comfortable air transport.

Rickenbacker shared this sense of progress. Had demonstrated it, in fact. He had recently flown from New York to Philadelphia and back in a DC-2, spending just fifty-seven minutes in the air. The first round trip, made in 1910, had required three hours, thirty-four minutes flying time. A daredevil named Charles Hamilton, competing for a ten thousand dollar prize, had taken off in fog and found his way to the Jersey shore by the smell of an oil-works chimney. After landing in Philadelphia, replacing a damaged propeller, and reviving himself with cigarettes and coffee, he nursed his sputtering Curtiss biplane back to Governor's Island before night fell. A man of large gestures, Hamilton collected his reward, took his friends to Atlantic City, and tossed a thousand dollar bill on the Hotel Chalfonte bar. He bade all to drink their fill.

Rickenbacker, though no stranger to hotel bars, had contented himself with publishing a celebratory essay. The difference between Hamilton's "chicken-coop" adventure and his own uneventful trip, he wrote, epitomized twenty-five years of aviation progress. An ongoing technological revolution had made possible "safe, sure, and regular transportation in the third dimension." Now, as he rose to address the Rockefeller Center crowd, he returned to this theme. Gazing at the Mailwing, his nostalgia leavened by his pride in aeronautical progress, Rickenbacker said that the days of the lone pilot battling the elements were over. Pilots, passengers, and mail flew about the country in enclosed, all-metal airliners. Though gallant in its time, events had made the Mailwing a museum piece, "marking the close of a romantic era in flying."

The ceremony itself ended with a romantic touch. Lily Pons, the diminutive Met coloratura, presented a bronze plaque to J. Shelly Charles, an Eastern Air Lines pilot representing those who had flown the mail. Charles accepted the memento dressed in a heavy flying suit, boots, helmet, and goggles, the antiquated gear synonymous with open-cockpit flying. Beside him stood a spry octogenarian, Bronco Charlie Miller, veteran of Buffalo Bill's Wild West and the last survivor of the original Pony Express. Bronco Charlie had also dressed for the occasion. He was wearing his spurs and Stetson hat.[1]

Frontier as Metaphor

The aviation literature is full of Bronco Charlies. By the 1920s and 1930s the American frontier, particularly the nineteenth-century frontier, had become an irresistible metaphor for the country's growing presence in the air. Writers spun variations on the heroic pioneers from aviation's "log cabin days" who had conquered the skies, dying with their flying boots on. Their sacrifices had expanded the next frontier, the high frontier, the air frontier, the new industrial frontier, and on down a long list. Airlines worked the metaphor into their advertising. Western called itself "America's Pioneer Airline." There were two Frontier Airlines, the second beginning operations out of Denver in 1994 after the first went broke during the 1980s airline wars. And space, of course, was the last, ultimate, or "final" frontier.[2]

Charles Hamilton lived to fly. Working as a circus acrobat and parachute jumper, he progressed through manned kites, gliders, dirigibles, and airplanes. He survived sixty-three accidents, including a crash that fractured his jaw, scalded his legs, and left him emaciated. In 1910, he won ten thousand dollars for a round-trip New York–Philadelphia flight. Ruined health forced him to quit flying two years later. When he died in 1914, he had a plate in his skull, two silver ribs, and pins in his shin. "There is little of the original Hamilton left," remarked Lincoln Beachey, another great stunt pilot of the era.

Most of the talk of air and space frontiers was superficial, nothing more than a casual evocation of an exciting past or a cliché of progress. Even writers who were familiar with frontier literature and who used the metaphor systematically seemed stuck in historiographical orbit, so many planets revolving around the dying star of Frederick Jackson Turner.

That star had once shone brightly. Turner, who lived from 1861 to 1932, was the most famous American historian of his generation. His big idea, the frontier thesis, held that the continuous settlement of free land along America's expanding western frontier had shaped the country's history, institutions, and character. The frontier had provided a means of escape for oppressed easterners, for whom the "free conditions of the frontier . . . promoted individualism, economic equality, freedom to rise, democracy. Men would not accept inferior wages and a permanent position of social subordination when this promised land of freedom and equality was theirs for the taking." That opportunity had diminished as the land frontier closed and economic power became concentrated in fewer and fewer hands.[3]

Turner's ideas, influential in their time but under increasing attack by historians since the mid-twentieth century, have thrived among space enthusiasts. In its palmy days, the National Aeronautics and Space Administration (NASA) sounded like a Turner seminar. NASA brass fretted about "running out of new frontiers to explore" and offered space exploration as an alternative. Robert Zubrin, the king of the space Turnerians, claimed that America—in fact, all of western civilization—would stagnate without a frontier experience to sustain it. Only human colonization of a terraformed (earthlike) Mars would permit the renewal of a free and prosperous society. Martian labor, Zubrin thought, would be more highly valued and dearly paid than its earthly equivalent.[4]

The historian smiles, recalling contrary precedents of forced labor in the New World. Still, the notion that frontier expansion determines a civilization's character has a plausible ring. Had not China stagnated when it turned inward? Had not contact with new environments reshaped immigrant cultures? Had not humans themselves evolved in wandering bands? Wernher von Braun and Carl Sagan, two of space exploration's boldest spirits, married Turner to Charles Darwin. If natural selection favored exploration, if the urge was instinctual, then terrestrial sedentism condemned our species to an unfulfilled existence, like bees stuck in the same crowded hive.[5]

These ideas have emotional appeal and political utility. They may even be true. But they are maddeningly vague. What does frontier revitalization mean? What do we get from the space-colony elixir? The problem with Turnerian usages is that they are too grand and speculative to be of practical value. If the frontier concept is to be salvaged, if it is to serve as an organizing idea for the history of aviation and space flight rather than as a cosmic sales pitch, it first has to be understood, more concretely, as a social process.

Frontier Types

In its most basic, ecological sense, a frontier is a shifting zone of interaction between indigenous and nonindigenous populations. While there were no human populations in the sky, there were insects and birds. Their presence would be affected by, and sometimes catastrophically affect, mechanical flight. It is a mistake to conceive the sky as entirely empty.

It is also a mistake to think of frontiers as being of a single type. Nineteenth-century American frontiers fell into two broad categories. Type-I frontiers were based on farming. They were found in fertile regions, such as Oregon's Willamette Valley, or in regions made fertile by irrigation, such as Mormon Utah. They attracted farm families, had relatively even numbers of men and women, a sprinkling of older people, many children, and high birth-rates. Indian conflicts aside, settlement was permanent and peaceful. Most men were married. Commercial vice was limited. So were opportunities for women.

Type-II frontiers looked very different. Found most often in grazing country or in the arid cordillera, their economies revolved around ranching, mining, lumbering, or other forms of extraction. They attracted unattached male workers, with ratios of eight or nine men to every woman. Children were scarce, as were those over the age of forty-five. Difficult access, harsh conditions, and grueling labor—conditions epitomized by the California gold fields—kept away all but the young and the fit. "The work is extremely hard," wrote one forty-niner. "I start at four o'clock in the morning and keep on till twelve noon. After that I rest for three or four hours, for at that time of day the heat is unbearable, and then I work again till eight o'clock in the evening." When they wrote home, they warned the old and frail to stay away. They could not stand such daily hardship, and would end up destitute or dead.[6]

For those who could endure it, life in the camps had compensations other than monetary. Relations among miners, when sober and unprovoked, were open, comradely, egalitarian. "We live a free life," the correspondent continued, "and the best thing of all, that which I have always considered one of the supreme blessings of existence, is that no human being here sets himself up as your lord and master." No one asked about social pedigree. The only question that mattered was, "Can he fill the position?" No place in America was more individualistic, more democratic, or more meritocratic than the California mining frontier in the late 1840s.[7]

And no place in America was more deadly. A fifth of the forty-niners died within six months of arriving in California, victims of disease, accidents, drunken violence, and hygienic neglect. The situation was so bad that insurance companies either refused to write policies for the California-bound or levied heavy additional premiums, tactics reprised during the gold-rush days of early aviation. Type-II frontiers had higher-than-expected death rates, given that most of their immigrants were young, fit workers. But youth offered no protection against scurvy, landslides, and errant gunshots. Death came in a hundred unexpected ways.[8]

Those who survived faced other dangers. Bachelor laborers fell prey to the whiskey peddlers, gamblers, and prostitutes who flocked to type-II frontiers. Saloons, gambling halls, and brothels served as flashpoints of violence that turned deadly when patrons and proprietors reached for their knives and guns. Vice siphoned off hard-earned dollars. Cowboys would sometimes blow months of wages during a spree, "drunk and dressed up and don't give a damn." Even sober workers were vulnerable to the boom and bust nature of ranching or extractive economies. Type-II frontiers offered little in the way of economic security.

Walter Nugent, the historian who coined the two types, contrasted the "colorless many" of the agricultural frontier, people "too busy trying to raise families and eke out a living to become legendary," with the "colorful few" of the mining camps and cattle towns, men who led more adventurous, if briefer, lives. Their world did not last. When the mines played out, when the timber was cut, and when the herds were gone, type-II settlements turned into ghost towns. Others survived, only to be transformed by an inexorable demographic process. The original influx of male workers moved on, went back east, or succumbed to accidents, disease, and advancing age. Eligible frontier women married young and bore many children. As the aging, supernumerary males disappeared, this rising generation took their place, married, and created a society that was more balanced, family-centered, and stable. In time, and in the absence of a stream of new male immigrants, the skewed masculine populations came to resemble the more normal populations of agricultural frontiers.[9]

Transportation improvements—here the analogy to aviation history becomes more exact—helped balance frontier populations. The cost and danger of transportation, as well as the difficult nature of the work, accounted for the mostly male immigration to the Far West in the mid–nineteenth century. Fewer women, children, and old people were willing to risk sailing around Cape Horn, or crossing Panama, or venturing over the prairies and deserts in wagon trains. Stagecoaches jolted passengers into a condition bordering on insanity. But steamships and railroads made it easier for the young, the old, and women to move into isolated regions. Some took advantage of the shortage of women. Lou Conway Roberts, the wife of a Texas Ranger who settled in New Mexico in 1882, saw an influx of eastern widows and spinsters. "They married," she wrote in her memoirs. "They didn't have to be attractive, just American women."[10]

Improvements in transportation technology worked a similar effect on aviation. Socially and demographically, early twentieth-century aviation resembled a type-II frontier. Young men risked their lives and health for adventure, prestige, and high wages in a novel environment and freewheeling social milieu that was simultaneously comradely and competitive, at times lethally so. Early passengers, like pilots, were overwhelmingly men. They traded risk for adventure, status, and economic advantage, paid in the coin of rapid business travel. Only in the late 1920s and early 1930s, with the advent of dependable, multi-engine passenger planes and a clever campaign to promote their use, did sizable numbers of women, children, and old people begin to fly. Males still predominated, in the cockpit as well as the cabin. But the broad trend for the rest of the century, after coach fares, jets, and deregulation lowered prices, was toward greater age, gender, and racial diversity. An airport waiting room in 1928 did not look like America. An airport waiting room in 1998 did, especially for anyone who happened to be near the Southwest Airlines counter.

All that lay in the future. Flying in the early days was a young man's game. Passengers of any sort were scarce. The pilots' culture, like that of the mining camp or bunkhouse, was masculine, competitive, and inclined toward risk. Young men showed off in one another's presence, doing things in groups that they would not do alone or in the presence of their families. Miners, men accustomed to spending their Sunday mornings in church back home, passed their California Sabbaths in boastful carousing, in gambling, and in acts of daring horsemanship, clinging to the sides of galloping ponies while pulling knives from the ground. The aviation equivalent was buzzing the control tower, showing off for "the boys," a term of juvenile connotation that runs through both frontier and aviation literature.

From the time of the Wright brothers, who worried (with reason) about their exhibition fliers, the reckless tendencies of young pilots have concerned their elders. A fool on a horse is one thing. A fool in a plane is another. On Sunday, April 29, 1929, Lt. Howard W. Keefer flew his Boeing pursuit plane into a Ford 5-AT-B Trimotor, which had been making a routine flight from San Diego. Keefer had been stunting. He performed a left wing-over, a steep, banking turn, trying to pass in front of the Trimotor. He misjudged the distance, killing himself, two Trimotor pilots, and the three passengers, who fell to messy deaths before hundreds of homebound churchgoers. A coroner's jury found Keefer guilty of criminal negligence, which was almost beside the point. The real, recurrent problem was how to discourage such behavior among those naturally inclined toward it.[11]

The simplest way to do so was to deny access to the sky, washing out the reckless or revoking their licenses. Airlines solved their problem by selecting the most mature and cautious pilots from the ranks of airmail and military fliers. Pan Am's Horace Brock said he wanted no cowboys, no show-offs, no prima donnas, and no Smilin' Jacks. The new hires were vetted, retrained for commercial flying, and dismissed if they failed to appreciate its sober realities. "The employer can't make money if his pilots take chances, crack up airplanes, bungle schedules, or annoy the passengers with anything steeper than a medium bank . . . ," the writer Beirne Lay Jr. explained. "Taking chances and getting away with them will win him, not a slap on the back, but an invitation to seek other employment." Pilots who made the transition, who accepted the routine and responsibility of hauling passengers, took on the attributes of their jobs. They were soft-spoken men, conservative in speech and demeanor, of an anticipatory turn of mind, and completely at home in the sky. "In a real sense the pilot does not 'leave the ground,'" Lay observed. "He 'returns to the air.' It is in the sky that he finds the real importance and meaning of living. Intervals on the ground are just that—intervals."[12]

Frontier Dimensions

If frontiers come in different types, they also come in different dimensions, including the fourth dimension of time. In 1978 the sociologist Murray Melbin published a brilliant article, "Night as Frontier," in which he showed how time, like space, was a niche that could be occupied by a species during its wakeful life. Few humans stayed up through the night until the nineteenth century, when artificial lighting—coal-gas lamps, incandescent cotton mantles, metal filaments, and, eventually, cheap electric lights—made possible the colonization of the world after dark. Novel modes of transportation—buses, subways, and cars—made it easier for people to get about at night. Factory hours expanded. Restaurants, radio stations, and other businesses extended their schedules to accommodate the nighttime activity.

The colonization of the night began in cities. Paris, the *ville lumière,* showcased the possibilities of life after dark. Then the United States took the lead in nighttime frontier expansion, both in its cities and in its electrified countryside. In all his decades of flying, Charles Lindbergh wrote in his *Autobiography of Values,* the most spectacular change he observed in the earth's surface was the sprinkling of myriad lights across the United States on a clear night.[13]

Who ventured out after dark? To find out, Melbin visited checkpoints in central Boston at different times of the day and night. He found the streets most crowded in the late afternoon hours, with an average of about seven passersby per minute, falling to one per minute from midnight to 2:00 A.M. Males were about as common as females during the day, but outnumbered them eight or nine to one after midnight. Melbin saw people of all ages during the day, but no one over fifty-nine between midnight and 5:00 A.M., and no one over forty-one between 2:00 and 5:00 A.M. The nighttime population—sparse, male, young—looked like that of a type-II frontier.

It certainly behaved like one. Melbin found less conformism, less deference to age, and less inclination to obey the law among late-night Bostonians. Fights peaked at midnight, despite the fact that most of the city's residents

Navy student pilots waiting for the ceiling to lift, Corpus Christi, Texas, November 1942. Pilots, like frontiersmen, enjoyed playing cards, smoking, and drinking with their comrades. They also loved to recount their experiences, a pastime known as ground or hangar flying. The stories they told could add to or detract from reputations, something about which all fliers were sensitive.

were asleep. The police did a brisk business after dark. "Our day begins when your day ends," the homicide detectives liked to say. Accidents also increased. Motor vehicle death rates quadrupled after dark, as more young, inexperienced, and intoxicated drivers took to the road.

Despite, and to some degree because of, the danger, late night populations exhibited more helpfulness and friendliness than their daytime counterparts. They were more likely to give directions, answer questions, and banter with strangers, traits Melbin noticed in accounts of the land frontier. As on land frontiers, human movement into the night occurred gradually, in recognizable stages. First came the isolated wanderers and social deviants, then graveyard-shift workers, then patrons of all-night restaurants and bars. The "rates of advance" could be erratic, as when the 1973–74 oil shortages temporarily diminished nighttime activities. Similar retreats followed crises on land and sky frontiers.

The colonization of the night came as a surprise, the by-product of new technologies. Municipal governments concerned themselves with problems of law and order, but otherwise had no night policy, no plan for its systematic exploitation. That changed during the twentieth century, as officials realized that the night was a basic economic resource. "Cheap," underutilized time was like cheap, supposedly underutilized frontier land. Expansion into the night offered the prospect of increased productivity, more efficient use of expensive facilities, fewer daytime traffic jams. By adding police patrols and extending public transport hours, governments made it safer and more convenient for people to be out at night. Sometimes, as when they imposed wartime triple shifts, governments mandated a nighttime presence, though corporations, anxious to increase productivity and tap a growing temporal market, expanded after-dark operations on their own initiative.

Those who were trying to get some sleep were not too happy about the nighttime rush. In Boston, citizens' groups lobbied the Massachusetts Port Authority to stop night flights at Logan Airport. An opposing coalition of politicians, boosters, airlines, unions, and airport employees managed to stave off the curfew. Melbin drew the obvious moral, that interest groups emerged and clashed as frontier activities expanded and matured.[14]

That was certainly true of aviation. Scheduled carriers fought charter operators, environmentalists fought jet manufacturers, regulators fought deregulators. These political clashes are among the many parallels between the development of airspace and nighttime—or of remote western lands. In all three cases the early social characteristics—youth, masculinity, risk, traumatic accidents, and high mortality—are the same. So is the basic pattern of development, with governments and corporations exerting more control over an increasingly valuable resource.

Frontier Synergisms

Thinking about frontiers in the plural reveals patterns of interactive growth. Frontiers touched. The sky was, literally, a superfrontier whose development affected, and was affected by, the land and night activities beneath it. The American frontier did not close. It became multidimensional, with continuous, technologically premised, socially constructed, and mutually reinforcing movement on the land, in the nighttime, and through the sky. The outstanding characteristic of modern American history has been its omniexpansiveness, the way it has spread out, up, over, and after dark faster than any civilization in history.

Aircraft performance offers a good example of this frontier synergism.

From the 1930s on, American commercial equipment was the best in the world. In 1934, more than half of American passengers flew at cruising speeds over 160 mph. The European airlines combined could muster just thirty-three planes that cruised at more than 125 mph. The best European long-distance racing planes could barely outperform the new generation of American airliners. When Neville Chamblerlain flew to Munich to meet Adolph Hitler in September 1938, he departed in American equipment, a twin-engine Lockheed. During the 1940s, American airlines acquired large, four-engine, pressurized planes capable of flying coast-to-coast above the worst weather. Why did British or German engineers, with a tradition of aeronautical excellence, fail to come up with something like the Douglas DC-3 or the Lockheed Constellation?

Historian Richard K. Smith argued that "the unique demands of a continental nation for a profitable high-speed transportation system" dictated American success. That is, the sheer size of the United States, the need to carry transcontinental cargos over mountain ranges and through unpredictable and often violent weather caused by warm and cold air masses clashing over its vast plains, helped produce, in Darwinian fashion, superior transport aircraft. Sixteenth- and seventeenth-century Western European sailing ships outperformed Ottoman Empire ships for the same reason: the storm-tossed Atlantic Ocean was a more demanding nautical environment than the Mediterranean or the Red Sea. By this reasoning, if there had been no nineteenth-century frontier expansion, if the United States had remained a littoral nation of thirteen former colonies, it would not have become the aviation hothouse of the twentieth century. Aeronautically, it would have been another Europe, with smaller, less powerful planes hopping from one coastal city to another.[15]

Russia offers an interesting parallel. Had it not been for the disruptions of war and revolution (which, among other things, sent the great aircraft designer Igor Sikorsky to the United States), Russia's mid-century air commerce might have rivaled America's. By 1939, the Soviet Union had almost caught up to Germany as Europe's air transport leader. After recovering from World War II, Aeroflot grew rapidly, jumped to twin-engine jets in 1956, and served a nation whose principal east-west cities, Moscow and Vladivostok, were nearly twice as far apart as New York and San Francisco. Even copies of *Pravda* went by plane. Land expansion had potentiated aviation expansion.[16]

The reverse was also true. When Turner declared the American frontier closed, he quoted a census official who said that by 1890 the unpopulated western area "had been so broken up by isolated bodies of settlement that there can hardly be said to be a frontier *line.*" Line or no, there were still huge swaths of unsettled land. Airplanes penetrated them. Equipped with pontoons and skis, bush pilots ferried explorers, hunters, geologists, workers, and their equipment into otherwise inaccessible locales. Also out of them. One reason why Arctic and oceanic drilling frontiers were more orderly than their nineteenth-century mining equivalents was that planes and helicopters permitted regular contact between male workers and their families, not to say tension-releasing excursions to Las Vegas.[17]

Airports and ground-support facilities required large-scale development. By the end of World War II, the Army Air Forces (AAF) had built up a network of domestic bases and training facilities that sprawled over 19.7 million acres, an area nearly as large as Connecticut, Massachusetts, New Hampshire, and Vermont combined. So massive was this network of training facilities, and so skewed were they toward the "sunshine belt" (a term of AAF coinage), that some claim World War II as the real end of the "traditional westward-oriented frontier." Wartime airfield construction pulled the compass needle of American development southward.[18]

Many cities gained army surplus airports as a peace dividend. Others built or enlarged fields farther from the central city. Idlewild (later Kennedy) Airport, under construction in the early 1940s and completed in 1948, eventually covered 4,930 acres on Long Island—as much land as in Manhattan from 42nd Street to the Battery. But the new suburban airports could not long escape the cities. Like an amoeba digesting its food, Chicago spread around two airports. First it surrounded Midway, nine miles from the Loop, and then O'Hare, built to replace Midway. By 1977 land next to O'Hare, which had once sold for $400 an acre, was going for $200,000.[19]

Aviation also expanded human activity in the night. Military night aviation was born during World War I. Commercial night aviation followed. To maximize their speed advantage over trains and ships, both of which operated after dark, planes had to fly at night. To do so safely required a network of lighted airways, radio beacons, and weather stations maintained around the clock. First mail planes took to the night skies, hopping along a network of relay fields illuminated with floodlights. Then came the trimotor transports, their nightbound cabins filled with fitfully dozing passengers, bathed in lambent blue light from the engines' exhaust plumes. Flying over the Great Plains at two thousand feet, watching the tiny, twinned headlights of cars crawling along unseen roads, covering in seven nighttime minutes a day's hard travel in covered wagons, those passengers were living, whether they knew it or not, at the intersection of modern America's three great frontiers.[20]

By the elemental yardstick of space and time, the twentieth century's most conspicuous change was the increase of human activity above the ground and after dark. First curiosity, and then profit and military necessity, drove the expansion, which occurred most rapidly during wartime. Here, tracers search out *Luftwaffe* attackers in the night sky above Algiers in 1943.

Airworld

Some might object that, save for the occupants of skyscrapers, people do not really live in the sky. They pass through it. They cannot settle it like the land. Perhaps they can settle the night. Some people—security guards, prostitutes, insomniacs, teenagers—do spend large amounts of waking time there. But is flying really analogous?

Two responses come to mind. First, permanent residence was the norm only in some frontier regions. Work on nonagricultural frontiers required mobile labor. Cowboys, lumberjacks, miners, and prospectors seldom stayed put. The city directory of one California mining town listed "drifter" as an occupational category. When the railroad came, itinerant men circulated from the "main stems," the downtown boardinghouse-and-saloon districts scattered throughout the United States. They rode the rails west to perform seasonal jobs, then headed back to the cities when idled by winter weather or unemployment. They were joined by immigrant laborers from Mexico, Italy, Greece, and other distant nations. These *padrone*-organized sojourners harvested the crops, broke the strikes, loaded the ore, and moved on. They may not have been settlers, but they helped develop the West.[21]

In 1902 the only people capable of controlled, heavier-than-air flight were two glider pilots from Dayton, Ohio, conducting experiments along the windy North Carolina shores. At the end of the century an average of five million people, including more than two million Americans, went aloft every day. They were not the same five million, and they could not stay aloft indefinitely. But they were a presence, incontrovertible evidence of expanding activity in a remote and difficult environment. The sky had become a purposeful, if transiently occupied, human space with its own distinctive culture. "So many people across the globe travel by jet plane that we can begin to speak of a *social life* in air space as a separate dimension of living," wrote the sociologist Mark Gottdiener. "We live in the air as well as on the ground. We are progressively *humanizing* a realm that was for millennia the sole province of birds and insects."[22]

The second response is that, by the mid-twentieth century, flying had become so common for some that it was no longer a transient experience, physically or psychologically. Pilots spent substantial portions of their waking lives aloft. Before retiring, United's E. H. "Ham" Lee logged more than three years in the air. Northwest's R. Lee Smith spent three-and-a-half. If graveyard-shift workers inhabit the night, it seems reasonable to say that aircrews inhabit the air.[23]

Pilots like Lee and Smith developed a sense of being at home in the air, of *belonging* there. Home is where your head is. Arthur Hailey, the author of *Airport,* catches this psychological reality:

> Among those who fly actively and professionally, there is a camaraderie which has no parallel in any other occupation. This has been true since aviation's earliest days. Among air crew on duty, there is a singular absence of pettiness, a fact well attested and proved both in commercial as well as military flying. I speak with firsthand knowledge; I was a pilot for six years and have since kept in touch.
>
> This camaraderie, this sense of unison and unity, are most evident during time spent in the air. When airplane wheels lift from the runway, there is an awareness of having left behind the smallness and trivia of the everyday world. This is no poetic fancy; it is a common, shared and consistent experience. There is a nobility of thinking, a dismissal of the

> unimportant, a shared pride in human knowledge and achievement, of which the conquest of the air undoubtedly is part. The future, viewed from high altitude, seems limitless, as in fact it is.
>
> And then, as earth recedes, becoming smaller, there is a second sensibility of the unimportance of the individual. Personal concerns become pathetically small against the vastness of space, the aeons behind us and ahead. Even passengers on commercial flights share at times this sensitivity.
>
> Returning to earth is precisely that. For airman and air traveler both, there are encumbrances, details, infuriating slowness, pettiness, perplexities. So often these things and others are in contrast to the swift untroubled flight which so short a time before preceded them.

The more candid aviation memoirs, peopled with prima donna captains, jet-lagged flight attendants, and aircrew so hung over they had to suck bottled oxygen, make Haley's account seem romantic. But all agree with his essential point, that professional pilots come to feel at home in the air. William Langewiesche recalls the precise moment it happened to him, on a westbound winter flight to California. "Once airborne I retracted the landing gear and rolled into an early left turn, and as I looked back at the leading edge of the wing slicing stiffly above the frozen prairie, I realized that no difference existed for me between the earth and sky; it was as if with these wings I could now walk in the air." He knew the sensation to be a dangerous deception, one that invited fatal inattention to detail. It was no less real for that.[24]

Passengers seldom flew as much aircrew, though there were exceptions. By 1978, Allen Rabin, a man who seems to have sold whiskey over most of the planet's surface, could claim five million air miles. South African golfer Gary Player had six million, more than any other athlete in the world. Johannesburg to New York added up fast. Travel writer Eugene Fodor, asked for his air mileage, said he had lost track of "the statistical aspects of what has become a permanent lifestyle." He marked his globe-trotting by counting the books—fifty-eight—that had resulted.[25]

Fodor began his career in 1930. By the end of the century, there were perhaps a half-million passengers like him, "road warriors" who booked more than fifty flights a year. Their unprecedented spatial and temporal mobility created a new social type, the "de-territorialized" individual. Armed with cell phones, laptop computers, and fax machines, working out of virtual offices in airplanes, airport lounges, and hotels, they could cut loose from their home bases, with which they kept in electronic touch. "My place of work is simply where I am," said Ellen Knapp, the chief information officer for a multinational consulting firm. She credited her lifestyle to constitutional immunity to jet lag, grown children, and two efficient office assistants who, in the manner of NASA flight controllers, kept her on course as she made her way through global airspace.[26]

Marshall Goldman, an executive consultant nominally based in San Diego, managed to accumulate seven million frequent-flier miles on American Airlines. Goldman's mind kept piling up miles long after his body deplaned. One night at the symphony his wife noticed him digging into his seat. He was hunting for his seat belt. On another occasion Goldman remarked, upon waking, that a picture bore an uncanny resemblance to one on the wall of his bedroom at home. His wife had to remind him that he *was* at home.

Or was he? Postmodern writers, attuned to the suppression of individual identities and relationships in the psychic new world of global consumer capitalism, have taken up the theme of airborne de-territorialization. Walter Kirn based an entire novel on it. Ryan Bingham, the passenger-hero of *Up in the Air,* is a jet-propelled Nowhere Man who passes his life in airports and airplanes, crisscrossing the familiar skies. "I call it Airworld; the scene, the place, the style. My hometown papers are *USA Today* and the *Wall Street Journal.*" Bingham's dream, achieved just before he goes around the bend, is to accumulate his landmark million frequent-flier miles.[27]

A century ago Bingham would have struck readers as a fantastic figure, worthy of the pen of H. G. Wells. Yet when Kirn published his novel in 2001, shortly before the attacks on the World Trade Center and the Pentagon, Bingham seemed all too credible, especially to the bleary-eyed readers in business class. In that imagined aesthetic distance, in that transformation from science-fiction character to believable figure of satire, lies the history of American aviation.

For some years I have been afflicted with the belief that flight is possible to man. My disease has increased in severity and I feel that it will soon cost me an increased amount of money if not my life.

—WILBUR WRIGHT TO OCTAVE CHANUTE, MAY 13, 1900

CHAPTER 2

The Worm Gets the Early Birds

In 1822, an aspiring inventor named D. B. Lee wrote to the aged Thomas Jefferson about the possibility of mechanical flight. Lee's letter has been lost, though a copy of Jefferson's reply survives. Balloons, Jefferson wrote, proved the possibility of artificial buoyancy. Birds demonstrated the possibility of controlled flight. But, he conceded, "to do this by macanacal means alone in a medium so rare and unassisting as air must have the aid of some principal not yet generaly known, however. I can realy give no oppinion understandingly on the subject and with more good will than confidence wish you success."[1]

"More good will than confidence" sums up the attitude of nineteenth-century Americans toward flight. They knew balloons could go aloft. The first American ascension, with George Washington and most of Philadelphia looking on, had taken place in 1793. By 1859, perhaps eight thousand American passengers had gone up in balloons. That same year John Wise, the country's preeminent balloonist, tried to reach the Atlantic coast from St. Louis. Caught in a storm as he drifted toward Lake Ontario, and desperate to gain altitude, Wise jettisoned everything save his three passengers, hatchet, grapnel, and rope. "The greatest balloon voyage that was ever made," as Wise styled the adventure, ended ignominiously in a tree outside Henderson, New York. Military ballooning fared little better. Thaddeus S. C. Lowe, Wise's aeronautical rival, organized a balloon observation corps for the Army of the Potomac. Union generals deployed the asset, like others at their disposal, with mixed results. They gave up on aerial observation in 1863.

After the war, balloons served as attractions at fairs and circuses. Showmen performed trapeze acts, parachute drops, and other risky stunts before morbidly curious crowds. Spectators paid to go aloft, either in captive ascents or, for bolder spirits, in free flights. Only their point of departure was certain. Americans called balloonists "professors," in deference to their aeronautical knowledge, rather than "pilots," which would have implied the ability to steer. Jules Verne took that inability as the premise of his 1870 novel, *The Mysterious Island,* in which five Union prisoners escaped their Confederate jailers in a balloon, only to be blown off course to an uncharted volcanic island. A balloon in the wind offered as much hope of practical transport, one skeptic wrote, as an iceberg caught in the Gulf Stream.[2]

Lighter-than-air flight remained a stagnant technology, attracting little capital or engineering talent during the last two decades of the nineteenth century. It was dangerous, too, or perceived as such. Accidents made good copy. The telegraph cable made them international news. *Sixteen dead in Hungarian balloon fire*—just the thing to spice up the provincial papers. The stories had a tongue-clucking, what-do-you-expect-if-you-leave-the-earth tone. Most Americans agreed with Mark Twain's definition of a balloon: "Thing to take meteoric observations and commit suicide with."[3]

Serious interest in lighter-than-air flight revived with the dirigible, made possible by the invention of the lightweight internal combustion engine. In 1901, Alberto Santos-Dumont, a Brazilian émigré flush with coffee money, rigged a 12 hp engine to a primitive dirigible and circled the Eiffel Tower, winning a 100,000 franc prize. Photographs of the feat appeared widely, as did the dapper Santos-Dumont, who toured Britain and America to public acclaim. Soon American airmen like Thomas Baldwin, Roy Knabenshue, and Charles Hamilton were entertaining crowds with their own dirigibles. Baldwin built the first airship for the Army Signal Corps, the cigar-shaped SC-1, powered by a 20 hp Curtiss water-cooled engine. He delivered it in 1908, the same year Orville Wright made his decisive airplane demonstrations at Fort Myer, Virginia.

Though airplanes superceded balloons and dirigibles over the next ten years, the era of lighter-than-air experimentation established expectations about the uses of flight. Entrepreneurs learned that people would pay hard money to observe flying machines in operation, and even more to go up in them. Someday they might even be able to travel long distances. John Wise dreamed of floating across the Atlantic, abandoning the attempt only when he lost his financial backing. Balloons could also be used militarily, to observe enemy movements, direct artillery fire, and communicate under siege. Sixty-sixty balloon flights bore more than 2 million letters, 102 passengers, and 400 carrier pigeons out of besieged Paris during 1870 and 1871. The balloons traveled only one way, and that erratically. The more reliable pigeons flew microfilmed letters back to Paris. But the lesson was clear enough. Anyone who succeeded in fully controlling "macanacal" flight could make aerial communication a regular, two-way activity.[4]

Speculation about the uses of a new technology both precedes and contributes to its actual development. Cartoonists imagined many applications for flight, among them fast transport, recreation, hunting, and combat. In 1907, four years after this airborne cannoneer appeared, *Scientific American* speculated that hydrogen-filled balloons might carry bombs over enemy lines. Zeppelins realized the prophecy in World War I.

The Breakthrough

That honor fell to Wilbur and Orville Wright. Raised in a middle-class Protestant family that provided personal discipline, deep affection, intellectual freedom, and a good library—always a powerful combination—the Wright brothers resolved three basic problems with heavier-than-air flight in the years from 1900 through 1903. To have overcome any one of them would have been a major achievement. Overcoming all three while fashioning a working airplane from private resources was the century's greatest feat of personal invention, if "personal" quite captures their unique state of fraternal mind-meld. The bachelor brothers were so close, and so absorbed in their mutual undertaking, that they would finish one another's sentences. "I never saw men so wrapped up in their work in my life," said one observer. "They had their whole heart and soul"—note the singular—"in what they were doing."[5]

Their first problem was to design and build a wing with a surface, curvature, and angle of attack that would generate sufficient lift. Realizing that previous lift calculations were inadequate, the Wrights worked out a solution experimentally, through glider flights and homemade wind-tunnel tests. The second problem was to generate enough thrust to get the plane into the air and keep it there. They solved it by designing a lightweight, four-cylinder gasoline engine. It drove two customized propellers, revolving airfoils whose shape, they realized, was as important as that of their wings. The third and trickiest problem was control in the air. This they achieved by wing-warping. The pilot adjusted guy wires attached to the pliable wood-and-canvas wings, "warping" their shape, altering their aerodynamic characteristics, and allowing him to bank the plane. The Wrights added a twin rudder and connected its wires with the wing-warping mechanism. The pilot could, with one motion, simultaneously manipulate both controls. Two forward elevators, which regulated pitch, the plane's climbing or diving motion, rounded out their ingenious system of control.

Following four brief but successful flights at Kitty Hawk, North Carolina, on December 17, 1903, the exuberant Wrights returned to Dayton and went to work improving their machine. Few noticed outside their circle of aeronautical correspondents. When their brother, Lorin, delivered word of the Kitty Hawk success to the local *Dayton Journal*, the editor reportedly said, "Fifty-seven seconds, hey? If it had been fifty-seven minutes then it might have been a news item."[6]

As it happened, public inattention, confusion, and skepticism suited the Wrights' purposes. Too much knowledge of the means of their progress—by 1905 they had built a machine capable of extended flights—might lead to the appropriation of their invention, for which they did not secure a patent until 1906. Royalties were much on the brothers' minds. As Wilbur explained in a 1905 letter to Octave Chanute, their fellow aeronautical pioneer and confidant, they had begun their investigations in a spirit of pleasure. But they had sunk so much time and money into the project that they had been "compelled to regard it as a strict business proposition until such time as we had recouped ourselves."[7]

Chanute told them to fly their new machine before the biggest crowd they could assemble, stun the world, and watch the governments come calling. That was good advice, but the distrustful Wrights rejected it. Regarding the military as the most likely purchaser, they attempted to negotiate on a no-peek basis. They wanted the government to first sign a contract specifying performance criteria, *then* they would demonstrate their equipment. If the trials proved successful, the Wrights would sell their machine, plus the training and necessary proprietary knowledge, for the agreed-upon price. It sounds reasonable. No performance, no pay. But, as historian Tom Crouch points out, the highest ambition of the average bureaucrat is to "avoid looking foolish." Negotiations with secretive flying-machine inventors would have seemed unpropitious under any circumstances. With "Langley's Folly" fresh in everyone's mind—the government had sunk seventy thousand dollars in the pet flying-machine project of Samuel Langley, the Secretary of the Smithsonian Institution—such negotiations would have seemed suicidal. The Board of Ordnance and Fortification turned the Wrights down. Having "taken pains to see that 'Opportunity' gave a good clear knock on the War Department's door," the brothers approached potential French, British, and German buyers with clear consciences.[8]

The Wrights knew that the Europeans operated in a more competitive military climate, and had more pressing need of an aerial scouting machine. They did not, however, arrive at satisfactory terms until 1908, when they reached a licensing agreement with a French syndicate. By then the U.S. War Department, urged on by Frank Lahm Jr., a young Signal Corps officer convinced the Wrights had invented something of military value, had reentered the picture. In late 1907, the Board of Ordnance and Fortification, with the Wright Flyer in mind, solicited bids for the construction of an airplane. Wilbur departed for Europe to demonstrate the machine for the satisfaction of the European investors. Orville departed to Fort Myer to do the same for the U.S. Army.

The brothers created a sensation on both sides of the Atlantic late in the summer of 1908. Wilbur's flights on the outskirts of Le Mans proved to awed onlookers that the Wright Flyer could outperform any of the European planes, which were unstable, difficult to maneuver, and capable of only short flights. "Nous sommes battus," admitted the French aviator Léon Delagrange. We are beaten.[9]

Orville, meanwhile, set one record after another. A flight on September 9, before three cabinet secretaries and a large crowd, occupied fifty-seven minutes—precisely the length of time the skeptical Dayton editor had pronounced newsworthy. Two days later he flew for seventy minutes. Wilbur wrote from Le Mans to say that Orville's "dandy" American flights had aroused as much excitement in France as his own performances. But the Fort Myer trials ended abruptly when, on September 17, a propeller blade broke and sliced the rudder-control wire. The plane plowed into the ground near the gate of Arlington Cemetery, badly injuring Orville and killing his passenger, Lt. Thomas Selfridge. He was history's first airplane fatality. The army board had seen enough, though, to realize that the Wrights had solved the fundamental problems of mechanical flight.[10]

The press was convinced, too. Before departing for their European and American trials, the brothers had returned to Kitty Hawk for some tune-up flights. This time the journalists in attendance, who privately regarded the

Wilbur Wright made 109 flights outside Le Mans between August 8, 1908, and January 2, 1909, carrying aloft 40 thrilled passengers. Airplanes were suddenly *à la mode.* Here, New Year's greetings arrive via the Wright Flyer, a Yankee contraption that had made the bird, hot air balloon, hydrogen balloon, and dirigible *vieux jeu,* antiquated. A new year, indeed.

Wrights as fakers, were won over by the strange-looking machine clacking over the dunes. "When one first looks up at an aeroplane sailing in mid air," wrote Byron Newton, "... it brings a singular exhilaration. It is different from the contemplation of any other marvel human eyes may behold in a lifetime. It awakens new emotions."[11]

Exhibition Flying

Glenn Hammond Curtiss, the Wrights' principal American rival, understood that people would pay a great deal of money to experience the awakening of new emotions. A crack motorcycle racer and designer, Curtiss also understood lightweight gasoline engines. He built those that powered the army's first dirigible and the first three airplanes of the Aerial Experiment Association (1907–1909), a research group assembled by inventor Alexander Graham Bell. Curtiss was the group's leading figure, but he pulled out in 1909 to concentrate on making money. He began building planes, training pilots, flying before paying crowds, and winning prizes, capturing the first Gordon Bennett racing trophy at Rheims in August 1909. Two hundred thousand spectators bought tickets to attend the historic air meet. Another hundred thousand freeloaded from the surrounding hills.

The Wrights, fed up and alarmed by Curtiss's success, brought suit for patent infringement. Historians still debate whether this was a legitimate defense of intellectual property or a selfish and vengeful attempt to stymie the real aeronautical talent. It may even have been a matter of family habit. Both Wilbur and his father, Bishop Milton Wright, had a history of righteous combat against rascals and swindlers, a role easily imputed to Curtiss. Only this much is certain: the suit proved an expensive mistake for everyone but the lawyers. The Wright Company spent $152,000 in legal fees. Curtiss, who refused to buckle, spent $175,000. The prolonged patent fights—Curtiss was but one of several competitors whom the Wrights sued—exacted more than a financial toll. The litigation distracted the brothers from their aeronautical work and may have hastened an exhausted Wilbur's death in May 1912. The suits dragged on until the government brokered a settlement in 1917. Meanwhile the Europeans, spurred on by military rivalry, surged ahead.[12]

The Wrights could not foresee any of this when they reviewed their options in 1909 and 1910. They had, however, come to understand one thing: that the ready money lay in exhibition flying. In 1910, crowd-pleasing so preoccupied aviators that the Census Bureau's labor statisticians classified them as showmen, along with minstrels, carnies, and sideshow freaks. No one had planned this indignity. It had happened by default. Peacetime military

Glenn Curtiss at the controls of the *June Bug,* the third and most successful plane built by the Aerial Experiment Association. On July 4, 1908, Curtiss captured the *Scientific American* trophy for the first straight-line public flight of more than one kilometer. Two weeks later, Orville Wright warned Curtiss, "If it is your desire to enter the exhibition business, we would be glad to take up the matter of a license to operate under our patents." Curtiss ignored the threat, fielded an exhibition team, and battled the Wrights in court.

demand amounted to a handful of planes. Private sport flying held some potential, but the costs of purchase, instruction, and maintenance limited the market. Air transport would not be possible until engines, the bane of early aviation, gained in power and dependability. Until then, Orville suggested, flights should be banned over large cities, the worst possible places for crack-ups and dead-stick landings. Curtiss for once agreed, saying he would not fly across Manhattan if given title to every building he passed over.[13]

That left, by process of elimination, professional exhibition flying at race tracks, fair grounds, and other open places. Exhibition fliers were the lineal descendants of the "balloonatic" aerialists who had performed above Gilded Age crowds. In fact, several early pilots, such as Charles Hamilton and Thomas Baldwin, had performed for years with lighter-than-air equipment. They simply switched to planes, whose novelty value, speed, and stunting possibilities promised to enlarge their gates.

The Wrights entered the exhibition business belatedly and with distaste. They knew it was driven by more than curiosity. Flocks of boys turned up, confident, as one later put it, "that nowhere on earth, between now and suppertime, was there such a good chance of seeing somebody break his neck." If necks were to be broken, at least they would not be the brothers'. They hired dirigible airshow veteran Roy Knabenshue to manage their exhibition team. The fliers got twenty dollars weekly base pay plus fifty dollars for each day they flew. The Wrights also offered to sell planes to exhibition fliers for five thousand dollars. But there was a catch. The new owners still had to pay them royalties of fifty dollars a day, or one hundred dollars when engaged in exhibitions or competitions. The Wrights were determined to remain technological rentiers. For once, they failed. Curtiss's exhibition pilots laughed at them and kept on flying, driving down prices, and then driving the Wrights out of exhibition flying in late 1911. "It is a life-long regret with me that this business has been ruined," Knabenshue wrote Orville. "Had there been a means of protection, we could have made several fortunes out of it."[14]

Exhibition flying engendered forms of competition other than price-cutting. Fair crowds soon demanded more than level flying around an oval track, and air meets offered prizes for speed and altitude contests. Though the Wrights warned against taking unnecessary risks (as well as drinking, gambling, and Sunday shows), their pilots were only too anxious to enter the game. Given the social dynamics and economic realities of exhibition flying in 1910 and 1911, it is hard to see how they could have acted otherwise.

Consider the six-month career of Arch Hoxsey, a mechanic and race-car driver who joined the Wright team in 1910. Hoxsey managed several headline-making flights, including one with Teddy Roosevelt above St. Louis's Kinloch Park. (Passing over the "Doughnaut," a faux battleship with smoke curling from its chimney, Roosevelt, seized by a characteristic inspiration, shouted, "Army! Army! Aeroplane! Bomb!") The young pilot proved a model of circumspection during the flight, warning the ex-president against waving too vigorously to the crowd. He feared that Roosevelt would hit one of the plane's control wires. "When we landed safely," he told reporters, "I felt as though someone had cut off the high pressure on my heart valve. Then the colonel reached his hand over and said, 'Hoxsey, you're all right.'"

When Hoxsey was on his own he flew by a very different code. He was an avid competitor, setting records for distance (104 miles) and altitude (11,474 feet), the last before a crowd of 75,000. Contrary to the Wrights' instructions, he and teammate Ralph Johnstone thrilled spectators by putting their planes into spiraling dives, pulling out just above the ground. Trying to best his own altitude record outside Los Angeles, Hoxsey climbed slowly to seven thousand feet, gave up on the attempt, put his plane into a steepening dive, lost control, and smashed into the ground before a gasping crowd. Knabenshue could not bring himself to describe the corpse, which had to be cremated. The press was less reticent. The impact had crushed the right side of Hoxsey's head and body beyond recognition. He was twenty-seven years old.

Hoxsey's death on December 31, 1910—coincidentally the same day that the celebrated New Orleans pilot John Moisant broke his neck—capped a very bad month. Ten men had died in eight crashes on three continents during December, bringing the international death toll to thirty-five. Some pilots were philosophical. "Funny luck," Charles Hamilton said, part of a bad run. "I guess we will all get it sooner or later," shrugged Eugene Ely, a prophecy he fulfilled by diving into the Georgia State Fairgrounds. Others deplored flying's circuslike atmosphere. "There is hazard enough without attempting anything extra hazardous," wrote Art Welsh, adding that Hoxsey had been too fond of stunting. He had died because of his competitiveness, his "mettle in wanting to do a little better than the other fellow."[15]

Rising in the Status Sphere

Welsh's remark about topping rivals provides an important clue to the social world of "the early birds," as American pilots who soloed before December 17, 1916, came to be known. It was, first of all, a masculine world, walled off by gender assumptions. The Wrights regarded women fliers as unsuitably nervous students. No American woman held a pilot's license until a striking, green-eyed journalist named Harriet Quimby earned hers in August 1911. The following April, Quimby soloed across the English Channel, only to see the news of her feat swallowed by the *Titanic* disaster. She flew briefly in exhibitions, but died when her Blériot monoplane pitched forward, throwing her and a passenger into the mud flats of Dorchester Bay. Matilde Moisant, America's second licensed female pilot, quit after less than a year. "My flying career didn't last awfully long because in those days that was man's work and they didn't think a nice girl should be in it," she later recalled—though four bad crashes, including one that set her clothing ablaze, may have had something to do with her quitting. Blanche Stuart Scott, a Curtiss student who performed as "the Tomboy of the Air," lasted six years, retiring in 1916. "In aviation there seems no place for the woman engineer, mechanic, or flier," she said. "Too often, people paid money to see me risk my neck more as a freak–a woman freak pilot—than as a skilled flier."[16]

Why would anyone, male or female, risk death in the exhibition game?

The few women on the exhibition circuit faced the same daunting odds as male pilots. Harriet Quimby died on July 1, 1912, when she and passenger William Willard fell from her plane into Dorchester Bay. Thousands witnessed the horror during a meet at Squantum, near Quincy, Massachusetts. Press photographer Leslie Jones was on hand to record the retrieval of her body.

There was, of course, the money. Each of Lincoln Beachey's performances netted him more than the average American worker earned in a year. Hoxsey, like many a young man who set out for the California gold fields, dreamed of making a fortune and getting out. He set a goal of $100,000 before quitting. Celebrity, which he did achieve, was another attraction. Exhibition fliers were like sports stars. They had their pictures all over the newspapers and on picture postcards, where they struck dashing poses at the controls of their planes. Pilots had all the women they could handle. Beachey did not even have to ask. Women simply showed up at his hotel rooms. His wife, seeking a divorce, listed all the cities in which Beachey had supposedly had affairs. She got through thirty-two before the judge cut her off and granted her petition. "Aviator's Conquest Not of Air Alone," headlined the local paper.[17]

Welsh's remark about Hoxsey, that he wanted to do a little better than the other fellow, gets at a more subtle reason why men risked so much in the exhibition game. Youthful male subcultures, especially those organized around hot-dog gadgets like skateboards, are highly competitive. They are, to borrow a term coined by Tom Wolfe, "status spheres" in which peer recognition depends on showing moxie and resourcefulness. As initiates master more difficult and dangerous challenges, their status grows. Wolfe likened a career in flying to climbing a pyramid with many steps. Moving up the pyramid meant always showing "the right stuff," the willingness to face danger in the air and the skill to master it. Failure brought death, success the uncounterfeitable coin of respect.[18]

Status competition emerged quickly in both American and European aviation. In 1912, a young Dutch pilot named Anthony Fokker, scion of another coffee fortune, set up shop at Berlin's Johannisthal airfield:

> Johannisthal was a thriving little cosmopolis. Aviation was a sport which had attracted daring spirits, ne'er-do-wells, and adventurers from all over the world. There were sober, industrious pilots and designers present too, but they were in the minority. Many of the amateur pilots were rich men's sons, who found this spot a fertile ground for the sowing of wild oats. Dazzled by the dare-deviltry of these men, beautiful women from the theatre and night clubs hung around the flying field, more than a little complaisant, alluring—unstinting of favors to their current heroes.
>
> Excitement out of the air centered in the gay, sportive little café, run by Papa Senftleben, attached to the field, where wine, women and song were permanently on the menu. My drink, 'Kaffe Fokker,' became famous, because it was so different, a tall beaker of warm milk with an inch of coffee. Pilots and their favorite girls spent most of the midday there, for actual flying lasted only an hour or two after sunrise and before sunset after the wind had died down. It was a hard, dangerous life, but a dashing and reckless one, attractive to youngsters barely out of their teens. There was something of a storybook quality about that heady mixture of brave men and fair women. At night, hastily organized parties raced into Berlin for a tour of all the gay spots. They drank to a 'quick life but a snappy one; a short life but a happy one.' Frequently these all-night affairs wound up at dawn with the bleary bravado of a half-drunken fight. The primrose path in the air sometimes ended in a screaming wreck. Everyone then had another drink, quick. But it was soon forgotten.

Not forgotten was where everyone stood on the status pyramid. Fokker, a nobody with a funny-looking monoplane, endured ridicule and cruel pranks, even sugar in his gas tank. One day Willy Rosenstein, the crowd-thrilling man of the moment, strolled into his hangar. He took a withering look at Fokker's plane, said it was "as good a way to kill yourself as any," and walked away laughing with his entourage. "I wanted to throw a wrench at his thick head," Fokker remembered, his anger still sharp after two decades. Fokker watched Rosenstein on his next flight. Pretty good, he admitted to himself. The man had a knack for airmanship. Showmanship, too. But Fokker knew he could make steeper banks and sharper turns. "Pretty soon I would show him."

When Fokker went aloft, he impressed the crowd with his control. Anyone who could fly an oddball plane without ailerons must be quite a pilot. The press wrote him up. Autograph-seekers crowded around. Women smiled fondly. He made longer and longer flights. The military took notice. He appeared in newsreels. He was on his way up.

Then came the *coup d'theatre.* In September 1913, a French flier, Adolphe Pégoud, looped the loop, repeating the stunt before crowds who paid thousands to see the astonishing feat. America's greatest surviving exhibition pilot, Lincoln Beachey, came out of retirement and began performing his version. Beachey had quit the circuit because so many young pilots had killed themselves trying to better his feats. (One Yale man's last words were, "I will show Linc a trick or two he has never thought of.") But the Frenchman's achievement rekindled Beachey's competitive spirit. By Thanksgiving he was performing the maneuver in his own specially designed plane, often taking home fifteen hundred dollars for a six-loop show. Even the professionals were impressed. "Beachey is making the LOOP in a very dignified but thrilling manner," Roy Knabenshue reported to Orville Wright in 1914, noting that his propeller seemed to carry him up and over without difficulty. Wings were another matter. The following year Beachey lost both of his while performing over San Francisco Bay. Schoolchildren commemorated the event with jump-rope sing-song:

Lincoln Beachey thought it was a dream
To go up to heaven in a flying machine.
The machine broke down, and down he fell.
Instead of going to heaven he went to _____
Lincoln Beachey thought it was a dream . . .

Fokker wanted to be the first pilot in Germany to accomplish the maneuver. He announced he would make the attempt in a monoplane of his own design, with a rectangular fuselage of welded steel tubes. In the air, he had second thoughts. Would the plane endure the stress? Would the wings buckle? He began to hope his engine would quit, so that he could descend with honor. It droned on. The audience grew impatient. He cast a glance at the mechanics below, craning their necks to keep him in sight. "I was simply in for it. So

I set my teeth and thought, 'Some day you must die, it might as well be now.'" He pushed the plane into a dive, waited until he heard the wind whistling through his guy wires, then pulled up hard on the elevator. Over he went, hanging upside down, feet slipping from the rudder pedals, falling back into a dive, from which he pulled out as quickly as he could, losing only two hundred feet before returning to level flight.

Fokker's loop made news all over Germany. Exhibition offers poured in. With practice, he learned to loop with less strain, pulling the plane up gently, nosing over easily, making perfect loops. "I found it was possible to thrill the public without really endangering myself," he mused. "The crowds sunburned their tonsils watching me loop the loop." It was easy money, and sweeter revenge. His tormentor Willy Rosenstein watched him enviously. Only his father objected. "Now you are famous," he wrote. "Now is the time to stop. The only thing you can do next is to break your neck."[19]

Sic Transit

Tony Fokker went on flying, though, like other exhibition fliers who made a lasting impact on aviation, he wisely gave up stunting. Fokker's real talent turned out to be aircraft design and manufacture. In 1915, his engineering team solved a problem that had defied five years of international tinkering, how to synchronize a machine gun to fire through a propeller arc. Fokker went on to design outstanding German pursuit planes. The Allies so feared one of these, the D.VII, that they placed it at the head of the list of German aircraft to be surrendered after the Armistice. Working both sides of the Atlantic after the war, Fokker set up a manufacturing company in the United States, where he introduced steel fuselages and innovative transport aircraft. He billed his planes as "the safest in the world." The claim held until 1931, when a flutter-prone wing broke off one of his trimotors, killing Notre Dame football coach Knute Rockne and seven other men.[20]

By then peacetime aviation deaths were rare occurrences, and becoming rarer. When Fokker himself died in 1939, aviation was incomparably safer than it had been in the early days. There were 148 accidents in 1909 and 1910, including 31 fatal crashes that claimed 34 lives. Six of the nine Wright exhibition fliers died in crashes, all but one of them before mid-1912. The military record was almost as dismal. Eight of the fourteen qualified pilots in the Army Signal Corps were dead by 1914. When Henry H. "Hap" Arnold received his invitation to train as a pilot, his commanding officer told him it was suicidal. Arnold disregarded the warning. Flying was a challenge, and more exciting than the Ordnance Department post for which he had been angling.[21]

Air show performers as gladiators: "We who are about to die salute you." It is an apt comparison. Exhibition fliers risked their lives before morbidly curious crowds. While they lived, they reaped the successful gladiators' rewards of fame, money, and sex.

The flying frontier for which Arnold volunteered was a classic type-II, sparsely populated and lopsidedly masculine. As of July 24, 1912, the day the diminutive Katherine Stinson received her license, America could claim just four licensed female pilots—and only two of them were still living. Prewar flying was a brotherhood, and a small one at that. Yet novelty, spectacle, and publicity gave these birdmen a cultural weight far out of proportion to their actual numbers, in much the way the Mercury astronauts heralded the arrival of the space frontier a half-century later.

The early birds left two important, and contradictory, legacies. The first was to inspire the rising generation of fliers and aircraft manufacturers, the men who would take the disreputable raiment of American aviation and turn it into the garment of empire. In 1909, ten-year-old Juan Trippe, the future founder of Pan American World Airways, watched Wilbur Wright circle the Statue of Liberty. He became enchanted with flying. The same thing happened to seventeen-year-old Donald Douglas, who saw Orville Wright perform in the 1909 army acceptance trials. In early 1910, a young engineer named William Boeing fell under the spell while watching the French aviator Louis Paulhan. Publisher William Randolph Hearst, privileged to fly with Paulhan,

The star of the 1910 Los Angeles Air Meet was the French aviator Louis Paulhan. The "Napoleon of the Air" set endurance and altitude records, the latter in this delicate-looking (and, in the Wrights' eyes, pirated) Farman biplane. Among the 226,000 spectators was a lanky young engineer named William Boeing. He tried for days to get Paulhan to take him up for a ride. Fifty years later, in 1960, the seventy-seven-year-old Paulhan would return to the site of his triumphs in a Boeing 707, as a guest on Air France's inaugural jet service from Paris to Los Angeles.

became a lifelong champion of aviation. Claire Chennault, of Flying Tigers fame, was a cadet at Louisiana State University when he saw a Curtiss pusher at the 1910 state fair. The sight of the frail biplane bucking the thermals inspired in him thoughts of a "new frontier" to conquer, a surrogate West for young men born too late to test themselves against the Indians. Curtis LeMay, the future head of the Strategic Air Command, spotted his first plane in the winter of 1910–11. Chasing the apparition across the sky, red stocking cap bobbing as he ran, LeMay yearned to know everything about the mysterious object in the sky. In 1912, Charles Lindbergh, accompanied by his mother, watched a plane race a motor car around an oval track. Fascinated, he decided he wanted to take up flying himself. The memoirs of almost every American pilot and aeronautical engineer born between 1880 and 1910 contain some version of this primal story. The early birds made an indelible impression on a young audience—an impression that would be reinforced, especially among boys, by the model airplane boom of the 1920s and 1930s.[22]

Unfortunately, the early birds made another lasting impression on many of the adults who watched or read about their performances. That was the association of flying with extreme and unwarranted risk. Editorialists called flying gruesome and deadly. They denounced stunting as "morally, if not legally, criminal." They called for rules to eliminate reckless feats from aerial shows. It was all in vain. The crowds demanded the frisson of danger. The young exhibition fliers, motivated by money, celebrity, sex, and peer rivalry, were happy to oblige. "You can go home now, I wasn't killed," was the way "Sure Shot" Kearney ended his shows. Then one day he too crashed and died.[23]

The necessary irony of the development of American aviation—in fact, of any frontier settlement process—was the dismantling of *both* of these legacies, that of fear and that of inspiration. Over the next four decades airplanes would become safer, but also humdrum, barely worth an upward glance. Though in some sense inexorable, the routinization of flight held a few surprises. The biggest of these was that public apprehensions about flying, already acute in 1914, would grow worse before finally beginning to recede in the late 1920s and early 1930s.

go west 1. To die. *Orig. cowboy and western use. Very common during W.W. I.*

—DICTIONARY OF AMERICAN SLANG

CHAPTER 3

Gone West

World War I marked a turning point in human history. It was effectively the end of the nineteenth century, the end of European supremacy in world affairs, the end of the old social and political order. Crowns rolled on the pavement in 1918, as Lenin had prophesied.

For aviation the war marked a new beginning rather than an end. Military necessity turned flying into a serious business, increasing the number of fliers, the significance of their activities, and the power of their planes. Yet, in another way, it narrowed access to the skies. More than ever, flying became a young man's job. The implications of aeronautical advances depended upon their political context. In peacetime, making planes bigger, safer, and more comfortable opened the skies to men and women, the young and the old, the fit and the unfit. But during wartime, technological progress had the opposite effect, at least for the duration of hostilities. High-performance military aircraft were best suited to young pilots and crewmen who could tolerate the hardships of combat flying.

Few anticipated these developments in 1914, or that the airplane would play much of a role in the war. But the sky's superfrontier status, its strategic transit above the shell-pocked land upon which deadlocked armies sacrificed more than nine million lives, forced the rapid development of military aviation. Aerial observers proved their value from the outset. They picked up the

German army's swing to the east of Paris, permitting the French army to mount a counterattack and save the city. German observers tracked Russian movements in the east, making possible the great victory at Tannenberg. When the war of maneuver settled down to trench stalemate, balloons and wireless-equipped aircraft played a critical role as artillery spotters. Though World War I is remembered as a war of machine guns and poison gas, artillery caused three-quarters of all casualties. Aerial observation improved its accuracy, so much so that armies moved their frontline supply convoys in the dead of night. (The Germans also made rail shipments at night, though Allied observers learned to judge their volume by counting the steam clouds rising into the dawn sky from the still-hot locomotives.) Aerial photographs, some taken from three or four miles up, gave military planners detailed knowledge of enemy fortifications and troop movements. The airplane took the element of surprise out of the war, and thus prolonged the stalemate.[1]

All of this made disruption of the enemy's aerial reconnaissance highly desirable. The disruptions were at first informal. Airmen attacked rival observers with brickbats and grenades, pistol and rifle shots. None of this proved effective. The front-mounted machine gun, which permitted concentrated fire along the plane's line of flight, was another matter. It became deadlier still with propeller synchronization and the addition of tracer, incendiary, armor-piercing, and explosive bullets. By 1915, both sides fielded pursuit (fighter) units whose primary mission was to destroy enemy balloons and observation planes, while defending their own. As the "war of the lenses" grew in importance, so did the role of these pursuit aircraft, which made up 34 percent of French, 42 percent of German, and 55 percent of British aircraft by August 1918. By then, both sides had also developed long-range bomber aircraft and tactics. Like pursuit planes, bombers evolved from spontaneous experimentation. They offered the hope of attacking otherwise invulnerable enemy forces, such as reserves massed outside artillery range. The Germans extended the logic to capital cities, using zeppelins to drop high explosive and incendiary bombs on "Fortress London."[2]

America Enters the War

The observation-pursuit-bombardment structure of military aviation was well established when the United States entered the war, obviously unprepared, in the spring of 1917. The army could field 56 pilots and fewer than 300 aircraft, none combat worthy. The navy had 48 aviation officers, 230 enlisted men, and 54 airplanes, mostly trainers. But the Allies counted on the United States for manpower, material, and money rather than advanced weapons. In July 1917, Congress responded with $640 million for army aviation, then the largest specific-purpose appropriation in American history. These funds, bolstered by further appropriations for naval aviation, ultimately translated into about 10,000 pilots, a like number of mechanics, 42,000 aircraft engines, and 14,000 airplanes. The wartime models were mostly Curtiss JN-4D "Jenny" trainers, DH-4 bombers built under license, and Curtiss flying boats for antisubmarine patrols. American pursuit planes were conspicuous in their absence. The rapid evolution of pursuit aircraft made it expedient for American airmen to fly the latest French and British models, in which they received advanced training overseas.[3]

The United States, like all other belligerents, had more than enough volunteers for its air services. Young men reasoned that it was better to defend the nation in the sky than in the trenches and collect flight pay in the bargain. No prejudice is more common in aviators' diaries and memoirs than that of infantrymen as dogs. "They say the army is worse than the navy," wrote one American volunteer. "I'd rather fly than belong to either."[4]

Because of its technical demands and lack of established traditions, aviation was the most meritocratic branch of the military. Instructors winnowed cadets ruthlessly. The slow, the timid, and the accident-prone were either killed or washed out, regardless of education or family connections. At Kelly Field, the largest American training center, cadets had to learn to hit twenty-three of twenty-five clay pigeons, on the theory that if they could not lead a moving target at the skeet range, they would never do it with a machine gun. Almost 15,000 cadets entered pilot training in the United States. Only 8,688 earned an aviator's rating. (A smaller number received their primary flight training in Europe.) Instructors sorted candidates by aptitude. The quickest went into pursuit, the next into bombers, then observation.[5]

Pilots who survived training were usually commissioned as officers, which raised many a European eyebrow. Regular U.S. Army officers also looked down on flying cadets and lieutenants, whom they regarded as immature, undisciplined, and irresponsible. "These little tin majors give me a pain," wrote ace-to-be Elliott Springs, returning the favor. "If we had to choose between fighting the Prussian Guard and the West Point Alumni Association, I know where at least two hundred and ten aviators would assemble."

Springs's fellow Pershing-haters were Americans shipped to England for training in September 1917. Their ranks included college boys, ne'er-do-wells, a full-blooded Sioux, and two cowboys, Bob Kelly and Allen Bird, who lit up the donnish precincts of Oxford. "They were both six feet three and would rather fight than eat," Springs wrote. "I had visions of them both being sent to Leavenworth in chains."[6]

Springs's rambunctious crew was overwhelmingly single and young. At the outset of the war, many aviators were cavalry retreads in their late twenties, thirties, or older. By 1917, flying was strictly a young man's game. "We walked off the playing fields into the lines," wrote Cecil Lewis, who applied to the Royal Flying Corps when he was sixteen and flew at seventeen. The average age of one British squadron was twenty. The faces in the photos seem much older, the effect of too many lost friends and fiery nightmares. "Here I am, twenty-four years old," wrote Springs. "I look forty and I feel ninety. I've lost all interest in life beyond the next patrol." In early 1917, George Squier, head of the Signal Corps' Aviation Section and military attaché to London, testified to Congress that he had yet to find an "actual flier" on the western front over twenty-four. He would be proved wrong on at least one count. Eddie Rickenbacker started flying at twenty-seven. A sympathetic doctor had lied about his age, writing "25" firmly on his physical examination form. Then again, Rickenbacker was a famous race-car driver, endowed with unusual eyesight, reflexes, and stamina.[7]

Of which he needed every ounce. Though pursuit planes evolved into high-performance, high-altitude aircraft, their cockpits remained open. The noise level, 125 decibels, exceeded that of pneumatic drills. "They can't use mufflers on the engines, as it reduces the power," the American aviator Josiah Rowe Jr. explained in a letter to his mother. "The noise is almost deafening, but you get used to it." At one point the Americans considered letting deaf men fly, reasoning that pilots could not hear anything anyway. Engine racket and high-altitude flying left a quarter of them with permanent hearing loss and grounded others. The German ace Ernst Udet built up so much pus in his ears that his doctor had to remove it with a spatula. Eddie Rickenbacker tried heated salt bags. He slept with one over his abscessed ear.[8]

Bitter cold numbed the body, thin air the mind. The Germans, equipped by 1917 with electric flying suits and oxygen bottles, coped best. Allied pilots rubbed whale grease on their faces and soldiered on. "I froze my nose and lips and both cheeks so bad that they all turned brown and peeled off," wrote observer Irving Sheely. Ace Ray Brooks said two hours at eighteen thousand feet made him feel like a frozen sick cow.[9]

Climbing for altitude drove blood pressure from a normal 120 systolic to a hypertensive 200 by the time pilots reached 6,000 feet. The higher they flew, the worse they felt. Teeth throbbed. Brains swelled. Vision blurred. At 18,000 feet the volume of abdominal gas doubled, a problem not helped by the castor oil spewing from rotary engines. The apparently simple business of patrolling, remarks historian Denis Winter, "caused more physical strain on more parts of the body than any fighting man had experienced in any past

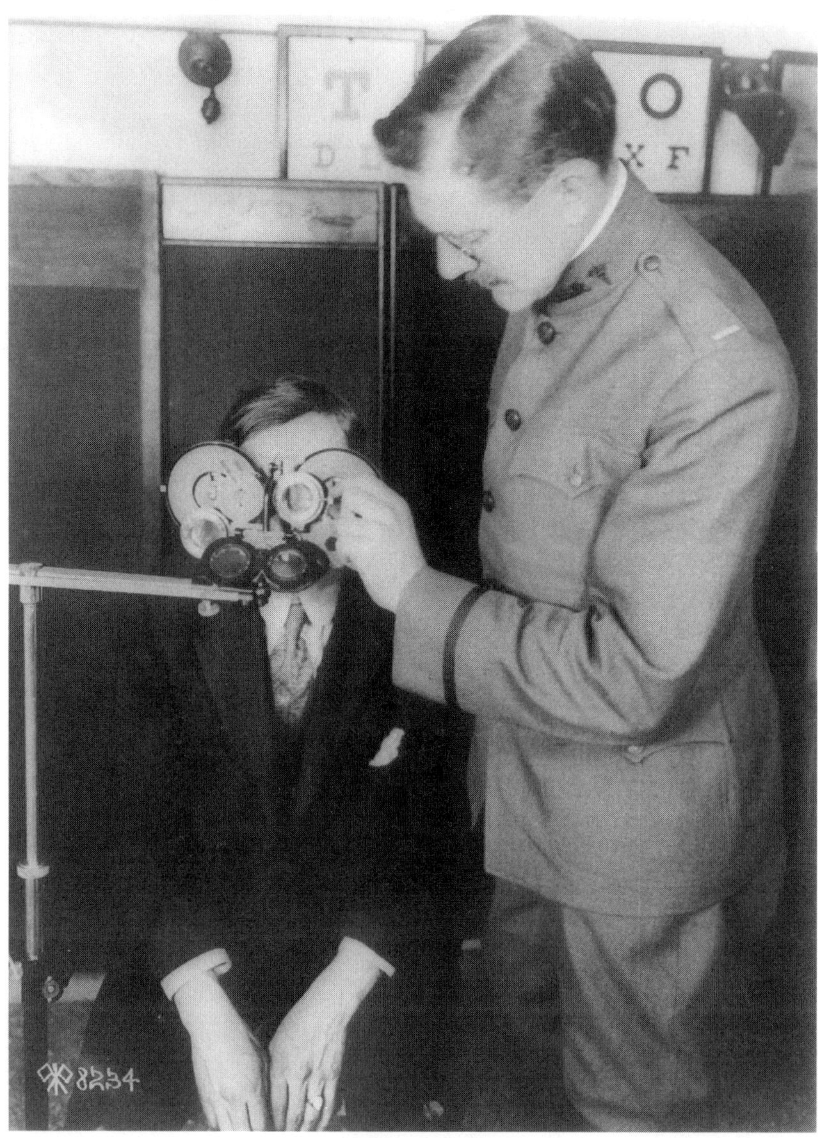

By 1917, recruiters accepted only the fittest young men for aviation training programs. Physicians tested for eyesight, balance, coordination, muscular development, and intelligence. The American Air Service also rejected applicants on the basis of age, marital status, and African ancestry, though two light-complected mulattoes reportedly passed by fooling their examiners. This recruit's dress, grooming, and lone signet ring indicate his preferred status—educated and single.

war." Half of all pilots developed serious neuroses during their tours. The prospects of recovery were better for bachelors than married men. The prospects of recovery for psychopaths were said to be excellent.[10]

Crazy or sane, the young fliers still managed to maneuver and shoot down their enemies. The experienced preyed on the inexperienced, whose usual end was sudden death at the hands of an unseen foe. The turnover among replacements was constant. "I'm frank to say we were rather brutal," wrote Allan Bonnalie, an American who flew with the Royal Flying Corps. "We paid no attention to a newly arrived man until he'd been around for three or four weeks." As on the western frontier, the killers got the glory. Men pencilled the names of the leading scorers on the mess walls. Downing the first enemy plane was a rite of passage: Brooks promised a case of good champagne to his mess. Bonnalie ran up a six hundred dollar bar bill the month he won his Distinguished Service Order. Abstemious souls like Percival Gates, the son of a famous Baptist minister, endured brawling drunks and kidding about their sober ways. The tone was strictly macho. Windsocks were "condoms," one "hunted" the enemy, turning "yellow" was the unforgivable sin. The five-victory status of ace, a term previously applied to sporting stars, was so prized that men took credit for doubtful kills. Allied aviators claimed 11,760 victories: 7,054 for the British, 3,950 for the French, and 756 for the Americans. According to postwar German calculations, the actual number of planes lost was only 3,000. Not enough Huns, apparently, to go around.[11]

The glory problem was acutest for the late-entering American pilots, most of whom got nowhere near the front. In June 1918, William Faulkner wrote his parents that he could become a second lieutenant—"leftenant they call it"—after three months in an Royal Air Force training camp. "It's a wonderful chance, for there's nothing to be had in the U.S. Army now, except a good job stopping *boche* bullets as a private." He enlisted and was sent to Toronto, where he composed a gushing poem called "The Ace" ("The sun light / Paints him as he stalks, huge through the morning") and found himself in ground school when the war ended. This was a common fate. Just one-third of the American aviators trained during the war made it to Europe and only six hundred saw any significant combat. "I've got to get a Hun some way or other," Rowe complained shortly before the Armistice, "and I've got to do it quick because it looks now as if we may have peace almost any day." He had to content himself with ground strafing. Others found themselves scattering propaganda or dropping cigarettes to grateful doughboys in advanced posts.[12]

Percival Gates, the pilot who refused alcohol, was another American who arrived too late to see much action. Assigned to the fabled 27th Pursuit Squadron in late September 1918, he never fired on a German aircraft. Yet, looking back, he was lucky to have survived. In just 140 to 150 hours of total flying time, he experienced eight forced landings, three of them crashes; a ground loop that wrecked his plane; and countless near misses. Fuel lines broke. Rudders froze. Engines quit. Any of these failures might have killed him. An American pilot's chance of dying in a training accident was 40 percent higher than his chance of dying in combat. Gates took it all stoically. "My policy is to never worry about anything until you get some good reason and definite information," he wrote home. "You have to be an absolute fatalist in this war."[13]

If the fatalism that had marked exhibition flying was evident in military flying, so was the competitive spirit. And it had the same effect, making a dangerous calling that much deadlier. Men died unnecessarily, both in training and in combat. Some stunted in trainers, pulling the fabric-covered wings from laminated wood frames. (Army regulations prohibited acrobatics except in advanced schools that specialized in combat tactics.) Other pilots returned to their bases, took on more fuel and ammunition, and returned obsessively to the air, laboring to build their scores. Frank Luke flew his last mission, in which he downed three German balloons before being shot down himself, against orders. The same clerk who had just typed his Distinguished Service Cross recommendation fed in another sheet and began typing his court-martial papers. (When Luke failed to return, having emptied his pistol at approaching German troops before dying, the army changed its mind again and gave him a Congressional Medal of Honor.) France's Georges Guynemer logged as many as seven hours a day on patrol. "The young hero cannot stay still," commented *Le Figaro.* "He sits down, he gets up, he walks about, he sits down again, all the time telling about his exploits in pieces and snatches, as if he were talking about a football game or a hunting episode."[14]

The most determined of the American air-combat sportsmen was a young Philadelphia aristocrat named Hobart Amory Hare Baker. A Princeton hockey and football legend, Hobey Baker "went to war as if it were an unusually satisfying Yale-Princeton game." He practiced dogfighting with Rickenbacker, gave acrobatic demonstrations for visiting generals, broke formation to risk individual combat, dove through tracers to attack observation balloons, flew five missions in a single day. "If I 'go west,'" he reasoned, "it would be a pleasant death, a quick and sure one." Instead he flew himself into command of a new squadron, the 141st, whose Spads he decorated with an orange and black Princeton tiger atop a German helmet. He claimed his second kill, then his third. He hunted for Fokkers. He prayed the armistice would not come too soon. When it did, he insisted on "one last flight in the old Spad" before departing his squadron. His friends begged him not to go up. He compounded his error by switching planes, taking up another Spad with a balky engine for a test flight. The engine quit shortly after takeoff, the plane crashed, and Baker split open his head. The newspapermen who reported his death promoted him to ace status, crediting him with fourteen kills.[15]

The War's Legacies

The war's end brought more than disappointment for would-be aces. It had consequences that would shape aviation's future, beginning with the fundamental question of who controlled access to the sky. Diplomats first addressed this issue at the 1910 Paris Aviation Conference. Should the sky be treated like the high seas, which nations could not legally claim, or should it be treated like a land frontier, over which nations could assert sovereignty? And, if nations enjoyed rights to their airspace, how exclusive were those rights? France favored a "right of innocent passage," Germany a policy of equal access for foreign and domestic planes. But the conferees failed to reach agreement because the British, anxious that the airplane threatened their insular security, insisted on complete control of national airspace.

The war settled the issue in favor of the British. Combat experience had demonstrated the growing offensive potential of aircraft and set precedents for the bombing of cities. The diplomats who attended the 1919 Paris Aviation Conference agreed that nations enjoyed "exclusive sovereignty in the air space above [their] lands and territorial waters." Access and landing rights could be worked out through bilateral treaties, but there would be no equivalent of an open-oceans policy. The 1919 convention failed to set an upper limit on airspace, a moot point until satellites arrived in the late 1950s. This time the great powers found it in their interest to allow orbital passage above the atmosphere, leading to the curious fact that airspace remains subject to national sovereignty, while "outer" space does not.[16]

The aircraft that provoked postwar anxieties were very different from prewar machines. The war brought rapid improvements in aircraft strength, stability, and control, as well as lighter, more dependable, more efficient, and more powerful engines. The last private aircraft purchased before the war, a Blériot XI, came equipped with a 50 hp Gnôme rotary engine. By 1918, the Liberty 12-cylinder engine, used in the DH-4 and other aircraft, could produce 400 hp. Air power advocate Billy Mitchell thought that more had been accomplished for aviation during four years of combat than would have been during five decades of peace.[17]

Eddie Rickenbacker was not so sure. Looking back from 1925, he wrote that the war had "forced a rapid development of aviation, but at the sacrifice of economy, durability, comfort, and carrying capacity for the sake of speed, altitude, and maneuverability." The industry had been left with too many of the wrong kinds of planes for peacetime commercial uses. Try imagining a Pullman carload of passengers, as another writer put it, going aloft in a dogfighting machine.[18]

If the situation of air commerce was unpromising in 1919, that of aircraft manufacturing was a disaster. The government virtually destroyed the industry by canceling $100 million worth of contracts and throwing surplus planes on the market. At the time of the Armistice, November 11, 1918, American aircraft manufacturers employed 175,000 workers capable of turning out 21,000 airplanes a year. Within three months, the industry had shrunk to 10 percent of its wartime peak. It kept right on shrinking. In 1922, it produced just 263 planes. The government's initial unwillingness to support commercial aviation, either through airline subsidies or the development of airports and navigational aids, kept demand low. Without sales, the industry could not afford research and development. Without research and development, it could not make much progress toward better planes. Without better planes, it could not win over reluctant passengers, who associated flying with combat, daredevils, and barnstormers.[19]

The Gold Rush

The barnstormers were themselves war surplus, mostly instructors and their students who had been bitten by the flying bug. Continued service was not an option. In 1919, the demobilizing army had little use for shave-tail aviators. The ground loomed with its ant-like routine. George "Buck" Weaver, one of the first barnstormers, thought of a way out. In March 1919, he and his brother-in-law, Charlie Meyers, bought two Curtiss Jennies, trainers of simple design and affordable price. Then they went barnstorming to recoup their investment and save up enough money to open a flying school.[20]

"Barnstormers" originally referred to actors who traveled the countryside performing in barns, with a repertoire of short, action-packed pieces suited to rustic tastes. Twentieth-century barnstormers provided the aerial equivalent of a Shakespearean duel with their mock dog fights, death's head–emblazoned planes, parachute stunts, and wing-walkers clad in pink tights. One bold spirit buzzed the 1920 Notre Dame–Northwestern football game in Evanston, flying over the field at grandstand level and then looping the Loop.[21]

There was nothing new about watching pilots risk their necks at county fairs and air shows. What was new, or greatly scaled up, was the ride busi-

Though the war had a narrowing effect on pilot demography—by 1917, aircrew were almost exclusively young men—it had a quite different effect on employment in the aircraft industry. In some plants, women comprised four-fifths of the workforce. Many of the planes they produced ended up in the hands of postwar barnstormers, who bought up surplus Curtiss JN-4D trainers and gave passengers joyrides in the plane's second seat.

ness. Barnstormers took up goggle-eyed first timers who paid a few dollars for five minutes in the air. Perhaps a million Americans, mostly men between the ages of eighteen and thirty-five, first flew in this fashion. The young had the fewest prejudices against flying and were quick to accept the barnstormers' come-ons. Eleven-year-old A. M. "Tex" Johnston got a free ride when a white-scarfed barnstormer landed near Emporia, Kansas, and offered him a spin. Johnston had a wonderful time. He urged all his neighbors to go for a ride. "Come on folks," the pilot cajoled. "See your hometown from the air."[22]

One of Charles Lindbergh's passengers had a better idea. He bought a ride so that he could urinate on his hometown. Lindbergh's barnstorming partner, "Cupid" Lynch, took off with a Montanan who pulled out two horse pistols and emptied them 100 feet above Main Street. As the plane taxied in, he grinned and shouted to Lynch, "I SHOT THIS TOWN UP A'FOOT, AN' I SHOT THIS TOWN UP A'HOSSBACK, AN' NOW I SHOT THIS TOWN UP FROM A AIRPLANE." "Well," said Lynch, "that sure ought to bring the passengers out if there are any."[23]

Barnstormers began systematically tapping the short-ride market in the spring and summer of 1919. By April, the American Flying Club, the memento-bedecked hangout for demobilized army pilots on New York's East 38th Street, buzzed with rumors. Fortunes awaited anyone who could get his hands on a surplus plane. At first the fares were steep, as much as $15 to $25 for a brief flight. Two pilots who started out with a single plane were able to gross $140,000 by the end of the year.

No one knows how many pilots tried to cash in, though a reasonable estimate of the initial rush would be about a thousand. The 1920 census counted 1,312 "aeronauts," including 1,304 men and 8 women. As the supply of barnstormers grew, and as joyriding's novelty faded, the prices fell, first to $5 a flight, then $2, then as low as $1—the asking price of the barnstormer who took Tex Johnston on his come-on ride in 1925.[24]

Which was exactly what had happened in California in the late 1840s and 1850s. The Gold Rush increased the state's non-Indian population sixteenfold between 1848 and 1852. Wages fell during those same years from $16 a day to $6 or $7 a day. They continued to decline, dipping to the $2.00 to $3.50 range by 1867, fueling a political backlash against Chinese immigrant labor. The nature of the mining industry changed, too. Forty-niners panning for placer gold needed little capital. But as the easy pickings diminished and gold extraction became more dependent upon sluices, irrigation ditches, hydraulic machinery, and tunneling, miners became employees rather than independent workers. They did not have the capital to run a mine, a task assumed first by business-oriented "engineers" and later by large corporations.[25]

Barnstormers' initial outlays were more manageable. They could buy surplus Jennies for five hundred dollars or less, a tenth of the plane's original cost. They could also save money by flying from town to town, avoiding the trouble and expense of packing their planes for railroad shipment, as prewar exhibition fliers had often done. But "gypsy flying" had a downside. As in the gold fields, income tapered off in November, when cold weather set in. Constant exposure to the elements could wear out a plane in six months. Accidents could claim them even sooner. Every time a barnstormer set down his battered crate in a pasture he prayed that rocks were not lurking in the rippling grass. Skimping on maintenance increased engine failures, dead-stick landings, and accidents. When a barnstormer was short on money he often pushed his luck, flying with a skipping motor and shimmying struts. He was always one uninsured mishap away from the loss of his capital and possibly his life.[26]

Chance, bankruptcy, and sudden death were the givens of life in the gold fields, where men saw little distinction between what they did for work—hunting for gold—and what they did for recreation—trying their luck at the faro table. "I have seen men come tottering from the mines with broken constitutions, but with plenty of the 'dust,' and sitting down at the gaming table, in ten minutes not be worth a cent," the forty-niner Alfred Doten wrote to his father. Even those who shunned gambling felt uncertain of their fortunes. "Took a walk among the diggings. Some of the miners are making good wages—others barely paying expenses," Bernard Reid noted in his diary. "All seems a lottery."[27]

A barnstormer's fate was just as unpredictable. Bad weather and accidents brought hardship, good weather and an untapped town brief prosperity. Basil Rowe devised a prospecting system. He flew low over a town and watched what happened. When the animals fled and the children tried to follow, he had found "virgin territory" and hunted for a convenient landing field. Offering its owner and his family free rides, he would set up a base of operations, lugging his gas cans to town for fuel. Roscoe Turner also worked the fresh veins. "As long as I could get passengers," he recalled, "there was no reason to leave a town." W. H. Parker ate beefsteak and slept in a feather bed when the trade was brisk. Then business would fall off, and he would have to make do with peanuts for supper and a bedroll under the wing.[28]

Barnstorming offered rewards other than intermittent prosperity. "For all their primitive knowledge and primitive equipment," Basil Rowe remembered, "the barnstormers had one thing in common—they loved to fly. . . . We lived flying, breathed it, talked it and slept it." Every hour of flying, Lindbergh agreed, had something worthwhile in it. He willingly assumed the risks, reckoning ten years spent as a pilot of greater value than "an ordinary lifetime."

Flying was socially as well as personally rewarding. Unlike most itinerant occupations, barnstorming conferred immense prestige. "I felt like a king," Walt Ballard remembered, "because that's the way people treated you." The barnstormer was always the center of attention, drawing curious farmers and children, dismissed from school to watch the flying. When they were not hopping from town to town, barnstormers enjoyed membership in an exclusive airmen's fraternity. Like most fraternities, it was both welcoming and competitive. A pilot who wandered into a late-night hangar bull session could expect practical jokes and salty gossip. But the bonds were lasting. Pilots formed friendships that survived frequent separations, the nature of their work ensuring that their paths would cross and recross over the years.

Women were another matter. "Many a barnstorming pilot slept with one woman one night, another the next, and never saw them again as he followed the wind and season," Lindbergh remembered. "A pilot I met in Nebraska was famed for his directness of approach on arriving at a new location. 'Do you or don't you? That's all I want to know,' he said as he canvassed a town's feminine possibilities." Barnstormers of a more subtle turn of mind relied on their planes, asking women if they would like to go up for a spin. "Aviation was romantic, adventurous, spectacular, and, except for timid creatures, the invitation seldom had to be extended twice."[29]

Lindbergh's candid account of barnstormers' sexuality, only hinted at in the euphemistic popular literature of the 1910s and 1920s, bears on a paradox of human nature. Unnecessary risk-taking is most common among young males, something that can be demonstrated statistically for all cultures. Unnecessary risk-taking leads, on average, to shorter lives, something that can likewise be demonstrated statistically. This seems like a contradiction. Should not natural selection weed out those of reckless disposition? It does—though not necessarily their genes. In Darwinian terms, what counts is an organism's reproductive success. Men who take big chances can reap big sexual rewards. Warriors or gladiators or barnstormers who lead short lives can still broadcast their genes. "Old, bold pilots" may be scarce, but that is not necessarily true of their descendants. Of course, the cocky young pilots of the 1920s were not thinking in such grand evolutionary terms. They simply understood that gypsy flying let them have their way with the ladies.[30]

Mean World

Barnstorming flourished in the early to mid-1920s. Then the novelty faded, the Jennies wore out, and the Commerce Department began requiring airworthiness certificates for planes. "I was as resentful of the law invading my

Pilot W. E. Callander takes his girlfriend Beatrice Whalen for a spin near Sioux City, Iowa. Her smile says it all. The airplane was the ultimate dating machine.

free flying as the early settlers of the West had been when the barbed-wire fences put an end to their free ranging," Basil Rowe wrote, adding that independent fliers all felt the same way. It did not matter. The market was disappearing anyway. Lindbergh's 1927 solo transatlantic flight temporarily revived the demand for joyrides, but it faded again and petered out during the Depression.[31]

Most of the gypsy pilots who managed to keep flying did so by settling down and becoming fixed-based operators. They found a hangar and a runway somewhere, overhauled engines and sold planes, gave flying lessons, took passengers on sightseeing and hunting excursions, contracted for aerial advertising, and provided taxi service for urgently needed parts and vaccines. During Prohibition, they sometimes delivered medicines of the 100-proof variety. But the typical fix-based operator had "little capital and makes only a fair living out of all his activities," Sherman Fairchild wrote in 1929. He persisted because he refused to give up the sky for "the humdrum ground."[32]

Many thought the ex-barnstormers' financial troubles were of their own making, that their harebrained stunts and crack-ups had made people afraid of flying. That was true, though only part of the story. After all, barnstormers had made a positive contribution to air-mindedness every time they had sideslipped into an alfalfa field and taken up a few curious passengers. Most people enjoyed their rides. Some became converts. "I love you and I'm going to be just like you," Tex Johnston told the pilot who took him above Emporia. Johnston went on to become a legendary test pilot, the man who put the 707 prototype into a slow barrel roll over the heads of astonished Boeing executives. Paul Tibbets, another barnstormer-struck kid, piloted the *Enola Gay* over Hiroshima. He remembered the mission as far less exciting than his first flight over the Hialeah race track. Young Howard Hughes, accompanied by his reluctant father, went on a five dollar seaplane ride. He later built the largest seaplane in history.[33]

Joyriding, however, was the benign side of the calling. In their exhibition performances, in their plane-swapping and death-dive acts, the barnstormers reinforced every stereotype of flying as a dangerous and disreputable sideshow. "We deliberately missed death by inches," admitted "Slats" Rodgers, "and we played the sucker wherever we could find him." Lieutenant Donald Duke, chief of the Army Air Corps' Airways Section, could barely contain his rage. The "nefarious practice of winged imbeciles," he wrote in 1927, had hurt public confidence and retarded air travel. The only thing they had proved was that "forced abuse" and negligent maintenance could wreck the best planes. Flying with fabric so rotten it broke to the touch; using control sticks loose enough to fall out during loops; taking off with a pint of gas; stunting at low altitudes; plowing into houses, power lines, and panicked crowds, barnstormers' accidents caused 196 deaths and 351 injuries from 1921 through 1923. Fixed-based operators, who owned approximately the same number of planes, exacted less than one-eighth of their toll.[34]

Barnstormers' stunts and mishaps were magnified by the newsreels, the silent (and after 1927, talking) cinematic tabloids that specialized in spectacles and disasters. Still seen in documentaries about the 1920s, these carnivalesque images of flight originated as stunts for hire. One newsreel company paid a Cherokee Indian named Whitefeather fifty dollars to hang from a plane by his braided ponytail. Dean Smith signed a contract with Fox Newsreel to loop the Brooklyn Bridge for five hundred dollars and land on the roof of the Pennsylvania Hotel for another twenty-five hundred. He never collected. City

"Folks came to events like this to see airmen killed," remembered barnstormer Roger Q. Wilson, "and went home disappointed if all crew members lived through the dangers of the day's work." Happy to play along, Wilson painted a large skull and crossbones on the fuselage of his plane.

officials nixed both schemes. Race officials were more accommodating. Set-course events, such as the National Air Races, offered drama, action, risk, crowds, colorful personalities, and easy production. Heavy cameras could be prepositioned near pylons and other strategic positions along the race course, simplifying filming.[35]

Flying attracted feature filmmakers, though their preferred subject was aerial combat over the western front. *Wings* (1927), featuring two dogfighting pilots quarreling over Clara Bow, won the first Academy Award. Highly realistic for its time, *Wings* producers had taken over the Air Corps Training School and used its student pilots for the mass-formation scenes. Barred from paying them directly for their services, the grateful filmmakers endowed the Kelly Field mess hall, leaving future cadets to marvel at breakfasts of steaks, oysters, and fresh eggs.[36]

Howard Hughes, an independently wealthy film producer and private pilot, had even deeper pockets. During the three years required to make *Hell's Angels* (1930), he assembled eighty-seven vintage aircraft, hired more than seventy pilots, and spent $3.8 million, a sum not surpassed until David O. Selznick pulled out the stops for *Gone With the Wind* (1939). Several of Hughes's fliers were stunt pilots and barnstormers. Roscoe Turner flew a giant Sikorski S-29 disguised as a German Gotha bomber. Another veteran, Al Wilson, piloted the big plane during its final crash scene. A prop man named Phil Jones, feeding lamp black into blowers near the tail, failed to bail out in time. He and the plane smashed into an orange grove. Three pilots also died during the filming, killed while making forced landings in the antiquated equipment or stunting for the amusement of the ground crews.

On May 27, 1930, *Hell's Angels* opened at Grauman's Chinese Theater, with a Fokker biplane hanging in its lobby and parachutists descending on Hollywood Boulevard. It played to packed houses for the next nineteen weeks. In a way, it kept on playing for years. Hughes shot more than three million feet of film, but selected only fifteen thousand feet for *Hell's Angels.* The unused footage turned up in at least seven other movies, including the dogfighting and bombing sequences in Hughes's own *Sky Devils* (1932).[37]

The social world of these movies was intensely masculine, at times misogynic. Aviation films of the 1920s and 1930s often presented the female lead as a greater threat to the aviator and his pals than enemy fighters. Women sparked feuds among pilots, mucked things up, and failed to appreciate the right stuff. They were incapable, wrote Robert Wohl, "of understanding the virile feelings and higher ethic that drive aviators to fly and risk their lives." The same was true of the classic Hollywood westerns, the plots of which featured collective masculine adventures set in ranching and Indian country. Respectable female characters applied civilization's brakes, fretting about wayward men and removing the ones they married from their old haunts and pards.[38]

Aviation action movies reinforced stereotypes of airplanes as dangerous, combustible, crash-prone, and minatory machines. Hollywood dogfighting represented an early version of the "mean-world syndrome," the tendency of sensational media content to foster pessimistic or fearful views. (Heavy viewers of television news, for example, worry more about stranger-perpetrated violent crime.) No one correlated frequency of movie attendance with attitudes toward aviation in the 1920s and 1930s, so the effect cannot be measured precisely. But reports of movie-inspired nightmares and angry complaints by aviation boosters, who groused about "hair-raising crack-ups and death every reel," hint that the effect was real. Film stunts heightened fears of what was acutally a rare form of death. The western genre had done the same thing with frontier violence, only retrospectively and on a grander scale. Buffalo Bill's Wild West, the dime novels of Prentiss Ingraham and Ned Buntline, the cowboy movies of William S. Hart and Tom Mix had magnified, ritualized, and ennobled the localized, transient, and often drunken violence of the post–Civil War frontier, repositioning it at the very center of national myth.[39]

Though political and moral ambivalence about World War I precluded a similar fate for dogfight movies, Hollywood appropriated wartime aviation no less surely than it seized on frontier violence. The movie ace's chattering machine guns and his victim's plunging plane were of a piece with the barnstormer's flying circuses and the newsreels' birdman antics. They all exploited flight to thrill mass audiences. The price of the entertainers' artifice, largely borne by others, was fear of real flying.

There was an exhilaration to flying an airplane in those days: their slow speed and light wing-loadings allowed short turns, sharp dives, and quick pull-outs that are impossible in faster planes. We did not rely on gauges and indicators; we flew by feel, noting the control pressures on our hands and feet, the shifting weight of our bodies, and the pitch of the singing wires.

—DEAN SMITH, *BY THE SEAT OF MY PANTS*

CHAPTER 4

The Next Thing to Suicide

One branch of postwar aviation required no artifice to impress the public of its risks. It did so simply by killing off most of its pilots. In the early 1920s, flying the U.S. Mail was one of the most dangerous occupations on earth. When Dean Smith, broke and desperate to keep flying, forsook barnstorming for the Air Mail Service in 1920, his friends at the American Flying Club threw him a farewell party. "Everyone considered the Air Mail the next thing to suicide," he remembered. With the pay, though, "you could at least be comfortable while life lasted."[1]

Smith's new line of work had begun as a philatelic sideshow. In the 1910s, exhibition pilots had carried specially marked cards and letters on short hops, flying a few miles from the local fairground to a nearby post office. Though the pilots took oaths as mail carriers and had route numbers assigned to their flights, the post office was just playing along with a gimmick. Still, it was a good omen. The post office had a history of using novel forms of transportation to speed the mails. Its patronage had advanced coaches, steamships, and trains. Some day it might do the same for the airplane.

On May 15, 1918, the U.S. Post Office started offering regular airmail service to Washington, D.C., Philadelphia, and New York. The army furnished the pilots, mechanics, and planes; the post office the fuel, mail, and stamps.

(Among them, the famous sheet of twenty-four-cent carmine-rose stamps with the inverted blue Jenny.) The project began inauspiciously. The first northbound Washington pilot took off late, got lost, and cracked up his plane. But Otto Praeger, the second assistant postmaster general, persisted. He acquired more planes and civilian pilots and pushed westward, reaching Chicago on September 5, 1919, Omaha on May 15, 1920, and San Francisco on September 8, 1920. Praeger pushed his pilots, too. His style, Ham Lee remembered, "was to look out his window and, if he could see the Capitol dome, you had to fly, no matter where you were." In February 1921, hoping to impress the incoming Harding administration, Praeger experimented with transcontinental night operations. Strictly a one-off affair—the pilots navigated by bonfires—the trial marked the beginning of a four-year struggle to add regular nighttime service.[2]

Major Reuben H. Fleet, the man in charge of the army's mail planes and pilots, points to a road map on his leg. He has just completed a ferrying trip to the old Washington Polo Grounds. Another pilot, George Boyle, took off on the inaugural mail flight to Philadelphia, flew in the wrong direction, and broke his propeller when he set down in a plowed Maryland field. With the exception of Boyle, mail pilots were fine as long as they could see the ground. The danger lay in poor visibility conditions, when pilots could stray from course, run out of gas, or become disoriented.

Flying the Mail

Day or night, airmail was scheduled mail. Pilots could not wait until they had accumulated a full load or fly only when conditions were good. Under post office pressure to demonstrate the service's dependability, and hating the thought that others might succeed in making a run they had abandoned, they often flew small loads through bad weather—or unexpectedly into it, weather reports being spotty and unreliable. Without instruments and radio beacons to guide them, pilots caught in clouds or fog could become disoriented and lose control of their planes. The westerly routes heightened the danger. Pilots flying from New York to Cleveland and on to Chicago passed through the worst spring-weather corridor in the country, and through one of the worst corridors for fall and winter weather. Ceilings often fell below one thousand feet, with visibility less than three miles.[3]

Some tried flying above the overcast. They used their clocks to judge the distance traveled, then dropped down through the murk, hoping to spot the tiny landing fields. Pilot James D. Hill smoked his way to a safe landing, reckoning the distance between Bellefonte and Sudbury, Pennsylvania, at one-and-a-half cigars. Others tried to fly under the weather, dodging steeples and telephone lines. Navigation meant memorizing visual landmarks, the same trick Sam Clemens had learned as a cub riverboat pilot in the 1850s. Follow the railroad switchback up Rattlesnake Mountain, Smith was advised. The town of Clearfield has three round reservoirs. The white gravel road leads straight to Du Bois. It was all fine and well as long as Smith could see.

And as long as his engine worked. The early airmail pilots mostly flew war-surplus DH-4s whose Liberty engines were prone to quit without warning. If an engine went out over western Pennsylvania, a pilot was in real trouble. Long stretches of ridges, mountains, and woods made finding a clear, flat place to land impossible. The same fate befell pilots who got lost and ran out of fuel over rough terrain. The DH-4, which carried "a hatful of mail and a couple of hours' gas," had a range of just 250 miles. Its open cockpit made winter flying an ordeal. Lean into the slipstream on a winter's night, Lindbergh wrote, and you felt as though a nail were piercing your forehead. Frozen pilots suffered lapses of judgment. Or they drank, subscribing to the fallacious folk remedy of liquor to ward off the cold.[4]

Waiting out bad weather was always an option, though any pilot who exercised it risked his reputation. The mail line's status sphere revolved around a simple maxim: nobody will fly over me, taking the mail through when I can't. One day Dean Smith and Wesley Smith, a cigar-smoking pilot known for his stubbornness, were both flying out of Cleveland. As Dean Smith told the story, they ran into fog. He returned to the field, and Wesley did the same—reluctantly, as he did not know whether his rival had landed. "First thing he said was: 'Where's Smith?' And he shot out his words: 'Gas her up, goddamn it.' Then he saw me standing there. And he smiled such a smile. He didn't try to go any further that day."[5]

But he did on other occasions, wrecking fifteen planes in the process. Competitiveness compounded the dangers of poor weather, inadequate airfields, and unreliable planes. All but nine of the original forty pilots were dead within eight years, and a total of forty-three persons had died by 1927. The early years were the deadliest. One in six pilots died in 1920—Russian roulette odds. Pilots addressed posthumous letters to their pals, with instructions that they be opened after their deaths. ("I go west, but with a cheerful heart . . .") Crack-ups were common. Few noticed unless someone was killed or crippled. The pilot simply transferred the mail to the nearest train and reported in: "On Trip 4 westbound. Flying low. Engine quit. Only place to land on cow. Killed cow. Wrecked plane. Scared me. Smith."[6]

As with exhibition flying, money tempted pilots to stay in the game. An experienced pilot could earn three hundred dollars a month in the early 1920s, four hundred dollars if he flew multi-engine planes. Not bad when a quart of milk cost fifteen cents. But Smith, who wrote the classic apologia of the pilot's life, chose to emphasize its nonmaterial rewards:

> People often asked me why I liked being a pilot, why I flew the mail and took such chances of getting killed. I would try to explain, but never could find the words to explain it all. I knew that I could fly and fly well, and this skill set me apart from the run of the mill. I certainly had no wish to get killed, but I was not afraid of it. I would have been frightened if I had thought I would get maimed or crippled for life, but there was little chance of that. A mail pilot was usually killed outright. Then, too, sometimes I was called a hero, and I liked that.
>
> One of the most rewarding things about a mail pilot's job was the high pay and the high percentage of leisure time, which made for a merry life, even if indications were that it might be a short one. As a normal thing we worked two or three days a week, five or six hours a day, plus standing reserve perhaps one day a week, which only meant keeping the field advised how they might reach us. I spent my time as unproductively as possible: learning to play golf, chasing girls, reading omnivorously and indiscriminately; investigating dives and joints in the area; and—an interest that has remained with me ever since—trout fishing.

> But what I could never tell of was the beauty and exaltation of flying itself. Above the haze layer with the sun behind you or sinking ahead, alone in an open cockpit, there is nothing and everything to see. The upper surface of the haze stretches on like a vast and endless desert, featureless and flat, and empty to the horizon. It seems your world alone. Threading one's way through the great piles of summer cumulus that hang over the plains, the patches of ground that show far below through the white are for earthbound folk, and the cloud shapes are sculptured just for you. The flash of rain, the shining rainbow riding completely around the plane, the lift over mountain ridges and crawling trains, the steady, pure air at dawn take-offs, and the smoke from the newly lit fires in houses just coming to life below—these are some of the many bits that help pay for the tense moments of plunging through fog, or the somber thoughts while flying cortege for a pilot's funeral. It was so alive and rich a life that any other conceivable choice seemed dull, prosaic, and humdrum.

Often cited to evoke nostalgia for open-cockpit flying, Smith's words also reveal a good deal about risk and masculine self-image. It is an offbeat sort of macho, hero-speak tempered by poetic receptivity, an awareness of the aesthetic possibilities of a new setting of human perception and action: the sky as frontier of the soul. Still, it would be hard to compile a more masculine list of reasons to chance sudden death than popular admiration, monied leisure, sexual opportunity, trout fishing, and godlike elevation above "the earthbound folk."

There is something else about this passage and the book from which it was taken that is not generally known. Smith's original manuscript ran to 807 pages and fleshed out the business about "investigating dives" in lurid detail. The draft title, *Pilot's Progress,* evoked *The Rake's Progress:* Smith in the cathouse, Smith in the gambling hell, Smith in the drunk tank, Smith in the barroom shooting scrape. He behaved no better in the cockpit. He tried his hand at smuggling booze—on federal time, no less—and just missed a grandstand to impress his pals. Smith's editors were wise to cut. They turned a sprawling, confessional memoir into a tight, nostalgic masterpiece. But the manuscript reveals a young man as prone to vice escapades and risky pranks as the prospectors and cowboys of the Western frontier.

He shared one other trait with them: a fierce independence. No occupation offered greater personal freedom in the 1920s. Smith liked to tell a story about Jack Knight, who once spotted a barbecue from the air. Knight landed, taxied over, and joined in, repaying his hosts with rides and an acrobatic show.

The Cheyenne mail was five hours late that day. Smith amused himself by running down gray geese, decapitating one with the inner strut of his wing. He thought nothing of interrupting his flight to claim his headless prize—or to visit his friends, or see unfamiliar sights, or relieve himself in a convenient pasture. Stretching his six-foot-four frame, unzipping himself where he pleased, his was truly an individualistic frontier life—or lives, his plane granting him free passage from America's open skies to its still open western lands.[7]

Reform and Expansion

Smith's adventurous life could not last, and he knew it. It was predicated on three things—excessive risk, wrecked equipment, and unscheduled leisure—that no modern administrative regime can abide. To survive, the Air Mail Service had to reform.

Safety came first. The most obvious danger was the DH-4 itself, a round peg of a high-altitude, short-range bomber in the square hole of a low-altitude, long-distance mail service. Only the price was right. The army had donated one hundred planes, with spare parts and extra engines. But the DH-4s had to be modified. Drastically. Mechanics converted front cockpits into mail holds, replaced fabric with plywood, and rebuilt the Liberty engines, using stub-tooth gears less prone to shearing. When they were through, the engineers had made more than six hundred changes.

Aircraft maintenance, slipshod in the early days, improved. During the first three years, 1918 through 1920, mechanical failure caused more forced landings than weather. From 1921 through 1923, mechanical failures caused just three forced landings for every eight due to weather. During 1924 through 1926, it was just three in ten. Though the post office could not do much about fog and storms, it could issue advance warning over its field-to-field radio network. Beginning in 1922, it made parachutes available to its pilots, a precaution that saved several lives. Charles Lindbergh bailed out twice while flying contract mail. The first time he suffered an anxious moment when his plane, still running, circled around him as he floated toward a cornfield.

Small improvements added up to a large gain in safety. Though forced landings and damaged planes remained commonplace, the key safety index, fatalities per million miles, dropped from 7.62 in 1920, to 3.66 in 1921, to just 0.57 in 1922. A celebrated run of no fatalities between July 1921 and September 1922, won the Air Mail Service the 1922 Collier Trophy, an annual award by the National Aeronautic Association for the greatest achievement in aviation.[8]

There was still the problem of foul weather. In the fall of 1924, mail pilots got a new instrument, the gyroscopic turn indicator. Used in conjunction with the bank indicator (originally a glass tube like a spirit level), it permitted disoriented pilots to regain and maintain level flight. Its effective use required them to learn a difficult trick, one that would be taught to later generations as a matter of course: in poor visibility trust your instruments. They were far more reliable than a pilot's sense of orientation, which could become confused whenver the horizon disappeared from view.

Instruments spared Lindbergh at least one parachute jump. Like other pilots trained during or immediately after the war, his instructors had taught him to distrust instruments. A "good pilot" did not need them. But Lindbergh, more cautious than most pilots and more technologically farsighted, had talked his employer into buying the new gyroscopic pitch-and-turn indicators. One night, en route between St. Louis and Springfield, the ceiling dropped too low for contact flying. Lindbergh pulled his stick back and studied the unfamiliar needles. At first he found coordination difficult. As he fought for altitude, his plane started skidding. When he concentrated on his turn and bank, he let his air speed drop, stalling the plane. He recovered, stalled again, recovered a little faster, and realized that if he could simultaneously keep the turn indicator centered and his airspeed high he would be fine. "I taught myself to fly by instruments that night," he recalled. He never forgot the lesson.

This was a common story. The old hands scoffed at the new gadgets. Then experience, often in the form of an unexpected encounter with blind weather, demonstrated their value. By decade's end, mail pilots were flying with confidence through night and fog. Now their problem became unmarked buildings. Twice in 1929, mail planes just missed colliding with the fog-enshrouded Capitol dome. It was still without warning lights.[9]

Improved lighting was another key to airmail expansion. In 1920, when the post office first offered transcontinental service, its pilots beat trains across the country by less than a day. But what would happen if they also flew after dark, passing over the mountains by day and the flat Midwest by night, hopping from field to field? Praeger's February 1921 experiment provided the answer. The total elapsed time of the first transcontinental day-and-night trip, thirty-three hours and twenty-one minutes, took a third of the time required to send mail by rail, despite the absolute priority given fast mail trains.

Like the transcontinental railroad it would one day supercede, the transcontinental airmail system took time to build. It required four years of appropriation battles, emergency-field construction, changes in plane design (landing and navigation lights, illuminated instruments, emergency parachute

Pioneer of the night sky, Jack Knight flew three legendary legs of the first continuous mail flight across the United States. Taking off from North Platte on the night of February 22, 1921, he flew to Omaha, then through a snowstorm to Iowa City, then on to Chicago, where he arrived exhausted the next morning. On November 21, 1922, Knight, shown here next to his modified DH-4, made another experimental flight, this time to test radio equipment. His is the face of a man who has seen a lot.

flares), and hundreds of beacons. The beacons rotated atop fifty-three-foot steel windmill towers, visible at up to seventy-five miles in clear weather. Every night, caretakers unlocked their generator shacks, checked for vandalism by the local boys, and fired up the engines. The most isolated beacons ran off windmill-recharged batteries and used tork clocks or sun switches to turn themselves on and off. When construction was completed in 1925, the post office could offer year-round service on a 2,669-mile transcontinental airway from New York City to San Francisco, lit all the way to Salt Lake City. It was a tunnel through the night unlike any other in the world.

Pilots loved it. On a clear, moonless night the rotating beacons stood out as pulsating sparks against the scattered lights of sleeping towns. Looking ahead from his droning plane, Dean Smith saw them lined up reassuringly far ahead. Looking above, he saw an unpolluted sky ablaze with stars. Sometimes a meteor startled him with its sudden luminance. When he tired of the astral sights, he turned on his cockpit lights and pulled out a magazine. Each time he finished a page he tore it out, paused to check his trimmed ship's progress along the beacon-lit course, and tossed it from his cockpit. Night flying—in good weather, anyway—had become that easy.[10]

Night airmail expedited the transport of important cargo. A traveler who discovered he had left his dentures in a Chicago hotel room could have them sent by airmail and pick them up in New York City when his train arrived the next morning. The most common use, though, was for business correspondence and financial instruments. Mail collected after business hours in New York City could now be in Chicago the next morning. It cost a fraction of a long-distance telephone call, $4.65 for three minutes at 1925 rates. Advertising agencies discovered they could dispatch their copy for less by airmail than by telegraph. Every time a banker in San Francisco sent ten thousand dollars' worth of checks to New York City for deposit, he gained two dollars in interest by using airmail, well worth a few cents extra postage. Volume multiplied the savings. The New York–Chicago airmail alone saved one hundred thousand dollars monthly in interest. The Air Mail Service began to resemble Wells Fargo. Pilots carried pistols, ground crews pump-action shot guns. Armed security and an improving safety record translated into an airmail loss rate half that of registered packages sent by rail.[11]

The Birth of the Airlines

The Air Mail Service's most lasting contribution, however, was to lay the cultural and technological foundations of the commercial airline industry. Had its personnel not pioneered night and instrument flying, built a reliable system of meteorological and navigational aids, and demonstrated the feasibility of continuous transcontinental service, the airline boom of the next two decades would not have occurred. The post office had managed—the analogy is historian F. Robert van der Linden's—to do for the airplane what the U.S. military had done for mass production at its Springfield armory in the nineteenth century. It had used public money to demonstrate the revolutionary potential of a new technology in which private enterprise was hesitant to invest.[12]

The cost was high. In addition to 43 fatalities, 25 serious injuries, and 200 crashed planes, the Air Mail Service lost $12 million flying the mail from May 1918 through August 1927. But few would dispute superintendent Benjamin Lipsner's judgment that the experience gained was worth every penny. Not least, the Air Mail Service bequeathed to the airlines a nucleus of seasoned pilots. "Unostentatious and mild-mannered, they nevertheless include some of the hardest white men there are, outside the Marines," wrote one appreciative passenger. "They are front-rank pioneers of our day, out on the frontiers of what has been a very dangerous game—the type of men the pioneers who opened up the West would have understood perfectly."[13]

Airmail also provided the initial financial impetus for the airlines. In 1925, Congress passed the Air Mail Act, better known as the Kelly Bill. It was officially intended to encourage commercial aviation, unofficially to placate the railroads, which had historically opposed post office efforts to transport its own mail. Scheduled government airmail mileage over aerial routes, which required no roadbed maintenance, had tripled between 1920 and 1925, and railroad officials were getting nervous. The Kelly Bill privatized this growing system. The postmaster general was to collect bids for the existing transcontinental service and several new feeder routes. The new routes would link cities such as St. Louis to the main transcontinental airway, while providing revenue to American carriers and aircraft manufacturers. Contractors would be required to use U.S.-built equipment and hire federally licensed pilots.

By January 1926, the post office had awarded twelve feeder routes, stretching from Boston–New York in the east to Los Angeles–Seattle in the west. Ten were up and running, in some cases just barely, by the end of September. The transcontinental trunk line remained under post office control, though it too was privatized in 1927. Aviation financier Clement Keys's National Air Transport got the eastern section. Boeing Air Transport, equipped with its own Model 40-A mail planes, got the western section. By 1930, both companies had been absorbed into United Aircraft and Transport Corporation, the predecessor of United Airlines. It became the largest of the holding companies that would dominate the industry in the early 1930s.

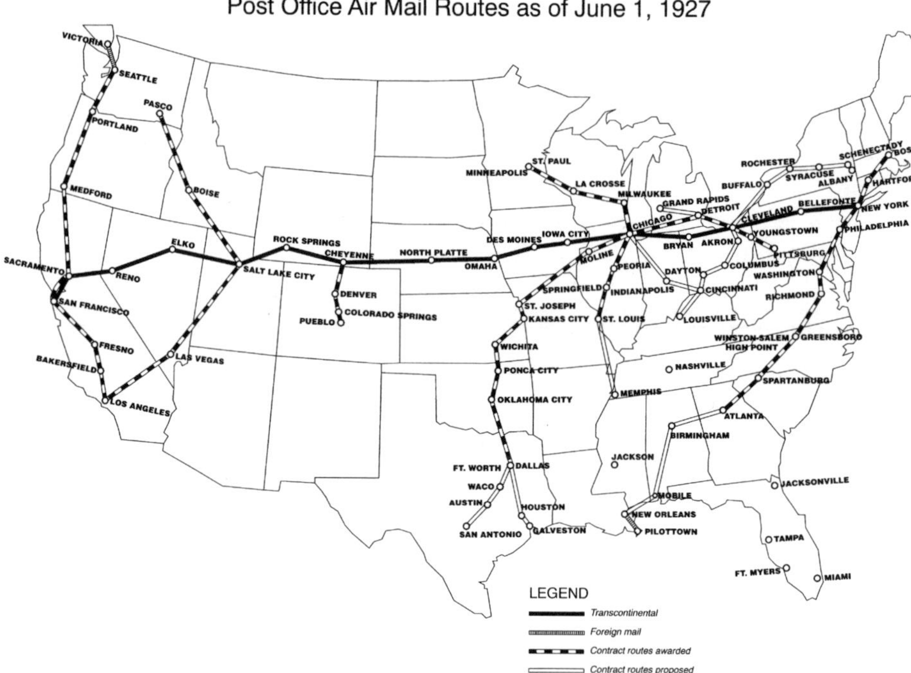

In 1927, the post office prepared a map showing the main east-west airway (the solid black line, roughly following the path of the original transcontinental railroad) and current or proposed contract feeder routes. Five of the feeder lines converged on Chicago, whose strategic position along the nation's lighted transcontinental airway assured its future as an air hub. Florida's cities were less fortunate. By the end of 1926, Florida Airways, which had connected Florida residents with Atlanta, had gone broke.

The going was a lot harder for the smaller feeder airlines. From July 1, 1926, all contractors had to operate on a poundage basis. The more mail they carried, the more revenue they earned. But airmail postage cost at least ten cents, and volume on the feeder routes was low. "A few dozen letters in, a few dozen letters out," was how Charles Lindbergh described the Peoria mail. He and other pilots on the St. Louis-Chicago route prayed for registered mail sacks. The brass locks meant a couple of extra dollars worth of weight. Flying time-sensitive freight like newsreels or machine replacement parts brought in some extra money, though air freight was still in its infancy in the late 1920s. It provided just 1 or 2 percent of the airlines' revenue.[14]

Contractors who invested in planes with cabins, such as the all-metal Ford-

Stout 2-AT, had another opportunity. They could add to their mail revenues by carrying passengers. Traveling salesmen, keen to stay ahead of the competition, and high-salaried executives, for whom time was money, were the natural market. William Stout, the designer of the 2-AT, pointed out that a $10,000-a-year businessman who averaged four months' travel could save $833 in "salary time" by flying. Riding in enclosed cabins, seated in comfortable wicker chairs, conversing with "little if any more" difficulty than in Pullman cars, these business travelers would become loyal customers.[15]

That was the theory, and time would bear it out. But in 1926, a year in which only 5,800 travelers bought airline tickets, the public still regarded airplanes as noisy, nausea-inducing, delay-prone, risky, and expensive means of transportation. The last two defects, fear and fare, were critical. Passengers would put up with some discomfort to save time (else the airline industry would have little history of which to write), but would refuse to fly if they regarded the enterprise as unsafe. Nor could they fly if ticket prices were out of reach.[16]

What happened to Florida Airways illustrates the problem. Despite modern equipment, good weather, and indirect subsidies such as prison labor for clearing landing fields, Florida Airways charged sixty dollars for a one-way Miami-Jacksonville ticket. With time savings of just a little over eight hours, that did not look like a bargain to many Floridians. Between June 1 and December 1, 1926, the airline flew only 939 passengers on its three seat-equipped planes: well under two passengers per plane per day. Total daily airmail seldom exceeded fifty pounds. Not all of that was kosher. The airline's agents mailed one another wet blotters to increase revenue. "Frequently this method was the only way Florida Airways could build up a pound of mail," cofounder Eddie Rickenbacker admitted in his memoirs. Before long, Rickenbacker's agents were mailing one another bricks. When a careless clerk dispatched an unwrapped specimen, bearing only stamps and an address label, a postal inspector put an end to Florida Airways' "airmail-augmentation program."

Ray Brooks, another ace turned Florida Airways executive, found the pilots' attitudes a sore point. "I wish there was some way," he wrote to Rickenbacker, "outside of getting hard boiled about it, to make all our pilots take a more personal interest in the company. They don't seem to care about the forms very much and as for getting things signed up in a hurry so that a mail [load] already half an hour late can be taken to town—no worry in the world. With two hours work a day, all they think of is getting down town to some confounded pleasure dive." Fed up with the informality, worn out trying to build airports in "cracker cities," and sensing financial disaster, Brooks bailed out in May 1926. Florida Airways, which never achieved significant passenger, mail, or freight volume, folded at the end of the year.[17]

Though it came too late to save Florida Airways, federal help for the struggling airlines was on the way. It took the form of regulatory legislation, something air-commerce advocates and business-oriented progressives had been lobbying for since the end of the war. What held them back was aviation's lack of credibility and financial clout. That changed in 1925, when Congress passed the Kelly Bill and Henry Ford announced he was going to build transport planes. Mail contracts and Ford money rekindled corporate interest. Outside the financial pages, Col. Billy Mitchell was making headlines with charges of aeronautical backwardness and mismanagement. Though Mitchell overstated his case and was court-martialed for insubordination, few Americans doubted aviation's strategic importance. Civil aircraft factories could quickly convert to war production; long-distance transports could link cities a continent apart. "But we are the aërial Rip Van Winkle of to-day," the navy's Clifford Tinker complained. "Bankrupt Europe is far ahead of us in commercial flying."[18]

It was in this atmosphere that Pres. Calvin Coolidge, a quiet friend of aviation, appointed a high-profile advisory commission to review the situation. The Morrow Board heard familiar testimony and made familiar recommendations for federal assistance. What mattered more than the contents of its December 1925 report was how it was said, and who said it. The chairman, Dwight Morrow, was a J. P. Morgan partner and close friend of the president. His board's blue-chip membership, moderate tone, and favorable publicity gave weight to the call to stabilize and promote the aviation industry.

The table thus set, Congress served up the 1926 Air Commerce Act. Southern Democrats, worried about expanded federal power, resisted, but lacked the votes to kill the bill. The final version charged the secretary of commerce with establishing airways and air-traffic rules; building, operating, and improving navigational aids; licensing pilots; registering planes and certifying their airworthiness; and investigating accidents. When the new regulations took effect, at midnight on December 31, 1926, air transport resembled the shipping industry. Privately owned companies operated under federal regulation and with federal navigational assistance. (Indeed, the new lighted airways fell under the management of the Bureau of Lighthouses.) Only the municipal airports, the "docks" of the system, remained under local control.[19]

Notable exceptions to the passivity of the Coolidge years, the 1925 and 1926 legislation had far-reaching consequences for American aviation. These laws did for national airways expansion what the 1785 Land Ordinance and 1787 Northwest Ordinance had done for expansion across the Ohio River: postal contracts and safety regulations served as the equivalents of cheap land and orderly political development. The 1926 law also tied up a strategic loose end.

It authorized the president to nationalize critical airspace, the secretary of war to designate military airways, and the secretary of the treasury to limit "ports of entry" for foreign aircraft, otherwise forbidden to operate within the United States. The skies above America were now sovereign territory.[20]

More legislation was forthcoming. When initial revenues proved insufficient to meet the airlines' operating costs, Congress cut airmail rates from ten cents for the first half-ounce to five cents for the first ounce. Volume doubled within a month. Airline revenue jumped from $4.0 million in fiscal 1928 to $11.2 million in fiscal 1929. The Foreign Air Mail Act, passed in 1928, set overseas contract rates. It authorized up to two dollars a pound, though only for "responsible" bidders who could "satisfactorily perform the service." Pan American, which had sewn up most of the key routes and landing rights in and around the Caribbean, exploited this provision to achieve a de facto monopoly. The airline asked for and got the maximum rate on most of its runs.[21]

Help for the infant airlines would also come from another, unexpected quarter. One moonlit night in September 1926, on a routine flight over the Illinois plains, a twenty-four-year-old mail pilot conceived a bold idea. Stuck in a lumbering DH-4, bored and looking for a challenge, Charles Lindbergh turned his mind to the fast and efficient new Bellanca monoplane. Aviation would have a great future, he thought, if people really understood the potential of such aircraft. Whisking mail and passengers from St. Louis to New York in eight or nine hours might make them forget the images of barnstorming and wrecked planes and the high costs that held aviation back. A plane such as the Bellanca, fitted with oversized fuel tanks, could fly through the night and into the next day. It could fly—the notion startled him—across the ocean, nonstop from New York to Paris. With the right equipment and the right plan it would not even be that dangerous. Not much more dangerous, anyway, than flying the winter mail.[22]

In my profession, you only fall once.

—CHARLES LINDBERGH, QUOTED IN *UNDER A WING*

CHAPTER 5

The Protestant Ethic and the SPIRIT OF ST. LOUIS

More than any single event, Charles Lindbergh's transatlantic flight of May 20–21, 1927, succeeded in making Americans air-minded. More than any single person, more even than Wilbur Wright, the combative visionary whose life was cut short by exhaustion and illness, Lindbergh came to personify American aviation. And more than any single plane, the *Spirit of St. Louis* came to symbolize the triumphant turn of American aviation.

"How did he make it in that thing?" Sen. Barry Goldwater wondered every time he saw the *Spirit of St. Louis* hanging in the museum. This was a common reaction, even among experienced fliers like Goldwater. Lindbergh himself, when he saw his plane in 1940, was struck by its size. "Such a small plane," he wrote in his journal. "I felt about it as I once felt about the old Wright biplanes." Weighing just 1,930 pounds empty, less than most compact cars, the plane has appeared to generations of visitors a precarious means for the heroic act that awakened millions to the possibilities of aviation.[1]

But there was something else there, something even more important than Lindbergh's personal determination and courage. Both the plane and the man embodied the two cardinal virtues, safety and efficiency, that revolutionized air transport in the mid-twentieth century. Lindbergh built, equipped, and flew the *Spirit of St. Louis* for just $13,500, landing in Paris three hours ahead of schedule and with enough reserve fuel for another one thousand miles. (He toyed with the idea of circling Paris, dipping his wings, and flying on to Rome, but wisely decided to land at Le Bourget Aerodrome.) When, in the triumphant aftermath of the flight, he became the great apostle of commercial aviation, Lindbergh made safe and efficient operation the foundation of his message. That he came to realize that rationalization was killing the profession he loved, and that aviation threatened the natural environment he valued above all else, adds a measure of tragic self-awareness to his heroic story.

The Pilot

Lindbergh's love of the land had its roots in his Minnesota childhood. He swam naked in the Mississippi, got his first rifle at six, and listened to his father tell stories of marauding Indians, woods full of animals, and skies black with ducks. Charles absorbed his father's rugged individualism and frontier-generalist outlook. "As a lawyer, my father harnessed a horse to carry on his business. As a young pilot, I unlashed my wings from fence posts, and pulled through my own propeller. But my father and I knew the feel of rain and the smell of the ground, and there was time for our thoughts to wander. When night came, our muscles put our brains to sleep."[2]

By circumstance and temperament, Lindbergh was an indifferent student. His father's congressional career interrupted his education; classroom instruction left him cold. Only two things interested him, nature and machines. As a boy, he lingered at the hardware store, studying the latest gadgets on the shelf. He drove his father's Model T at eleven, owned an Excelsior motorcycle at eighteen. He ran the family farm at sixteen, hooking the gang plow to the tractor and pulling it through the western forty. One evening the lift mechanism jammed, upsetting the plow. The share missed his head by inches. Machines saved labor, he realized. But when it came to safety, they were unforgiving.

Lindbergh studied mechanical engineering at the University of Wisconsin. Inattentive and tired of drafting boards, he flunked out in his second year. Still fascinated with planes, he enrolled in a Nebraska flying school. The sky was his safety valve, his escape from the hated indoors. "Trees become bushes; barns, toys; cows turn into rabbits as we climb," he wrote of his first flight. "I live only in the moment in this strange, unmortal space, crowded with beauty, pierced with danger." He was smitten. "Science, freedom, beauty, adventure: what more could you ask of life? Aviation combined all the elements I loved."

Though Lindbergh never entirely lost his enthusiasm for flying, his romantic perception of it soon gave way to a cool professionalism. As he put it, experience calloused the senses. Cows no longer seemed like rabbits, barns no longer like toys. The sky itself became familiar, altitude a matter of calculated distance. "I can read the contour of the hillside that to the beginner's eye looks flat. I can translate the secret textures and the shadings of the ground. Tricks of wind and storm and mountains are to me an open book."

These words, from *The Spirit of St. Louis,* echo literature's most famous expression of professional disenchantment. In *Life on the Mississippi,* Mark Twain described a riverine sunset so astonishing it left him speechless. When Twain learned his piloting craft, however, he judged the sunset only for what it told him of tomorrow's winds, studied the water's marks only for signs of a fatal reef. The passenger might see charm and beauty in the scenic book of the river, but for the pilot it was "the most dead-earnest of reading-matter," with life and death in its italicized passages.[3]

Lindbergh learned to read the corresponding dangers in the sky. He knew he could not entirely avoid them. Nor did he wish to. He regarded danger as the essential spice of life. Nothing worthwhile could be accomplished without risk. Yet risk was something that could be anticipated, measured, and to some degree controlled. Like the Wright brothers who preceded him or the astronauts who followed, he specialized in "dangerous situations, tackled rationally, with risk factors correctly analyzed and judgment unclouded by fear." It was his judgment, rather than any extraordinary piloting skill, that carried him safely across the Atlantic.[4]

That judgment was in evidence from the unpropitious beginning of his career as "Daredevil Lindbergh," parachute jumper and wing walker. Like most aviators of the day, he made his living by entertaining crowds. He thought he could do so safely if he used proper equipment, proper technique, and flew with a proper pilot. He knew it was not a parachute jump or simian stunt, done with cables invisible to the gasping crowd, that would kill him. It was a doofus in the cockpit, someone from the bottom of the status heap:

> I studied every pilot who passed through Lincoln. Was he a "mechanical" flyer, or did he have the "feel" of his plane? How many hours had he logged? How many times had he crashed? What standards of maintenance did he hold? Was he afraid of wind and weather? Did he fly when he was drunk? Visitors who landed on our field never realized the care with which each detail of their lives was watched. And how we admired their qualities and criticized their defects: "He skids on his turns." "His tail's too high taking off." "He over-controls—did you see

those ailerons flap when he was coming in to land?" "Boy, *he* always makes 'em three-point!" This man I would be willing to fly with; that man, I would not.

When Lindbergh acquired a Jenny in 1923, he solved the problem by becoming his own pilot, an arrangement he would prefer for the rest of his life. Endowed with unusual stamina, quick reflexes, 20/15 vision, and steady nerves—in college he had been the best marksman on the best rifle team in the nation—he became a proficient flier. At a time when many barnstormers showed up in the morning "so hung-over they just felt around the fuselage till they found a hole and climbed in," Lindbergh neither drank nor smoked. He did not even take coffee with him on his Paris flight. His abstemiousness was one thing everyone remembered about him, the virtue being as rare in the piloting fraternity of the 1920s as it had been among cowboys and miners fifty years before.[5]

Barnstorming gave Lindbergh a chance to hone his mechanical skills. He served as his own mechanic and rigger, cleaning spark plugs, adjusting valves, replacing propellers, stitching torn fabric, and attending to a hundred other tasks, any one of which, if botched or neglected, could wreck his ship. He got his education in aeronautics at the most practical level. But he knew empiricism had its limits. He got tired of flying a patched-up, underpowered plane, tired of trying to make a buck in towns that had been "barnstormed out." A chance acquaintance suggested he joined the Army Air Service. He could fly a DH with a 400 hp engine and leave the maintenance to someone else. Lindbergh hesitated. He loved the "world of clouds and sky, and the great geographical expanses of the West," the freedom to point his plane in any direction on the compass. But the prospect of hot planes and no financial worries won out. He lined up the necessary recommendations through his father, took the tests, passed them, and reported for duty at Brooks Field in San Antonio on March 15, 1924.[6]

Lindbergh and the army were made for one another. Motivated now, as he had not been in his schoolboy days, he excelled in flight school, finishing at the top of his class. He mastered navigation skills that would prove indispensable to his transatlantic flight. Graduating as a second lieutenant in 1925, he rose to the rank of captain in the Officers' Reserve Corps in November 1926. (After his 1927 flight, he got a colonelcy and a Medal of Honor, capping the most spectacular two-year career rise in the army's peacetime history.) The officers who examined him for his reserve captaincy described him as frank, capable, and engaging, "a man of good moral habits," likely to "successfully complete everything he undertakes."[7]

What he undertook, after winning his wings, was another round of barnstorming. There were no active-duty slots available in the army's peacetime squadrons. He printed up a business card, touting midair plane changes and high-altitude "deaf flights" to cure the hearing-impaired, evidently on the homeopathic principle of "like cures like." In late 1925, he signed on as chief pilot for the St. Louis-based Robertson Aircraft Corporation, which had won the contract for the St. Louis–Chicago mail route. Lindbergh did his usual conscientious job, surveying the terrain, hiring the pilots, promoting the service before Chamber of Commerce luncheons. He and his fellow pilots completed 98 percent of their scheduled flights, despite some of the most unpredictable weather in the country. Then he grew restless. Routine flights offered nothing against which to match himself. "You simply sit, touching stick and rudder lightly, dreaming of the earth below, of experiences past, of adventures that may come." It was in one of these reveries, droning through the Illinois night, that he realized the right pilot, flying alone with the right equipment, could negotiate the 3,600 miles from New York to Paris and capture the Orteig Prize.[8]

There was no doubt in Charles Lindbergh's mind who the right pilot might be.

The Planner

"Some people believe the most important thing Charles Lindbergh contributed to the field of aviation was not the flight in the *Spirit of St. Louis* but the safety checklist," Reeve Lindbergh wrote in her memoirs. "As a pilot my father habitually kept comprehensive lists on all his equipment and all his flying procedures. He checked and rechecked these constantly to make sure that everything he did before, during, and after each flight was appropriate, and the aircraft was kept in top condition. It was a habit that saved his life more than once, and it most likely saved the lives of many other fliers who followed him." A man so obsessed by checklists that he assigned them to his own children, Lindbergh naturally began his great adventure by reaching for a pad.

At the head of his list, right after "plan," came "propaganda," "backers," and "equipment." Lindbergh knew that securing local financial backing and organization would be his greatest challenges. He began laying out his arguments:

> ADVANTAGES:
> 1. Revive St. Louis interest in aviation
> 2. Advertise St. Louis as an aviation city
> 3. Aid in making America first in the air

4. Promote nationwide interest in aeronautics
5. Demonstrate perfection of modern equipment

RESULTS:

1. Successful completion, winning $25,000 prize to cover expense
2. Complete failure

To guard against the latter, Lindbergh knew he needed more than the right equipment. He needed a different approach. His rivals were raising large sums to equip large planes crewed by up to four men. Too heavy, Lindbergh thought. Too complex. One pilot in a stripped-down plane stood the best chance.[9]

It was a hard sell. Single engine, single pilot? "That's *some* flight, Slim." He persisted, said he was prepared to invest his own money. By dint of compulsive thrift—Lindbergh never hesitated to move to cheaper digs to save a few dollars, or give flying lessons to pick up extra cash—he had saved two thousand dollars from his barnstorming and cadet days. He pushed it all into the pot. By year's end, his St. Louis backers had pledged another thirteen thousand. He had fifteen thousand dollars, enough for the new Wright-Bellanca he coveted. In February, he took the train to New York, delivered his cashier's check to the manufacturer, and was told that the company reserved the right to select the crew for the transatlantic flight. Lindbergh stalked out the door.

He had a backup. Ryan Aeronautical, a small San Diego company that built high-winged monoplanes, would assemble a modified version for the Atlantic competition. With several other groups preparing for spring flights, construction time was critical. Ryan agreed to complete the plane in sixty days for $10,580. Lindbergh camped out in the factory. He worked closely with the company's chief engineer, Donald Hall. At his drawing board for as much as thirty-six hours at a stretch, Hall was the one man who lost more sleep over the *Spirit of St. Louis* than its pilot.

"No airship will fly from New York to Paris," Wilbur Wright had prophesied in 1909. "What limits flight is the motor. No known motor will run at the requisite speed for four days without stopping." Had he lived to see the Whirlwind J-5-C air-cooled engine, he would have thought otherwise. Hall and Lindbergh knew the engine's average time-to-failure was nine thousand hours, or roughly 270 times what the pilot needed to reach Paris. Premature failure, and with it a forced landing or ocean ditching, could be catastrophic. But it was a low-probability risk.[10]

The graver danger was that the engine would run out of fuel before Lindbergh reached a safe place to land. That was one of the reasons he chose to fly alone: "I'd rather have the extra gasoline than the extra man." Hall agreed. One less pilot meant fifty more gallons. The plane he and Lindbergh designed was a flying tanker with oversized wings, "nine barrels of gasoline and oil, wrapped up in fabric." But fuel was heavy, six pounds a gallon, and a mortal danger in an overloaded plane. A pilot sandwiched between the engine and the fuselage tank would be just that if the plane crashed on take-off. So put the main tank in front of the pilot, Lindbergh instructed, and fair in the rear cockpit. Make the top of the fuselage the top of the cockpit, cutting drag. All he needed was a window on each side. "I think we ought to give first consideration to efficiency in flight," he told his engineer, "second to protection in a crack-up; third, to pilot comfort."

The preoccupation with fuel reflected Lindbergh's uncertainty about the length of the flight. If he encountered adverse winds, or got lost in a storm, or drifted off his dead-reckoned course, it might take him much longer than expected to reach land. His fuel reserve was his margin of safety. To maximize it, he stripped excess weight. "From the start, I've planned this flight on the principle that nothing can be wasted, that no detail is too small to be considered. I've made my own flying boots out of light material. I've bought small flashlights for my pocket, so that two would weigh no more than one of ordinary size. I've cut unneeded areas from my charts to gain some extra ounces."

Lindbergh and Hall paid close attention to the pilot's comfort and working environment, using the principles of what would one day be called ergonomic design. Lindbergh crossed the Atlantic in an air-cushioned wicker chair, instrument board within easy reach, in a cabin whose roof rib had been precisely hollowed to accommodate his helmeted head. "There's room enough, no more, no less," Lindbergh boasted. "My cockpit has been tailored to me like a suit of clothes."[11]

Lindbergh was just as fanatical about construction details, telling the mechanics to redo anything that was not to his liking. "Why does this damn plane have to be so perfect?" one of them asked.

"Because I'm a damn poor swimmer, that's why."

On another occasion Lindbergh told a mechanic to shorten up the oil lines. "Don't make any oil line more than 18 inches long and reconnect them with rubber hose."

"What for?"

"Well, most forced landings I've heard about on long hops were caused by a break in the oil line. From vibration."

Lindbergh's demands—backed by Hall, who held all work to a 1/32-inch tolerance—caused a good deal of grumbling among the Ryan factory workers. They did not need curt instructions on top of a seven-day week. But they came to respect Lindbergh's unwillingness to compromise and found themselves drawn into his quest. Before it was done, they had painted "We are sure with you" and all their names inside the plane's spinner cap. "There was no chatter now," a mechanic remembered of the last, busy days in April. "Everyone talked in low voices. Lunches were forgotten until 3:00 and 4:00 in the afternoon. Most of us thought, 'He can't miss now.'" Lindbergh was not so sure. He stayed in San Diego until he was certain he had a plane capable of spanning the ocean. He made a series of test flights using progressively heavier loads of fuel. He quit at three hundred gallons, reasoning that further tests posed more of a risk than a safety advantage.[12]

Charles Lindbergh made four nonstop flights of extraordinary length in 1927. He flew from San Diego to St. Louis, St. Louis to New York, New York to Paris, and Washington, D.C., to Mexico City. The first of these revealed a danger he had missed during the test hops in San Diego's balmy air: carburetor icing over the mountains. The engine's sporadic coughing came as bad news. The air over the North Atlantic, he thought, would be even colder. Staying a step ahead of disaster, he installed a carburetor heater when he reached New York. "He knew, when he took off, all that was possible to know," pilot Bob Buck wrote admiringly, "and he was as well prepared for it, relatively, as Neil Armstrong was when he blasted off for the moon."[13]

The ISOLATO

The plane performed flawlessly on its transatlantic flight. The pilot did not. Lindbergh made one serious miscalculation, a miscalculation born of competition. Hearing a report of clearing Atlantic weather, and anxious to steal a march on his rivals, he decided to take off early in the morning of May 20. He had hardly slept the night before. He knew he should be fresh for such a difficult flight. Then again, he had flown the mail without much sleep. His reserves of energy had carried him through other emergencies. He reasoned they would do so once more.

By the time he left the coast of Newfoundland, Lindbergh found himself in a tantalizing predicament. His engine was singing. He had plenty of gas and a good tail wind. Everything was perfect, except for his growing drowsiness. It soon became a torment, a monster he battled for the next sixteen hours across the Atlantic. Sleep invited two sorts of disaster, sudden and gradual. If he dozed off while flying blind (Lindbergh was to do as much instrument flying as during all his previous flights), he would lose control and crash. If he closed his eyes and drifted off his compass course, as he often caught himself doing, the cumulative navigational errors might take him hundreds or even thousands of miles away from his anticipated Irish landfall. That would leave him low on fuel and over unknown terrain.

Where, for that matter, was Charles Augustus Lindbergh? His body was traveling along a great-circle course, so many feet above the ocean, so many miles an hour, duly noted in his log until he could write no more. But his mind was somewhere else, somewhere on the very edge of human experience. If the sky was a frontier, Lindbergh became in those hours its ultimate *isolato.* "I weave in and out, eastward, toward Europe, hidden away in my plane's tiny cockpit, submerged, alone, in the magnitude of this weird, unhuman space, venturing where man has never been, irretrievably launched on a flight through this sacred garden of the sky, this inner shrine of higher spirits. Am I myself a living, breathing, earth-bound body, or is this a dream of death I'm passing through? Am I alive, or am I really dead, a spirit in a spirit world?"

The remarkable answer was that he *had* entered a spirit world. In his twenty-second hour, passing in and out of fog, staring at his instruments, simultaneously awake and asleep, Lindbergh began communing with ghosts. They filled his fuselage, glanced over his shoulder, kibitzed his flight. He showed no surprise. He felt at one with them, disembodied, independent of physical laws. The only difference, he thought, was that he maintained a tenuous hold on life.

He clung to that kernel of reality through the long, hallucinatory hours. Brain swimming, eyelids involuntarily shutting, still a thousand miles from Paris, he flexed his long limbs, bounced up and down, stamped the cockpit floor. Nothing worked. The alternative to wakefulness was failure and death. But that knowledge, the mere thought of dying, could not alter his neural chemistry, could not clear his exhausted brain. It took the electric current of a crisis—Lindbergh blacking out, losing control of his plane, thrusting his head into the slipstream to gulp reviving air, praying to God to give him strength—to regain control of his dulled senses. Lindbergh proved Dr. Johnson right. He required the imminence of death, what he called the very sight of it, to finally concentrate his mind, draw out his last reserves of energy, and break sleep's spell.

When at last he caught sight of a fishing fleet, drowsiness left him. Hope proved a more potent elixir than death. He was close to the European coast now, close to the safety of land. But whose land? He might be anywhere from Scotland to Spain. He studied the terrain's features, searched the chart spread across his knees. He had struck the southwest coast of Ireland, almost exactly on his dead-reckoned course! He had expected to be at least fifty miles

"Sea, clouds, and sky are all stirred up together—dull gray mist, blinding white mist, patches of blue, mottling of black, a band of sunlight sprinkling diamond facets on the water." Flying above, between, and below the clouds, sometimes so low the breakers' foam splashed his wheels, Lindbergh droned on, fighting the elements and his own overwhelming desire for sleep. Painting by William J. Reynolds.

off, and that with perfect conditions. He had flown through every sort of weather, semi-comatose, and had been off by three miles. "What was it?" he wondered. "Before I made this flight, I would have said carelessly that it was luck. Now, luck seems far too trivial a word, a term to be used only by those who've never seen the curtain drawn or looked on life from far away."[14]

For the rest of his life, Charles Lindbergh bridled at the most famous of his many nicknames, "Lucky Lindy." The tag has its defenders. Floridly hallucinating navigators do not, as an invariable thing, make their landfalls with such precision. And, precautions or no, Lindbergh had had several close calls in his barnstorming and airmail days. He was lucky to have made it as far as Long Island. Still, he had a point. He was always more of a planner than a gambler. He took calculated risks, but emphasized the calculation—a trait of character he shared with such aviation giants as Wilbur Wright, Juan Trippe, Donald Douglas, and Boeing's Bill Allen. Lindbergh's calculations had helped him through this, his greatest crisis. He and Hall had consciously built a slightly unstable plane, one that began turning every time the pilot relaxed the pressure on the stick or rudder pedals. That instability startled the dozing Lindbergh back to momentary alertness and forced him to recheck his course through the soporific hours of night and fog. Even if he had not managed so precise a landfall, he still had ample fuel reserves to scout out a safe place to land or adjust his course and fly on to Paris. That reserve was no lucky accident.[15]

Ireland, England, the Channel, Cape de la Hague . . . he could relax now. Darkness was falling again, but the weather was clear. At two thousand feet, one hundred miles out of Paris, he spotted a flashing beacon. His course was converging with the lighted London–Paris airway. His epic flight had resolved itself into the last, uncomplicated leg of a mail run on a clear night. He approached Paris, pitched his urine can, found Le Bourget, circled, and landed. His first words were not "I'm Charles Lindbergh," or "Well, I made it," or any of the other gush invented by the press. He said, "Are there any mechanics here?"

His words were lost in the surging, delirious crowd, already ripping souvenirs from his plane. Spirited off to the American ambassador's residence, he climbed into bed at 4:15 A.M. Paris time, some sixty-three hours after he had last slept. He awoke at 1:00 in the afternoon, "a little stiff but well rested, into a life which could hardly have been more amazing if I had landed on another planet instead of at Paris."[16]

The Hero

These last words, from the last paragraph of the last chapter of *The Spirit of St. Louis,* hint at another level of meaning, hint that Lindbergh intended his epic as a parable of death and rebirth. For surely he understood, as he reflected in middle age, polishing his book's ten drafts, that celebrity had imposed upon him a kind of death, ending his first life as abruptly as a plunge into the frigid sea. Charles Lindbergh—plain Slim, Carl, or Charlie to his barnstorming pals—did die during that ghost-haunted Atlantic crossing, only to be reborn into a new life as the Lone Eagle.

The reaction to his flight was astonishing. Taxis ten abreast jammed the boulevard to Le Bourget. Revelers passed libations from cab to cab, danced through the night, remembered the thrill for the rest of their lives. American newspapers ordered an extra twenty-five thousand tons of newsprint. One clipping bureau amassed 300,000 stories in twelve days, and those just from the New York papers. Poets ransacked myth's cupboard, apotheosizing Lindbergh in the name of every divine or heroic figure in the western tradition. Four million cheered his New York return; another thirty million, a quarter of the American population, saw him during his forty-eight-state tour in the *Spirit of St. Louis.* Hardened journalists wept with emotion. Old women and children, barely able to glimpse the hero's passing motorcade, wept with frustration. When Lindbergh spoke on radio, listeners had to turn down the volume to quiet the tumultuous applause. *Time* named him man of the year, the magazine's first. Some spoke of amending the Constitution to permit the twenty-five-year-old to run for president.[17]

Lindbergh disliked exhibiting himself—an odd feeling, he admitted, for an ex-wing walker. But that had been a show of rehearsed skill, of team coordination. The lone-hero act violated his sense of modesty and personal reserve. He felt more at home in the air than among jostling crowds. He took to idling down his engine (still running, he noted proudly, on the same transatlantic spark plugs) to rest and reflect between his goodwill stops. "I was astonished at the effect my successful landing in France had on the nations of the world," he later wrote. "To me, it was like a match lighting a bonfire. I thought thereafter that people confused the light of the bonfire with the flame of the match, and that one individual was credited with doing what, in reality, many groups of individuals had done."[18]

Historians have had the same thought. Why all the fuss over one pilot? Before May 1927, 117 airplanes and airships had crossed the Atlantic. But none had flown directly between major continental cities, and none had made the crossing with such speed and precision. Most critically, Lindbergh had flown alone. He had won the Orteig Prize as a dark horse, challenging more famous, better-financed, and larger teams in a dangerous race that had claimed four lives. He was, said one who witnessed his Paris arrival, "a real life hero, who exemplified all the attributes of the heroes of history and literature, the thrust for achievement, the individual accomplishing the impossible against all odds."[19]

That Lindbergh denied the lone-hero business, sharing credit with his St. Louis partners, his engineers, and his plane; that he used the plural pronoun when he spoke of his triumph; that he did all of this for the sake of truth and modesty was beside the point. Lindbergh's fate, as John Ward pointed out, was to be a type. His personal attributes (taciturn determination, self-discipline, rural upbringing, WASP ancestry, lanky frame: a better-looking Lincoln) and circumstances (improbable solo victory in a technologically progressive competition, free of militaristic taint) linked him to the core American traditions of self-sufficient individualism and mechanical mastery of nature. Americans were celebrating more than Lindbergh, sociologist Robert Merton observed. They were celebrating themselves—or what they imagined themselves to have been in a purer, simpler past, before the grafters and gangsters and flappers seized the day. "A young Minnesotan who seemed to have nothing to do with his generation did a heroic thing," F. Scott Fitzgerald wrote of the flight, "and for a moment people set down their glasses in country clubs and speakeasies and thought of their old best dreams. Maybe there was a way out by flying, maybe our restless blood could find frontiers in the illimitable air."[20]

The Promoter

Fame aged Lindbergh. Dean Smith, who in 1930 ran into Lindbergh in Panama, was startled by how "serious, reserved, dignified, definitely self-conscious" he had become. Lindbergh's carefree, practical-joking side—he had once daubed a sleeping barracks braggart's private parts with green paint—was gone, replaced by a dignified wariness. "There were more perils in being a hero," Smith realized, "than those that made you a hero."[21]

The most obvious peril was money. Endorsement offers poured in. There was nothing unusual in this, save for the sums involved. Charles Kingsford-Smith, Frank Hawks, Roscoe Turner, Lloyd Child, and other well-known fliers of Lindbergh's generation pulled up their goggles, smiled for the camera, and cheerfully lied about this or that cigarette. Amelia Earhart, who had her own line of travel clothes and luggage, milked the lecture circuit. Lindbergh refused all such offers. He turned down $500,000 to star in his own biopic opposite Hearst's mistress, Marion Davies. He was as incorruptible as Gandhi, and just as determined. He meant to use his celebrity for his cause, not for himself. The cause was the same one he had emphasized in his 1926 list of advantages. He would devote himself to promoting commercial aviation.[22]

His flight had already had a tonic effect. The stock of Wright Aeronautical, the manufacturer of his engine, jumped $2.5 million in value. The short-ride business prospered in the month after his Paris landing, as more first-timers stuck their toes in the air. Private airmail contractors enjoyed 200 to 300 percent gains by year's end. Aircraft stocks rose proportionately. Applications poured into flying schools, orders into factories. Ryan, which built the *Spirit of St. Louis,* added one hundred workers and still fell two months behind schedule. Twenty-three new passenger lines, most short-lived, began service in 1928. Passenger volume quadrupled over 1927. The Yellow Cab Company trademarked the name "Yellow Airways," just in case.[23]

Lindbergh worked to keep the momentum going. After hurriedly setting down his memoirs in *"We"*, a book that would sell 635,000 copies, he embarked on a cross-country tour. The tour's sponsor, the Daniel

Guggenheim Fund for the Promotion of Aeronautics, had provided the seed money for the gathering revolution in American aviation, creating or expanding the university programs that produced most of the country's senior aeronautical engineers. The fund's president—Daniel's son, Harry Frank Guggenheim, an enthusiastic ex-navy flier—wanted to encourage public air-mindedness. For this, Lindbergh was perfect. Stopping in eighty-two cities, arriving late only once in foggy Portland, Maine, he told his awed listeners to install beacons, paint their towns' names on roofs, use the airmail, and improve their local airports. The lack of good landing fields, Lindbergh knew, limited the plane's potential in the same way the lack of paved roads had limited the car's.

Though Lindbergh preached America in the air, his vision was international. Aviation, he thought, offered the prospect of breaking down prejudices among nations. He followed his American tour with a two-month Caribbean swing, part self-financed adventure, part aviation propaganda, and part last fling with the *Spirit of St. Louis.* Returning to the United States, and tiring of the relentless attention—admirers stole his clothes, the press his privacy—he decided to change promotional tactics. Henceforth he would play a behind-the-scenes role. He went to work as a route surveyor and technical advisor for two new airlines. One was Transcontinental Air Transport (TAT, called TWA after a 1930 merger created Transcontinental and Western Air). The other was Pan American.[24]

Lindbergh stressed safe and efficient operation. He planned the TWA routes with 180 emergency fields, 83 weather-reporting stations, 23 radio ranges, and beacons every 16 miles. He insisted that the new plane TWA ordered from Douglas Aircraft, the DC-1, be able to take off, fully loaded, from any TWA field, climb, and fly over the highest mountains, all on one engine. "I'll call you back," Donald Douglas said. But he delivered.

Lindbergh took a different tack with Pan Am. He initially recommended flying boats for its Caribbean and Latin American destinations, which had few good airports. Igor Sikorski's S-38 amphibian and S-40 designs reassured passengers. They liked a plane that carried its landing field in its bottom. But Lindbergh foresaw the limitations of heavy hulled airplanes. He wanted the unwieldy flying boats retired as soon as long-range land planes and concrete runways became available, a shift largely accomplished by the end of 1945.[25]

While surveying TAT's transcontinental route in 1928, Lindbergh's restless, anticipatory mind turned to another limitation, that of the airfoil itself. Was it possible, he wondered, to use rockets to travel through the vacuum above the atmosphere? When he met the rocket pioneer Robert Goddard the following year, Lindbergh at once became an enthusiastic supporter. He secured

Mexico's president, Plutarco Elías Calles, welcomes Charles Lindbergh after his twenty-seven-hour flight from Washington, D.C. Dwight and Elizabeth Morrow smile above their clasped hands. The American ambassador and his wife entertained Lindbergh over the 1927 Christmas holidays. When Lindbergh considered marriage the following year, his mind returned to their pretty, blue-eyed daughter, Anne. Inevitably, he made a checklist: good health and form, intelligence, honesty, a liking for planes. Anne filled the bill, both as his wife and flying partner.

Guggenheim funding for the reclusive scientist, and championed his work during the difficult Depression years. If humans were to realize speeds of more than a few hundred miles per hour, he wrote in 1937, they must look to the rocket, which had the potential to span continents, possibly planets. As the plane had conferred "freedom from the earth," the rocket promised freedom from the atmosphere itself.[26]

The Disenchanted Innocent

Charles Lindbergh's promotional activities on behalf of aviation and rocketry formed only a small and, as time passed, diminishing part of a remarkable career. He pursued medical research, explored naturalistic philosophy, campaigned against America's entry into the European war, flew combat missions in the Pacific theater, and wrote six more books. He traveled, relentlessly and frugally, sleeping in his Volkswagen, flying economy class. He toted his possessions in a single suitcase, stowed under the seat to avoid the baggage claim line. His globetrotting convinced him of the fragility of the world's wild places and tribal peoples, on whose behalf he spoke out. The uncomplicated hero became complicated, controversial. Americans attributed all sorts of new roles and values to him: press victim, racist, copperhead, patriot, conservationist. One, two, many Lindberghs. It required a two-page obituary in the *New York Times* to encompass his life.[27]

The bright thread running through Lindbergh's polymathic career was his growing wariness of technological advances. The thought had first come to him on the eve of his triumph, in the twenty-ninth hour of his transatlantic flight, winging over St. George's Channel, confident of his Paris arrival. If a single pilot could make it from New York to Paris, he mused, aviation's possibilities were endless. Planes might one day replace cars, as cars had replaced horses. Everyone could travel by air. The thought gave him pause. What would happen to the sky's comforting solitude if it became cluttered with planes? He was, he realized, like the "western pioneer" who had just caught his first glimpse of barbed wire. The very success of his pathfinding mission might entail the end of the open frontier he loved.

Over the next two decades this premonition hardened into a conviction. Self-starters, enclosed cockpits, radios, and automatic pilots made flying more efficient and commonplace but also more intellectualized and denatured. "As speed and completed schedules improved," Lindbergh complained in 1954, "pilot and engineer alike lost touch with the hayfield's sun. The yielding sod of the early days gave way to concrete aprons, while open cockpits were streamlined into fuselages until our cheeks no longer felt the turbulence of air." A decade later, watching a stewardess serving meals in the pressurized cabin of a North Atlantic flight, he said he found it hard to believe the water thirty-five thousand feet below was the same ocean he had struggled across in 1927. Modern transport aircraft had severed space and time, diminishing the experience of, and respect for, nature's barriers.[28]

The plane's annihilation of space made it a formidable weapon. Lindbergh himself had wielded that weapon in 1944, adding streaming tracers and falling bombs to his store of aviation memories. "I have seen the science I worshiped, and the aircraft I loved, destroying the civilization I expected them to serve, and which I thought as permanent as the earth itself," he wrote in 1960. It was his conviction that mechanized warfare threatened western civilization, together with his fear that the *Luftwaffe* gave

Germany an unbeatable edge, that had inspired his opposition to America's involvement in the European war. Regarding that war as a body blow to western culture and its "genetic heredity," and a preview of worse horrors to come, he never recanted his opposition.[29]

Nor, he made clear, did he regard aerial warfare as the worst of aviation's evils. He saw that the conquest of one frontier, the sky, had entailed the subjugation of another, the earth's wild places. The plane had become an airborne version of the snowmobile, a device he detested. A lifetime of flying had given him a bird's-eye view of environmental carnage, of disappearing forests, eroding hills, vanishing species, and smoggy megolopoli spilling over the countryside. "Obviously, an exponential breakdown in our environment was taking place; and, just as obviously, my profession of aviation was a major factor in that breakdown," he wrote. "Aircraft had opened every spot on earth to exploitation, carried developers into wildernesses that had been inaccessible before. I realized that the future of aviation, to which I had devoted so much of my life, depended less on the perfection of aircraft than on preserving the epoch-evolved environment of life, and this was true of all technological progress."[30]

Lindbergh's conviction that aviation threatened civilization and the environment makes much of his conduct after 1941 seem puzzling, even hypocritical. He did, after all, volunteer to fight in a war he had sacrificed his reputation to prevent. The brotherhood of pilots made sure a fighter was available for him wherever he traveled in the Pacific. Though nominally a civilian adviser, and, at forty-two, old enough to have fathered most combat pilots, Lindbergh never hesitated to climb into the cockpit. He continued to advise the air force after the war, participating in ballistic-missile and strategic-bomber studies, even flying on B-52 patrols over the Arctic. He stayed on Pan Am's payroll, instructing the airline on everything from employee morale to in-flight meals. He worked with Boeing to develop its 707 and 747 models, odd behavior for someone who complained that aircraft had opened every spot on earth to exploitation.[31]

It is tempting to write off the contradiction as a triumph of nostalgic hope over bitter experience. Men seldom forget anything associated with heroism. The last job Ronald Reagan could remember, as he succumbed to Alzheimer's disease, was that of lifeguard. The airplane had made Lindbergh the century's greatest hero, and it would have required an act of superhuman discipline to repudiate it entirely. But he had other reasons for pursuing its development. The most basic fact of life, he wrote in the privacy of a letter to Harry Guggenheim, was competition. Without it there could be no evolutionary progress. Christianity's problem was its "blindness" to and, in times of war, hypocrisy toward the inevitability of human conflict. Given the nature of modern war and the Soviet threat—Lindbergh despised communism—the United States had to maintain its aerospace edge. It was up to its citizens to rein in the worst features of these technologies. Whatever Lindbergh's personal feelings ("If I had to choose, I would rather have birds than airplanes"), he understood power. Anne Morrow Lindbergh, who knew him better than anyone, caught him in a sentence: "He was interested in facts, and saw them clearly." His integrity was such that he stated all the facts, even when they stood in opposition. He frankly admitted their contradictions.[32]

There is a deep resonance here. Calvinists, in Max Weber's famous rendering of history, believed that success through dedicated, systematic labor revealed God's favor. Yet, being ascetics, they could not spend the profits of their enterprises on transient pleasures. So they reinvested them. Pools of capital accumulated, the economy grew, society prospered. But that very prosperity eroded the religious spirit that underpinned capitalist enterprise. As riches increased, so did love of the world. Like a spent booster rocket, the Protestant ethic fell away from the capitalist payload it had launched into historical orbit.

Charles Lindbergh's eventful life described a similar trajectory. It should be read, in fact, as a Weberian parable of unintended consequences. For what was Lindbergh, really, but a secularized version of Weber's Puritan innocent? As a young man he believed that progress in aviation would be an unqualified boon for humanity. Flight would expand the range of human experience, improve its character, and bring prosperity to those who attended its peaceful gospel. No cause has ever had a more appealing evangelist. Yet, the more Lindbergh accomplished, the more he realized that flying was turning into a job and that the airplane itself had become an agent of cultural leveling, military destruction, and environmental degradation. Ultimately, he saw aviation as part of a malignant technological order that, left unchecked, threatened the quality and the very existence of human life.

The historian Arthur Schlesinger Jr., noting Lindbergh's refusal to recant his prewar isolationism, said that he was a person of "unrepentant obstinacy," laboring under the conviction that "he enjoyed a monopoly of morality and wisdom." There is some—but only some—truth in this view. Lindbergh could be stubborn, aloof, and self-absorbed, traits magnified, as he grew older, by his flying-induced hearing loss. Few men have been as content with their own silent company. Yet he also acknowledged error, as when he switched from supporter to vocal opponent of the fuel-gulping supersonic transport. Reflecting on the global consequences of aviation technology, he came to question the wisdom of the path he had chosen in adult life. He expressed his reservations with such persistence and clarity that, by 1974, when his unembalmed body was lowered into its grave—his death certificate filled out in advance, his checklist of funeral arrangements carried out to the letter—he had become aviation's most forceful critic as well as its most celebrated champion.[33]

Part II

The Age of Mass Experience

There are only two emotions in a plane: boredom and terror.

—ORSON WELLES

CHAPTER 6

Assisted Takeoff

After Lindbergh reached Paris, aviation enthusiasts heralded a prosperous new era. Passenger volume was bound to increase. If Lindbergh could make it across the ocean on one engine, the average person would feel confident flying above the land on three. "Lindbergh," boasted one amateur pilot, "has killed the bogy of American aviation—fear."

In fact, he had not. Lindbergh's flight, and the public relations campaign built on its foundation, never succeeded in killing the fear of flying. That primal force continued to exert its drag on commercial aviation. In 1969, when the comedian Jackie Gleason cracked that "the best way to fly is by train," he spoke for millions of still-nervous Americans.[1]

What the 1927 boom did do, however, was to reframe the public's understanding of aviation. Before Lindbergh, most Americans regarded flying as dangerous and expensive. It might do for a once-in-a-lifetime thrill, or in the pinch of a family emergency. Otherwise, why take a chance? After Lindbergh, the attitude shifted toward hopeful ambivalence. There was still some risk, but the time saved might be worth it if ticket prices came down. The task facing the industry's leaders and its government supporters was to resolve the ambivalence in favor of flying, to get more Americans to venture into the sky.

It was a formidable task. Resistance to flying was rooted in two basic fears, that of falling and that of the unknown. First-time passengers entrusted their lives to a stranger piloting an unfamiliar machine in an insubstantial medium. They would have little control in an emergency situation, and less chance if things went badly wrong. When you covered a flood, as one journalist put it, you saw bodies. When you visited a crash site, you "just saw faces." Sometimes less. A ghoulish treasure hunter found a bone in the Rockne crash debris and claimed it was the coach's shin. Fire was a worse fate than dismemberment. "I resolved that, if the plane started burning, I would open my mouth and suck in the flames," Eddie Rickenbacker wrote of the 1941 crash that almost took his life. "It's quicker that way." Comforting advice.[2]

The chance of disaster was remote and becoming more remote all the time. But the mean-world effect persisted. Aviation pulps recycled dogfighting stories. Comics like *Scorchy Smith* featured crack-ups and hair's-breadth escapes. Newspapers reported aviation's statistical progress on the inside pages, its disasters on the front. The staid *New York Times* ran "KNUTE ROCKNE DIES WITH SEVEN OTHERS IN MAIL PLANE DIVE" above the fold, next to its lead story on the 1931 Managua earthquake. Crashes of lesser note still produced banner headlines. One American Airlines official wondered why the company bothered with newspaper advertising at all. Competing with scare headlines, he said, was like "trying to put out a forest fire with a garden hose." Seven people were killed in a grade-crossing accident, Will Rogers remarked, and the newspaper did not even publish their names. Five people died in a plane crash and got headlines everywhere. "It looks like the only way you can get any publicity on your death is to be killed in a plane." Rogers more than fulfilled the prophecy when he went down with Wiley Post in 1935.[3]

In May 1939, Gallup pollsters asked adults, "If it did not cost you anything, would you like to learn to fly an airplane?" Fifty-eight percent said no. Half the men declined, two-thirds of the women. There were, however, two conspicuous exceptions. Two-thirds of those who had flown before said they would not mind learning how to fly, as did nearly two-thirds of those under thirty. The older the respondent, the greater the reluctance. The results confirm the truism that the young are more open to new experiences. But they also hint at a more specific, generational effect. Someone born in 1900 associated flying with birdmen, dogfighters, and barnstormers, types disposed to crash and burn. Someone born in 1920 grew up with Lindbergh, model airplanes, and a string of speed and distance records. Flying seemed a more promising means of transport to the young.

AGE AND THE FEAR OF FLYING: 1939 GALLUP POLL

Would you accept free flying instruction?

	Yes	No
18–29 years	62%	38%
30–49 years	39%	61%
50 years +	23%	77%

Source: George H. Gallup, *The Gallup Poll,* vol. 1, *1935–1948* (New York: Random House, 1972), 156.

Parents and children sniped across aviation's generation gap. Palmer Holmes, enrolled in a new aviation course at his Georgia military academy, wrote his sister to say that twenty-five boys had signed up. "But I think there will be a few of them drop out real soon as some of them have plenty of trouble with their parents. Some people think if you put your hand on the side of a [*sic*] air plane that you will get killed." Worse that they should go near military aircraft. In June 1942, at the request of the U.S. Navy's Bureau of Aeronautics, the J. Walter Thompson advertising agency surveyed parents of boys of enlistment age. Fully a third of the parents said they would "emotionally object" to their sons joining the air services. It was just too dangerous.[4]

J. Walter Thompson did another study in 1945, this time of businessmen and -women. Sixty percent of the sample had traveled by air. Forty percent had not. Though the interviewees acknowledged the airlines' service and timesaving value, many still expressed reservations. These ranged from stark fear ("You couldn't drag me into a plane") to complaints of tension, ear aches, and nausea. Sickness worries turned up in other surveys in the late 1940s, though basic safety fears always ranked first among those who had never flown.[5]

Boiled down, the market research showed sales resistance to be concentrated in three overlapping groups: the inexperienced, the aged, and women. Married women's fears carried extra weight, in that they lobbied their husbands against flying, particularly in winter weather or immediately after a crash. Asked to picture themselves going down in a plane, men in research focus groups said that the thought of dying did not so much bother them as much as the thought of how their wives would react: "The darned fool, he should have gone by train."[6]

Ford Trimotors offered a safe but rough ride. The three uncowled engines increased drag, as did the wing struts and fixed landing gear. The plane poked along at 105 to 110 mph, prolonging the ordeal of the ten to twelve passengers in its drafty, vibrating cabin. Pilots disliked the nose engine, which "introduced fire hazard, sent vibrations into the cockpit, provided terrible visibility, and splattered oil all over."

Federal Policy in the 1930s

None of these anxieties would have mattered much if the fledgling industry had stuck to hauling mail, its chief business in the late 1920s and early 1930s. Rockne dead in "mail plane dive" may seem an odd locution, but it made sense in 1931. The plane's passengers were ancillary cargo. When weight constraints forced airlines to choose between mail and passengers, the passengers got bumped. But events were already in motion that would change the airlines' priorities, forcing them to center their operations on passenger service and giving them every incentive to win over ambivalent customers.[7]

The man who triggered the change was the postmaster general, Walter Folger Brown. A progressive Republican of New Nationalist leanings—Gore Vidal once called him a "Herbert Hoover socialist"—Brown hated unrestrained competition. He knew that intense rivalries had distorted the nation's railroad system, plagued by over-dense construction, parallel routes, and other absurdities. What he had in mind for the airways was very different. He wanted a stable, regulated oligopoly in which a few consolidated airlines carried the passengers and mail. Their large, modern transport planes would fly on approved routes that made national sense.[8]

In 1930, Brown asked for and got changes in the Air Mail Act. The post office would henceforth pay its contractors for space available rather than poundage. The change eliminated the incentive for fraud—no more clerks pasting stamps on bricks—and favored airlines with larger equipment. The law also empowered the postmaster general to extend and consolidate routes and issue ten-year route certificates, with the proviso that he could adjust future rates to reflect aeronautical advances. Brown meant to wean the airlines from mail revenue as they began flying more passengers in improved planes, the ultimate requirement for an efficient national air transport industry.

Armed with the new legislation, Brown convened a series of meetings, later dubbed the "spoils conferences," in which he imposed his plan of orderly progress. He made offers that representatives of selected large airlines could not refuse. He told Western Air Express to merge with TAT or forget about carrying the U.S. Mail. The corporate result of this shotgun merger, Transcontinental and Western Air (TWA), got the central transcontinental route. United ended up with the northern cross-country route, a newly consolidated American Airways the southern. Eastern Airways got the New York-Atlanta-Miami run.

The complaints of small operators might have gone unnoticed had it not been for the 1932 Democratic electoral sweep. New Dealers, led by Alabama's Sen. Hugo Black, investigated Brown's allegedly fraudulent practices. In February 1934, Franklin Roosevelt ordered the domestic airmail contracts canceled. (Pan American, operating under the separate Foreign Air Mail Act of 1928, managed to hang on to its monopoly until the 1940s, when the war brought overseas competition.) Rather than simply shipping domestic airmail by rail until such time as a new and more competitive system could be devised, Roosevelt assigned the Army Air Corps the job.

That was a mistake. Young army pilots, trained for combat maneuvers and tight formations, had little experience flying cross-country through night and winter weather. Suddenly it was 1920 again, with wrecked mail planes and dead fliers. Eastern's Eddie Rickenbacker called it "legalized murder" and told reporters to quote him. The *New York Evening Journal*, which needed no prompting in the matter, decried the "senseless butchery of young Army aviators." The New Dealers had suffered their first major political embarrassment.

"The best way to handle a red-hot poker," wrote journalist Henry Ladd Smith, "is to drop it." The administration went back to airmail contracting, but in a way that accelerated the industry's movement toward the passenger business. Under the terms of the 1934 Air Mail Act, the domestic "big four" of United, TWA, American, and Eastern recovered most of their routes. But they had to separate from their parent holding companies and purge the officials who had supposedly connived with Brown. Most critically, the law reduced domestic airmail rates, which had already declined under Brown's regime. The new rates, set by the Interstate Commerce Commission, could not exceed forty cents per mile.[9]

The remarkable thing about this imbroglio, typical of Roosevelt's habit of pursuing contradictory policies while grandstanding against big business, was that he initiated programs to help the airline industry before, during, and after his high-stakes quarrel with its leaders. No fewer than four New Deal relief administrations set the unemployed to work on landing facilities and municipal airports, the crucial choke points in the emerging air transportation system. The 1938 Civil Aeronautics Act, designed to promote commercial aviation, consolidated federal regulatory authority in the Civil Aeronautics Authority. (Reorganized in 1940, it became the Civil Aeronautics Administration, or CAA.) Even Rickenbacker, who hated the New Deal, grudgingly admitted the CAA did a good job managing the "technical details" of commercial aviation. The new authority, and the Civil Aeronautics Board (CAB) that spun off from it in 1940, had the power to set fares and routes and thus manage competition. That was exactly what Brown had set out to do in 1930. Government-sponsored oligopoly, the issue that had started the New Deal aviation brawl, ended up getting a four-decade lease on life. The CAB became, in all but name, the manager of an airline cartel.[10]

The more nervous the administration became about war, the more money it lavished on aviation. Annual expenditures on military aircraft rose from $13 million in 1934 to $68 million in 1939. Defense spending, coupled with growing overseas demand, lifted the aircraft manufacturing industry out of the Depression. Then, in May 1940, Roosevelt startled the nation by calling for the production of fifty thousand planes a year. "I was called crazy," he said. The number, picked from a hat for its big, round-number effect, did seem far-fetched. The entire American output from the time of the Wright brothers had been about fifty thousand planes, and they were not exactly B-17s. But the announcement also signified something quite real, a flood of money for aircraft factories. The investment would total $4 billion over the next five years, with $3.5 billion coming from the government itself. In 1938, there were just fifteen plants making airframes, engines, and propellers in the United States. By 1940, there were forty-one. No American industry, *Fortune* reported the following year, had ever grown as rapidly.[11]

New planes were useless without places to land them and people to fly them. The buildup included $40 million more for airport construction in 1940, followed by another $95 million in 1941. National (now Reagan) Airport rose from the Potomac, courtesy of dredging and filling by the Corps of Engineers. Federal spending on aerial navigation and communication doubled during 1938–41. Meanwhile the CAA launched its Civilian Pilot Training Program (CPTP). This was a vocational education scheme and stimulus for the light-plane industry that evolved, under the threat of war, into a huge preparedness program. By mid-1942, it had produced over 125,000 pilots, 3,565 of them with commercial licenses. The CPTP pilots who flew for the airlines, and the ex-military aviators who joined them, had their basic training costs picked up by the government.[12]

It always helps to follow the beam of money through the fog of politics. Despite the political *contretemps* of the mid-1930s, and despite the inevitable cuts in the airmail rates, the federal government continued to provide the means of aviation's expansion. Together with local governments, which built and maintained municipal airports, it absorbed costs the industry would otherwise have found impossible to meet.

The Modern Airliners

The same was true of research and development. The military's demand for high-performance aircraft, and the growing appropriations for the government's principal research arm, the National Advisory Committee for Aeronautics (NACA), brought rapid aeronautical advances. Talented engineers at Boeing, Douglas, and Lockheed used the knowledge to help design the first modern airliners. These fast, dependable planes enabled the airlines to solve the problem of falling mail revenue by increasing passenger volume.

The economic situation was simple. In the early 1930s, business and professional travelers made up from 60 to 80 percent of the airlines' passengers. Short flights did not interest them. Flying from New York to Philadelphia hardly saved enough time to justify the added cost and risk. Flying from New York to Chicago or to Los Angeles was another matter. Planes to these destinations could save days, as well as meal and lodging expenses. With cross-country equipment, airlines could siphon business passengers from Pullman railroad cars, their main long-distance rivals.[13]

What made this possible was the development of more powerful radial engines, powerplants with air-cooled cylinders arrayed in a circle around the crankshaft that drove the propeller. The impetus came from the navy. It needed compact, lightweight carrier planes, uncluttered by the radiators, cooling jackets, water pumps, and hoses of the heavy (and failure-prone) Liberty engines. Inventor Charles Lawrance designed and Wright Aeronautical built the navy's new radial engines. In 1924, the company brought out an improved version, the 220 hp Whirlwind. Rival manufacturer Pratt & Whitney introduced two formidable radial engines of its own, the 410 hp Wasp and the 525 hp Hornet. The race was on. Wright countered with the Cyclone, a more powerful version of the Whirlwind. Further refinement doubled the Cyclone's horsepower, from 550 hp in 1930 to 1,100 hp in 1939.

The growing power and efficiency of lightweight engines doubled airplanes' maximum range during the 1920s. Lindbergh knew what he was doing when he put the latest model of the Whirlwind in the *Spirit of St. Louis.* Improved radial engines ended the biplane's supremacy. Biplanes were lighter and could lift more than comparably sized monoplanes, weighed down by their thick single wings. But biplanes had one crucial disadvantage. They were slow. Equipped with the new engines, monoplanes could outfly them and still carry an ample payload. In 1931, the Army Air Corps introduced the B-9, a single-wing bomber with twin Hornet engines. None of its pursuit planes could catch it. The implications were obvious for the airlines. Big, fast monoplanes meant a decisive advantage in the long-distance passenger market.[14]

Radial engines had one drawback. Their cylinder heads, shrouded in cooling fins, stuck out in the air to dissipate heat. That increased drag, slowing the plane. NACA researchers studied the problem at Langley Field, the government's aeronautical research complex near Norfolk, Virginia. Their experiments in a new, full-scale wind tunnel showed that a completely cowled, or covered, engine permitted cooling while reducing drag. Despite the added weight, planes fitted with "NACA cowls" gained as much as 20 mph, equivalent to an additional 100 hp. Aerodynamic efficiency improved range, too, extending the gains achieved by lightweight engines. More wind-tunnel work showed the best place to situate these engines on a large plane. It was in nacelles, or engine housings, mounted directly in line with the wing.

NACA's budget, just $200,000 in 1921, grew during the 1920s and on through the Depression, reaching $4.4 million in 1940. The money was an industry subsidy in all but name. As a publicly funded agency, NACA made its research available to all interested parties, convening an annual conference to brief manufacturers and the military services. Aircraft manufacturers used the NACA findings, as well as the experience gained in making military aircraft and engines, to help design a new generation of transport planes.

The first of these to enter service, in 1931, was the Northrop Alpha. A sleek, cowled monoplane with a strong, multicellular wing, the Alpha was essentially a fast mail hauler that could squeeze in a half-dozen passengers. The Boeing 247, which took to the air in early 1933, had a better claim as the first modern airliner. Based on the twin-engine B-9 bomber, the streamlined 247 carried ten passengers at a cruising speed of 155 mph, half again as fast as most trimotors. A year later, in 1934, Boeing brought out an advanced version, the 247-D, featuring more efficient engines and Hamilton Standard's new two-speed, controllable-pitch propeller. By setting the blades at a shallow angle of attack and piling on the rpms, a pilot could produce maximum thrust for takeoff. While cruising he could increase the pitch of the blades and throttle back his engine, conserving fuel and extending range.[15]

Roscoe Turner entered a 247-D in the 1934 MacRobertson Air Race, flown between London and Melbourne. He finished third. First went to a De Havilland DH-88 Comet, one of three lightweight, twin-engine wooden racing planes specially built to compete in the race. Second went to a new American competitor to the 247, a Douglas DC-2. The plane flew with a crew of four, three passengers, and thirty thousand letters, much of it souvenir mail. The British were stunned. "Preconceived ideas of the maximum speed limitations of the standard commercial aeroplane have been blown sky high," commented the *London Morning Post*. "America now has in hundreds, standard commercial aeroplanes with a higher top speed than the fastest aeroplane in regular service in the whole of the Royal Air Force."[16]

The DC-2 was a byproduct of the Boeing 247's success. Boeing had pledged its 247 production to United, which was part of its parent corporation. TWA, stuck with obsolete equipment—the Rockne crash had tainted its fleet of F10 Trimotors—approached Douglas Aircraft with specifications for a new airliner. Douglas produced the DC-1. It was larger than the 247 and, as Lindbergh had insisted, capable of taking off on one engine and flying over the highest mountains on TWA's route. Douglas tinkered with the prototype, extending the fuselage to add two more seats, and brought out the DC-2 in early 1934.

The plane was fast, cruising at 175 to 180 mph. (TWA claimed 200 mph, but that was a stretcher.) Weather permitting, fourteen passengers could board a DC-2 in Newark at 4:00 in the afternoon and land in Los Angeles at 7:00 the next morning. The service marked the beginning of "bi-coastalism," a peculiarly American form of space-time compression. For the first time in history, passengers could cross the country without losing part of a normal business day.

Not that they would feel like doing business after eighteen hours in an

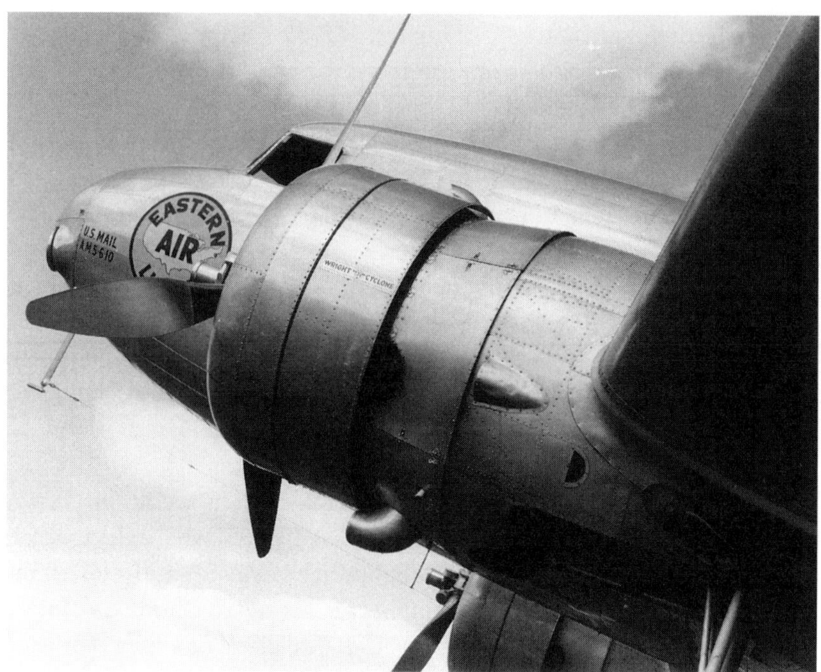

The Douglas DC-2 combined a streamlined, soundproofed fuselage with twin cowled engines, variable-pitch propellers, and landing gear that retracted into the nacelles of its low, internally braced wings. It easily outflew the old trimotors and just about anything the Europeans put into the skies.

airplane seat. American Airlines president C. R. Smith asked Donald Douglas to develop a larger version of the DC-2, one capable of carrying fourteen berthed passengers at night or twenty-one seated passengers during the day. Smith got his planes, paid for with a loan from the government's Reconstruction Finance Corporation. More importantly, the industry got the DC-3, the dayplane version of the Douglas Sleeper Transport. The DC-3 was to flying what Ford's Model T was to driving, the affordable breakthrough vehicle that introduced millions to a new form of transportation. The DC-3 carried half again as many passengers as the DC-2, but cost only a tenth more to operate. Later versions, equipped with up to twenty-eight seats, were still more efficient. Smith and other airline executives realized they now had enough fast-plane capacity to make money by hauling passengers, ending their dependence on federal mail payments. Introduced in 1936, the new plane proved so successful that, by late 1941, four of every five American airliners were DC-3s. Its only real two-engine rivals were Lockheed's Electras and Lodestars, faster but smaller-capacity planes that competed on shorter routes.[17]

Improvements in instrumentation and control kept pace with increases in size and speed. The key development was the melding of radios and airplanes into an integrated transportation system. Radios enabled pilots to receive information from dispatchers, including frequent updates on weather and landing conditions; to estimate the position of the plane; to follow a course marked out by radio beacons through night and fog; and to report the plane's position in the event of a forced landing or other emergency. There were bugs. On a bad night the Newark weather report sounded like "... garble garble ... three garble ... viz garble one garble ... light blowing ... garble ...." But an experienced pilot like Ernie Gann could decipher the meaning: ceiling three hundred feet, visibility one mile in light, blowing snow. He could use his altimeter to descend and hunt for the runway lights from a safe minimum altitude. (The official limit was three hundred feet, though pilots often "cheated" by dropping lower for a closer look.) If he could not find the lights, he would fly on to another field where the radio dispatcher reported better conditions.

In 1942, Charles Lindbergh, doing his wartime bit as a test pilot and quality controller at Henry Ford's Willow Run bomber plant, found time to reflect on the radio revolution:

> In a sense, I am learning to fly all over again here at Willow Run. The procedures used are very different from those I have used in the past, in that they are based largely upon radio control and precisely laid-down rules and regulations that depend on constant contact with the ground and knowledge of what lies beneath, behind, and ahead, regardless of whether the ground is covered with fog or not. Here, one's safety depends upon ground facilities.
>
> In most of the flying I have done, safety depended upon *independence* of ground facilities. To have counted on any assistance from the ground after I once started on a flight would sooner or later have been fatal for me. During my early flights radio was so unreliable that I did not carry it at all; and during the later ones I used it as an added safety and convenience but never counted on it greatly in planning my flights ...
>
> Flying was at first more of an art than a science. Now it is more a science than an art. It has passed from the era of the pioneer to the era of the routine operator, from the time when a 'good pilot' forgot his instruments in an emergency to the time when a 'good pilot' turns to his instruments in an emergency.[18]

These were the musings of someone who had proved himself an adaptable, safety-conscious instrument pilot. The real old-timers hated the new ways. They groused about sitting behind Plexiglas, surrounded by gauges and switches, earphones perched on their heads, tending the plane as it droned along its acoustical railroad in the sky. But woe to those who could not, or would not, make the transition. They were either fired by the airlines or flunked by federal inspectors, who in 1932 began testing transport pilots on radio navigation and instrument flying. Novice pilots found it easier to master blind flying than veterans. Instructors drilled students in the new Link flight simulators, so realistic that one "lost" pilot "tore the top hatch off the trainer and jumped out." Link trainees learned well the first commandment: thou shalt not place your instincts above your instruments. The veterans adjusted, but they never escaped their preference for navigating by familiar landmarks, never quite freed their flying from the need for visual contact with the earth.[19]

What was lost in independence was gained in passenger confidence. All-metal, multi-engine, radio-equipped planes operating on government-regulated airways achieved an unprecedented safety record. Insurers dropped restrictions and extra premiums. Only frequent fliers paid more for life insurance, and by 1936 some insurers were waiving even that surcharge. By 1940, insurance companies felt confident enough of the airlines' soundness to invest in their commercial paper.[20]

Aviation advanced in every category that mattered. A typical 1930 passenger paid a little more than eight cents a mile for a trip spanning 224 miles. Averaging about 110 mph, in a plane about 40 percent full, he ran about a 1 in 14,000 chance of dying en route. Those were long odds, but not so long as to encourage regular flying. (Imagine whether you would buy a lottery ticket with the same winning chance, then reverse the logic.) A typical 1941 passenger paid five cents a mile, flew at more than 160 mph, and rode in a plane nearly two-thirds full. He had only a 1 in 116,000 chance of a fatal accident, despite traveling farther, 367 miles, per average trip. He also had more company at the airport. More than ten passengers flew in 1941 for every one who had flown in 1930. They did so—this was the remarkable thing—using fewer aircraft. More flights with higher "load factors" (percentage of seats filled) on bigger, faster, and more reliable planes had enabled the airlines to cut fleet size by a third.[21]

The American airline industry, in short, took off in the 1930s. A post office satrapy at the beginning of the decade, it had become a self-supporting, modestly profitable, technically advanced, and world-leading enterprise by decade's end. All this had happened in the midst of the Great Depression. The market still had tremendous potential. Fares remained high in 1940. A one-way, cross-country ticket cost $150. That was down from $400 in 1930,

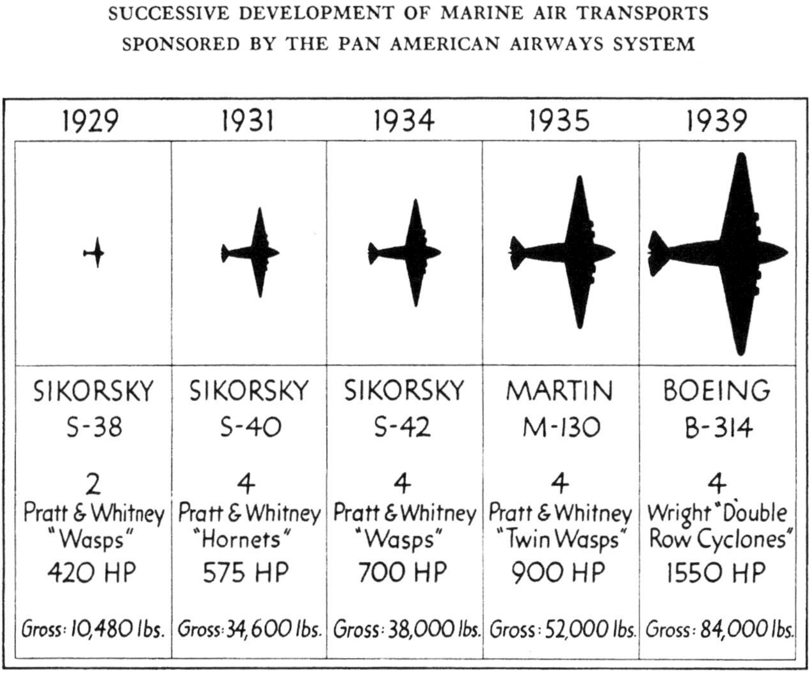

SUCCESSIVE DEVELOPMENT OF MARINE AIR TRANSPORTS
SPONSORED BY THE PAN AMERICAN AIRWAYS SYSTEM

1929	1931	1934	1935	1939
SIKORSKY S-38	SIKORSKY S-40	SIKORSKY S-42	MARTIN M-130	BOEING B-314
2 Pratt & Whitney "Wasps" 420 HP	4 Pratt & Whitney "Hornets" 575 HP	4 Pratt & Whitney "Wasps" 700 HP	4 Pratt & Whitney "Twin Wasps" 900 HP	4 Wright "Double Row Cyclones" 1550 HP
Gross: 10,480 lbs.	Gross: 34,600 lbs.	Gross: 38,000 lbs.	Gross: 52,000 lbs.	Gross: 84,000 lbs.

Airplane inflation, real and augmented. In 1940, Juan Trippe used this chart to show how Pan Am's planes had grown from eight-passenger mail-haulers like the Sikorsky S-38 to the giant Boeing B-314 "Clippers," capable of carrying seventy-two day or forty berthed passengers on transoceanic flights. Notice how the chart's icons overstate, for added visual effect, the actual gains in gross weight. Illustrators used similar tricks in airline ads, drawing planes to a larger scale than the passengers.

but still out of reach for anyone without a trust fund, executive salary, expense account, or Hollywood contract. And there was still the fear factor. Though the risk per mile flown had diminished tenfold, people still worried about crashes and, with better reason, discomfort and sickness. "Rough air" turned even experienced fliers green. "There were drops and slips at all angles," a NACA engineer wrote of a bad forty-minute flight. "I think everyone was sick except the pilot." Some aircrew never adjusted. Stewardesses ate airsickness pills and carried on, helping worse-off passengers retrieve their dentures from their erp cups.[22]

The DC-3, for all its sturdiness, failed to banish airsickness. Its slightly swept wings tended to wallow in rough air, swinging the tail back and forth.

Engineers nicknamed this form of yaw "Dutch Roll," after the method of skating on alternate feet while leaning from side to side. "It made the ride in the cabin uncomfortable and caused much of the airsickness that was routine stuff in those days," wrote Bob Buck, who flew for TWA. "A good pilot could combat this tail swinging by using the rudder, but the heaviness of the control and the effort of pushing one's feet forward and back on the rudder pedals for long periods was tiring, so much of the time the pilot rested his feet on the floor while the tail swayed through the sky and passengers heaved and retched."[23]

Pilots seldom encountered bad weather above 12,000 feet, and almost never above 20,000. Their new airliners could fight their way up to that altitude, and more. The DC-3 had a ceiling of 23,100 feet. But passengers could not tolerate the thin air. Without supplemental oxygen, anoxia set in at 10,000 feet, sometimes less. One woman behaved normally until her pilot, trying to avoid a storm, climbed to 8,000 feet. She became disoriented and began breaking out windows. She could not explain her actions when she reached the ground. Others suffered intestinal upsets and headaches. One man likened the feeling to a bad hangover.[24]

The solution, obvious to industry leaders in the late 1930s and early 1940s, was to invest in a new generation of pressurized, four-engine equipment. Pan American, which flew long, island-hopping legs on its growing Pacific and Atlantic routes, already had four-engine flying boats. But none of these was pressurized. A big land plane with a pressurized cabin could carry passengers above the worst weather. With four supercharged engines (piston engines outfitted with compressors to force additional air into the cylinders), it could take off with more passengers and fuel. Climbing to a high altitude, it could fly farther and faster, taking advantage of the diminished drag in the rarefied atmosphere. Result: more and happier customers, larger and blacker bottom line. "The successful formula for making money in running an airline," summed up a Wall Street analyst, "is to carry as many passengers and as much cargo load as quickly as possible from one point to another and to keep all equipment in operation a maximum number of hours daily—meanwhile, of course, keeping costs in line with service rates."[25]

In 1940, TWA introduced the pressurized Boeing Stratoliner. A derivative of Boeing's successful B-17 bomber, it could fly 33 passengers in relative comfort as high as 14,000 feet. TWA's new master, Howard Hughes, had his eye on something grander, a 280 mph Lockheed design that could carry 54 passengers above 20,000 feet. On April 17, 1944, he showed what the sleek Constellation could do. He flew nonstop from Burbank, California, to Washington, D.C., in just under seven hours. Though promised to the military for the duration, the plane's bright red markings made plain Hughes's postwar plans. So did TWA's ads, which promised "air-conditioned, over-weather comfort at pursuit-plane speeds." This was literally true. Designer Kelly Johnson had derived the Constellation's wing from the P-38 fighter. Military innovation had again paid commercial dividends.[26]

Beyond the Field of Dreams

An economist, looking back on the golden age of 1925 to 1941, would conclude that supply-side factors drove commercial aviation's expansion. Government policies, military needs, and technological progress changed the quantity and quality of a product, air transport, and brought down its price. Though still ambivalent about flying, Americans could purchase more seats at lower cost on safer and faster planes flying from more and better-equipped airports.

Some version of this story appears in every history of American aviation. Their authors differ on the weight they assign to political, military, and technological developments, differences that can be detected by scanning their illustrations. But the basic idea remains the same. Build them better and they will come. Once the airline industry, kick-started by government subsidies and rationalized by federal regulations, provided Americans with decent equipment, safe airways, and improved airports, the passenger business flourished.

The "field of dreams" story has one flaw. It leaves out the demand-side forces that also determined the airlines' success or failure. Industry insiders paid close attention to, and worked hard to augment, the shifting demand for passenger service. Flying still had to be sold to a reluctant public. The key was persuading people to go up for the first time. Those who had flown once were more likely to do so again.

In 1938, a natural experiment in the form of a hurricane confirmed this statistical fact. A mighty storm engulfed southern New England, severing road and rail links between Boston and New York. With no alternative, passengers crowded into airport terminals. When the crisis passed, however, the traffic remained above pre-hurricane levels. "The people who used to travel back and forth between the two cities by train, bus, or car had seen what flying was like, and the time and effort it saved," one pilot remembered. "I've often thought that the hurricane of September 1938 was the real beginning of mass air transportation."[27]

Lacking the means to conjure hurricanes, industry leaders resorted to more mundane tactics to crack the first-flight barrier. TWA offered "courtesy hops," half-hour joyrides to travel agents, businessmen and -women, and other likely prospects. Colonial Air Transport gave seats to journalists, hoping for publicity. Several airlines offered complimentary tickets to wives who accompanied husbands on winter flights, which always had vacant seats. Harold Crary, United's vice president for traffic, thought the wife who "put her foot down" had likely never been on a plane. If she became acquainted with air travel, she would quit objecting to her husband's flying and might even consider it herself. As a further inducement, United offered free seats to children under two and baby food served by stewardesses.[28]

To pacify adult passengers, airlines provided coffee, cold chicken, and Chesterfield cigarettes, fifty per complimentary tin. In February 1929, Universal Air Lines (soon to be part of American) showed the first in-flight movie. "Save for the drone of the three motors," the *New York Times* reported, "the passengers lost all sense of air consciousness." The following year Boeing Air Transport introduced the first stewardesses. Originally trained nurses, they quickly became all-purpose morale builders and found work throughout the industry by the mid-1930s. Personable young women (on Pan American and Eastern, young men) greeted passengers, calmed the anxious, and assisted the sick, lending a domestic touch popular with regulars as well as first-timers. Businessmen began scheduling flights with their favorite stewardesses. The airlines noticed and stepped up their hiring.[29]

They would, in fact, go on to hire about forty thousand stewardesses over the next quarter century. Careers were short. Stewardesses were unmarried women in their twenties who met exacting standards of education, tact, and appearance, working in close personal contact with accomplished and affluent men. They married quickly and well, often to pilots or professionals. May Bobeck, who worked for American, had thirty proposals during her seven-year career. Hers was an unusually long one, the average being two years before marrying up and out. No more weight checks and girdle inspections.[30]

Something similar happened along type-II land frontiers, where governesses and school teachers attracted suitors from the moment they stepped off the stage coach. The newcomers often married army officers, judges, or others above their social station in the East. Women in the California gold fields had, as one wrote home, a "first rate chance" to marry rich men. Hypergyny (women marrying up) is a universal characteristic of social environments in which a coterie of young, single women find themselves in heavily masculine company. That was certainly the case in the aviation milieu of the 1930s and 1940s, where three-quarters of the passengers and nearly all the pilots were male.[31]

Put another way, stewardesses enjoyed a symbiotic relationship with the airlines. Those who made it through the rigorous screening and training got the social equivalent of a ticket out of Amarillo: travel, glamor, and the best marriage market south of Alaska. The airlines got dedicated workers whose calm, conscientious professionalism pleased existing customers and attracted new ones. Stewardesses memorized names by associating them with tie colors, then flattered their charges with attentive conversation. "Answer all questions positively and quickly, then turn the conversation back to the passenger," American Airlines advised its trainees. "Always remember, people want to tell YOU what THEY think." The charm siege worked, and not just on the flight deck. In a price-regulated market, where superior service offered one of the few competitive edges, airlines were quick to feature stewardesses in their advertising strategies. Paralleling, signifying, and to some degree contributing to the sexual revolution, the preferred corporate image of the stewardess would evolve over the next four decades from smiling helpmeet to bombshell. For a time National Airlines hired only blonds, TWA only the light-complected, Southwest only those who looked good in hot pants.[32]

Airline manufacturers could not sell sex, but they could sell modernity. The first big campaign began in 1928, when the N. W. Ayer agency, inventor of the coffee break and "I'd walk a mile for a Camel," launched seventeen eye-catching ads for Ford airplanes. The ads targeted passengers and city planners, those whose investments in tickets or airport improvements would ultimately sell Trimotors. The message was simple. Flying was safe, practical, and up-to-date. The joyriding days were gone. Now people flew to stay ahead of the competition.[33]

The airlines played the same angle. Circulars left in clubs, banks, brokerage houses, and the pricier barber shops stressed flying's speed advantage. For women, an untapped but promising market, the airlines stressed safety and comfort. "Tell them how comfortable they'll be, how delicious their meals are, how capable the stewardesses are, how luxurious their surroundings will be, and you can 'sell' women on air travel. Leave the 'revolutions per minute' to the men," advised Helen Stansbury, director of United's women's traffic division. Stewardesses pitched women's clubs. Female dietary consultants advised the airlines on linen, china, silver, and "tempting menus."[34]

Newspaper publicity helped the industry build demand. The Lindbergh phenomenon and a string of "firsts" kept aviation in the public's mind, as did features like "Woman of 90 Has First Air Ride." Despite the crash headlines, newspapers maintained a favorable editorial line on flying, as did the twenty aviation periodicals that had sprung up by 1930. Ads for products as diverse as cigarettes and shirts used flying as a backdrop, signaling public acceptance and reinforcing the link to modernity and consumerism.[35]

Nor did it hurt that celebrities flew. Will Rogers, who accumulated a half-million air miles before his death in 1935, was an enthusiastic champion of aviation, one of the few non-pilots inducted into the Aviation Hall of Fame. Eleanor Roosevelt, the political eyes and ears of the crippled president, visited all forty-eight states by air. Getting to know half the airline pilots in America, pecking out her "My Day" column as she flew, she joined Rogers in the small but growing group of Americans who spent a substantial portion of their professional lives aloft.[36]

The Myth of Independence

The pioneer myth that Daniel Boone, Davy Crockett, "and men of that type played out a lone hand and made America" no longer cuts any ice with western historians. They have emphasized that governments and corporations, working in concert, provided the means of access and exploitation. "In Western affairs," wrote Patricia Limerick, "business and government were interdependent and symbiotic, and only a pathologically subtle mind could find a line dividing them." Without a chain of protective forts; without pools of capital for fur, mining, and timber operations; and without assistance for railroad and water projects, as well as subsidies for farmers and ranchers, these regions would not have developed, however resourceful individual westerners may have been. No cattle drives, no cowboys. No railroads, no cattle drives. No land grants, no railroads. No Congress, no land grants. "More than any other region," summed up Richard White, "the West has been historically a dependency of the federal government."[37]

More than any other region, save the sky. During the 1920s and 1930s, flying, once the province of a few thousand military aviators, mail pilots, crop dusters, and showmen, became accessible to hundreds of thousands of ordinary mortals. Expansion on this scale was possible only because governments and corporations invested heavily in commercial aviation. Private philanthropy, notably the Guggenheim fund, had played a timely role in the late 1920s. But the main thrust came from public spending on airports, airways, aeronautical research, mail subsidies, military contracts, and pilot training. Directly or indirectly, these activities benefitted airlines and aircraft manufacturers, which pursued their own complementary schemes to build passenger volume.

Eugene Vidal—West Pointer, engineer, pilot, airline executive, father of Gore Vidal, friend (some say lover) of Amelia Earhart, and director of the Commerce Department's aviation operations from 1933 to 1937—was the New Deal official who had the most expansive view of the government's role in the air frontier. Vidal knew that aviation, "with all its past romance and color," needed federal help to become a real industry and effective military reserve. Far from wrecking the airlines, he insisted, the administration was increasing revenues and lowering costs. He even thought the New Deal should work to democratize private flying, turning "a rich man's hobby" into a "daily utility" as common as the car. "The pioneers of aviation have conquered the air," Vidal said in 1934. "Our task is to develop that conquest into a national heritage." No advocate of Manifest Destiny could have put it better.[38]

The government-industry collaboration had its tensions. Airline executives never forgot, or forgave, Hugo Black's and Franklin Roosevelt's sensational attacks. William Boeing was so disgusted he sold his stock and quit the business, leaving only his name to the company. Nor did the fault lay solely with the politicians. Eddie Rickenbacker and Juan Trippe devoted much of their careers to scheming against the federal aviation bureaucracy. But quarrels over this route or that fare should not obscure the basic mutuality of interest. Vidal was right. The industry needed the government. The government needed the industry. Together they opened airways above the nation and extended them across its surrounding oceans.

And they did it just in time. Shortly before 6:00 in the morning of December 7, 1941, at a point 230 miles north of Pearl Harbor, six aircraft carriers turned into their launch positions, signal flags beating against the stiff easterly wind. Vice Admiral Nagumo Chūichi of the Imperial Japanese Navy was about to touch off a war that would demonstrate exactly how important the partnership between the American aviation industry and its government had become.

We are determined that before the sun sets on this terrible struggle, our flag will be recognized throughout the world as a symbol of freedom on the one hand, and of overwhelming power on the other.

—GEORGE C. MARSHALL, 1942 WEST POINT COMMENCEMENT

CHAPTER 7

The Rome of the Air

Like most journalists who covered commercial aviation, the *New York Times'* Frederick Graham speculated about future trends. Aeronautics got most of his attention, but in May 1941 the war loomed even larger. What would happen if America entered? Graham thought the mass production of planes and pilots would stimulate postwar flying, as it had after World War I. That was an easy call. Wartime conditions were another matter. Would private pilots, he wondered, have trouble flying? Would airlines' progress be interrupted? Or would the airlines actually lose ground, at least for a while?

The answer to all of Graham's questions turned out to be "yes." After December 7, 1941, restrictions on flying disrupted general aviation and airline service. But in the long run—in fact, well before it ended in 1945—the war proved a boon to the airlines. The war supercharged commercial flying, making possible its rapid expansion. It did the same for military aviation, which emerged from the war with great strategic weight. Lindbergh thought the country had become an aerial Rome, a preeminent nation with expanded frontiers and dependent allies that required a powerful fleet of military aircraft to deter attack. The airlines, for their part, gave the armed forces a reserve airlift capability. Though their primary postwar mission was flying ever-growing numbers of civilians, they remained "America's merchant marine of the air," ready in the event of a national emergency.[1]

Wartime Flying

The war hit general aviation, the operation of mostly small aircraft for private and business purposes, harder than any other branch of the industry. A volatile business, general aviation had flourished during the Lindbergh boom, stagnated when the Depression stuck, and regained its vigor in the four years before the war. Light planes, like airliners, had evolved rapidly during the 1930s. The newer, single-wing models featured enclosed cabins and efficient radial engines. Improved designs, a flood of CPTP pilots, and a reviving economy spelled boom. Americans owned twenty-four thousand private planes in 1941, up from ten thousand in 1938.

Then the CAA, in the anxious days following Pearl Harbor, grounded all flights save those of scheduled airlines and revoked all airmen's certificates save those of airline pilots. Reinstatement required proof of citizenship, fingerprinting, security clearance, a loyalty oath, lack of Japanese ancestors, and submission to a host of new regulations. The CAA kept tabs on every plane in the country, and cleared all takeoffs and landings. Flights from unapproved airports, even from private farms and ranches, were forbidden. I'll-fly-when-I-please individualists faced fines, injunctions, and license suspensions.

Equipment was scarce. The CAA's War Training Service and the AAF bought up most of the private planes. Light-plane manufacturers like Piper ceased civilian production and began building training, observation, ambulance, and liaison aircraft. The new planes went to the army, navy, and marines. Companies engaged in essential war production hung on to a few older aircraft. Otherwise, private flying stagnated.[2]

The armed forces leased or purchased half the commercial airliners. They took the best and the biggest, the pressurized Stratoliners and Pan American's giant Clippers, as well as DC-3s. Workers ripped out upholstered seats and soundproofing, cut larger doors for cargo, and sprayed on olive drab or blue paint. (The airlines had preferred unpainted planes of polished aluminum because they were lighter and more aerodynamically efficient; military versions sacrificed up to 12 mph for camouflage and uniformity.) Seats on the remaining commercial airliners went on a priority basis. White House staff topped the list, followed by military ferry pilots, military personnel with air-travel orders, essential military equipment, civilian government employees on urgent business, then everyone else. The term "VIP" was born of wartime flying. So were "standby" and "bumped," the fates of ordinary civilians hoping for an unclaimed seat or forced to surrender one to a priority passenger. Some, like missionaries bound for Africa, could not purchase tickets at all. (Their travel agent denounced the Pan Am sales representative as

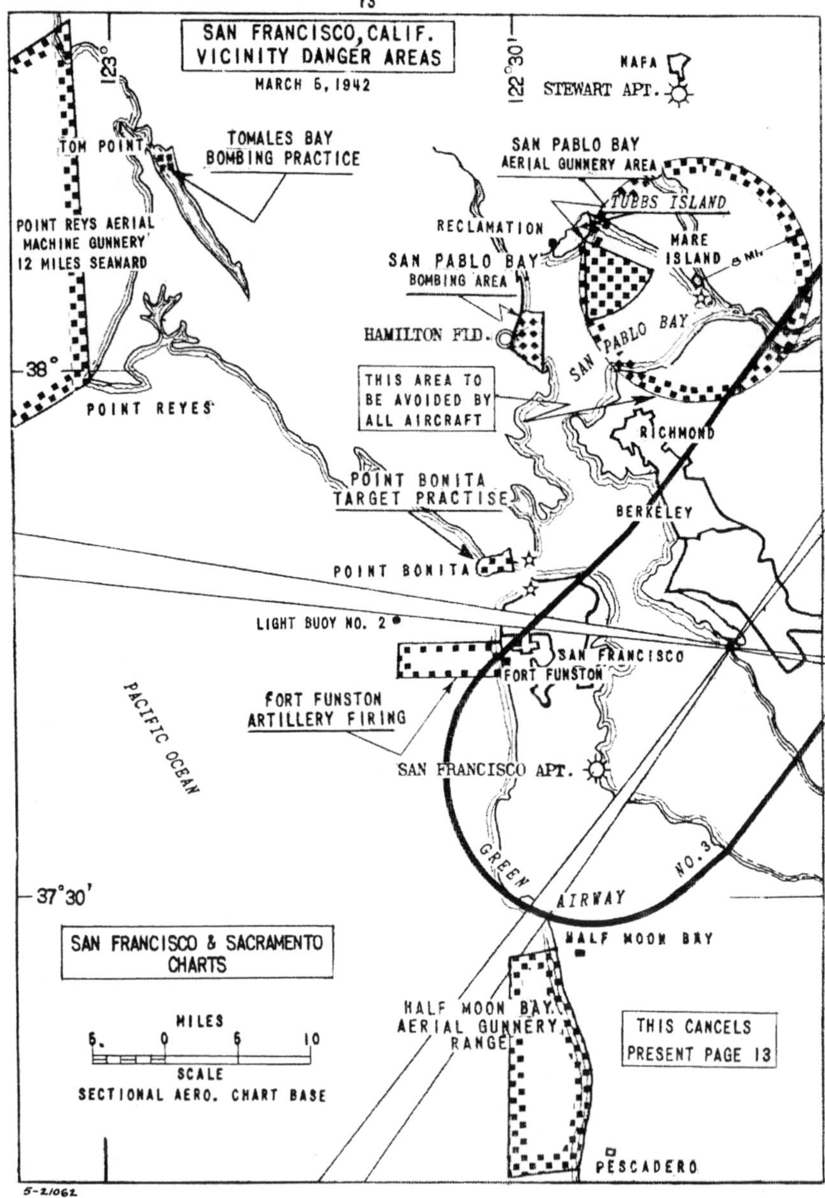

The war accelerated the trend toward the segmentation and regimentation of airspace. One pilot who blundered over a defense plant at Alton, Illinois, had his plane riddled with bullets. Updated CAA charts like this one for the San Francisco Bay area marked danger areas as well as navigational aids. The intersecting lines represent the Oakland radio range, part of the system of acoustical "rails" that guided pilots along the airways.

"godless," the theological equivalent of shooting the messenger.) Washington, D.C., was the hottest domestic ticket. General Curtis LeMay's wife, Helen, could not even get one to join him there during one of his rare stateside visits.[3]

Although the airlines lost a third of their personnel, half their equipment, and all their new orders to the military, the number of revenue passengers slipped just 16 percent between 1941 and 1942. Left with DC-3s and Lodestars, the airlines made virtue of necessity, standardizing maintenance operations, keeping planes in the air longer, and flying with more seats filled. The load factor at National Airlines, 43 percent in 1941, shot up to 84 percent in 1943. Mail poundage on National and other U.S. carriers doubled. Then, in mid-1943, with aviation manufacturers gorging on a quarter of the military budget, the army began returning planes to regular airline service. Passenger volume rose again, hitting new records in 1944 and 1945. "The plane, of course, is full," Lindbergh wrote of one his wartime flights. Sold-out flights meant profits and dividends. Airline stocks climbed steadily after April 1942, outperforming the Dow-Jones Industrial Average.[4]

The airlines' wartime prosperity was part of a larger, global story of American aerial expansion. After Pearl Harbor, the army's Air Transport Command (ATC) and the Navy Air Transport Service (NATS) scrambled for planes and personnel. With the help of experienced airline executives, mechanics, and pilots (many of whom were reservists), and by retraining crop dusters and bush pilots to ferry planes, the military transport commands made do until an influx of new pilots, bases, and aircraft permitted them to ramp up operations. Carrying scientists and generals, blood plasma and submarine parts, ATC and NATS sped key personnel and cargos to every theater of the war. They returned with wounded soldiers, workers for labor-starved farms, and strategic materials like quinine, cobalt, and tungsten. They even rearranged nature, importing twenty tons of rubber seeds from Liberia and beetles from the Fiji Islands. The beetles ate root weevils attacking the Honduran hemp crop.

The airlines, operating under cost-plus contracts with the military transport commands, carried their share of vital cargoes. Westbound Pan Am planes rushed antitank shell fuses and engine sand filters to the British in North Africa. Eastbound planes ferried uranium-rich pitchblende from the Belgian Congo. American Airlines delivered the spare parts that enabled many B-24s to take part in the 1943 Ploesti raid. When Ibn Saud demanded gold sovereigns as Aramco royalty payments, TWA crews flew them to Saudi Arabia. They landed, tossed the boxes out the cargo doors, and took off, confident that the local custom of chopping off thieves' hands would protect the gold until collected.[5]

The Hump, the most fabled of the long-distance supply lines, stretched from Assam over the main ridge of the Himalayas to Kunming. Scared kids with seventy hours flew above Japanese-occupied jungles and mountain passes littered with wrecked planes, coping with monsoons, icing, false radio beacons, and flooded runways. They carried everything from ammunition to OSS personnel, including one imperturbable young woman who would become known to the world as Julia Child. It was as close to frontier conditions as anything that might be imagined. The flying was so difficult, and the loss of life so high, that the ATC's India–China Wing became the first purely logistical organization to receive a Presidential Unit Citation. Hard-won experience, better equipment, and navigational aids finally diminished the toll. By August 1945, only 1 in every 2,309 flights was lost. Those were unattractive odds for pilots in the saddle, but a vast improvement over January 1944, when 1 in 218 went down.[6]

Safety and volume improved on the Pacific and Atlantic runs, and for the same reasons: more powerful planes, better communications, and more accurate forecasting along increasingly familiar and heavily traveled airways. Before 1939, American pilots had made just a few dozen flights across the Atlantic. By 1943, they were making tens of thousands annually. "There is no more mystery about flying the oceans . . . ," wrote aeronautical engineer Grover Loening. "I was present at an airfield in Scotland one afternoon last fall when seventy-six American planes arrived from across the Atlantic in one short hour. To those pilots, largely youngsters with only two or three hundred hours of flying, this flight was just an extra-long one—no romance, just tedious routine."[7]

That was an oversimplification. The first North Atlantic crossing could arouse strong feelings even in veteran pilots, who knew they would be facing treacherous weather with limited fuel. Weldon "Dusty" Rhoades, a by-the-book United pilot, found himself enjoying the unaccustomed whiff of danger. But Loening was right about the unprecedented volume of transoceanic air operations. Had spy satellites existed during World War II, they would have registered two extraordinary changes in the planet's built environment, one radically delimiting human space, the other radically expanding it. These would have been the archipelago of barbed wire-enclosed camps, more than ten thousand in Nazi-occupied Europe alone, and the archipelago of new air bases, within and without the United States, from Goose Bay to Guam, that sped the flow of men and *matériel* to all battle fronts against the Axis powers.[8]

Who Flew

The aircrews who made their way across the oceans came from a narrow section of the population. They were exclusively men, commissioned and noncommissioned officers drawn from a volunteer pool. "I never had a bad officer," *Catch-22* author Joseph Heller, of all people, said of the Twelfth Air Force. Good or bad, few who flew in combat did so past their mid-twenties. As in World War I, the demands of high-performance aircraft ruled out all but the young and the fit. "Those controls weren't hydraulically operated, and at 400 mph they became extremely heavy," fighter pilot Chuck Yeager recalled, "After a couple of minutes of dogfighting, your back and arms felt like you had been hauling a piano up stairs." A fighter cockpit could also be an exceedingly cold place, though bomber crews suffered the most. "Thirty-three thousand feet with no heat is the coldest I've ever been," wrote B-24 gunner Edward Diemente. "We had two pairs of gloves and we had to field-strip a cal. 50 machine gun in the turret. We could only take off one pair or our hands would freeze to the metal."[9]

The military selected combat aircrews by the criterion of masculine gender as well as sex, a bias apparent in aircraft nose art. German fighter pilots, a B-17 pilot joked, must have thought they were homing in on "flying underwear catalogs." Interviewers rejected applicants who showed the least sign of homosexuality or effeminacy. They asked candidates whether they favored their mother or their father, and which handle of a motorcycle held the throttle grip. (The right.) Motorcycle riders were considered good bets, as were boys who liked hunting and fishing with their dads. Athletic interest was a strong plus. Naval aviation cadets listed football as their favorite sport. Their favorite reading matter was Superman comics and daredevil adventure pulps—a sobering detail, considering that they averaged more than two years of college education.

It was not that the services were looking for daredevils. Their ideal candidate was someone who displayed a disciplined masculinity, was "frank, open-faced, pleasant-mannered, and co-operatively-inclined"—a little Lindbergh. The overtly reckless, those who would not "straighten up and fly right," were washed out. Yet this gave rise to a dilemma. If instructors weeded too vigorously, they might eliminate good combat pilots. They knew risk-taking and aggressiveness were two sides of the same psychological coin, and that "weak sisters," pilots who lacked resolve, could freeze up under fire. "There were guys who became so terrified being in the same sky with krauts that they began to hyperventilate and blacked out," Yeager wrote. "A few actually shit their pants."

Instructors sometimes winked at infractions if they thought an errant, buzz-happy candidate had the makings of an effective combat pilot.

Robert Morgan, who got one of the buzzing reprieves, vindicated their judgment. He flew the B-17 *Memphis Belle* on twenty-five daylight missions over Europe, returned home a hero, and found he had the sky in his veins. He took one look at a B-29 Superfortress, said give me a squadron, and flew another twenty-six missions in the Pacific. Morgan was unusual in another way. He was married—more than once, in fact. Most who flew in combat, four in five, were single. Married and engaged pilots were more safety conscious, but also suffered more anxiety and higher rates of combat failure. Single men faced flak and 20-mm shells, if not quite with equanimity, then at least with less to lose.[10]

As they evolve, frontier populations typically become larger and denser, more evenly balanced between men and women, more inclusive of children and old people, and less afflicted by premature and traumatic mortality. The war altered this pattern. It increased density, the number of people in the air, but it also temporarily reversed the intertwined trends toward safety and diversity developing since the late 1920s. The war remasculinized the sky, and not only in combat zones. The airlines' priority system worked against children and women. Female passengers declined from 25 to 15 percent. One stewardess was startled to see a man board her plane with his wife and teenage daughter. "It was unusual to have women passengers during wartime," she recalled. "Most of our passengers were military ferry command pilots, or military personnel being transported on leave or to duty stations."[11]

An exception to the rule of male dominance was the Women Airforce Service Pilots (WASP) program. Prior to the war most licensed pilots, and virtually all commercial pilots, were men. In 1940, only fifty-one American women told census takers they worked as "aviators." That was less than 1 percent of those who claimed flying as a full-time job. Fear and prejudice held women back. When Eleanor Roosevelt began taking flying lessons from Amelia Earhart, Franklin told her to stop. "I was doing quite well," Eleanor confided to seaplane pilot Bob Fogg, who obligingly let her take over the controls. "He said he had enough on his mind to worry about. He said he didn't want me taking any more flying lessons because he'd become a nervous wreck worrying about me flying around in the sky." The sheer hypocrisy of the complaint—Eleanor's political travels yielded her more hours "in the sky" than any other female passenger in the 1930s—underscores its prejudicial character. FDR let his wife fly as long as there was a man in the cockpit. This familiar bias was compounded by an institutional one. Airlines tended to hire ex-military pilots, all of whom were men.[12]

It was an exclusive club—in wartime, too exclusive. The country would need more pilots, aviatrix Jacqueline Cochran warned Eleanor Roosevelt in September 1939. Cochran wanted the army to recruit women for "back of the lines work," freeing up male pilots for combat. General Hap Arnold initially opposed the idea, but Pearl Harbor had a way of changing minds. In 1942, the AAF activated its first squadron of female ferrying pilots, mostly experienced fliers, and began setting up facilities to train new ones. Reorganized in 1943 and placed under Cochran's supervision, the WASP program attracted twenty-five thousand applications. "I am physically fit; have a college degree; can sing the Star Spangled Banner; have never been a nazi spy; and would gladly take out U.S. papers if only it were possible," pleaded one Canadian. No luck. United States citizens only.

More than a thousand WASPs, some as young as eighteen, saw duty. They delivered the advanced aircraft pouring from factories, towed targets for aerial gunnery practice. Thirty-seven died in accidents, yet had no right to a military funeral. Despite a record equal or superior to that of male pilots, and despite Arnold's strong endorsement, Congress refused to militarize the program. In 1944, it killed WASP funding. The end of the war was in sight, the CAA was closing down its training operations, and male pilots were writing outraged letters about women bumping them into the "walking Army." But the experiment had convinced skeptical officers and flight surgeons that women could do the job. And it had produced, however briefly, an influx of female professional pilots into America's skies.

Other women found their way into the air as flying nurses and stewardesses. Eastern and Pan American ("as much a male preserve as the Marine Corps") had resisted the trend toward hiring female cabin crew before the war. Eastern had tried stewardesses, then switched back to stewards. Rickenbacker, never shy about voicing his prejudices, said men "can do more work and aren't forever quitting their jobs to get married." They did get drafted, though, and, during the war, Eastern and Pan Am had to hire women. Pan Am opened ground jobs as well, training women as mechanics, radio telegraphers, traffic controllers, and airport clerks. The CAA went down the same road. Ninety percent of its wartime communications and air traffic control trainees were women.[13]

The war also created opportunities for African Americans, the most earthbound people in the country before the defense buildup. In 1936, every licensed black pilot in America could have been seated in a single DC-3, with none left over to fly the plane. But the CPTP inaugurated aeronautics courses at several black colleges, and the AAF began training black pilots at the Tuskegee Army Air Field in late 1941, graduating nearly a thousand by war's end. Though the effort owed more to political pressure than AAF desire to train black pilots, Tuskegee Field alumni proved themselves in combat. The all-black 332d Fighter Group developed a reputation for protecting bomber formations. Attacked over Berlin by twenty ME-262s, its pilots shot down three of the jets without losing any of the vulnerable bombers. A black medium bombardment group, the 477th, made its mark in a different way, when 101 of its officers got themselves arrested for protesting a segregated officer's club. The men of the Freeman Field mutiny went on to make civil rights history, though no combat history. The 477th languished stateside when an exhausted Japan surrendered in August 1945.[14]

Air Power

At the outset of the war the United States, like its British ally, possessed only a small standing army. Prewar doctrine and funding favored the navy. Building up the army and invading Europe would require time, as well as air superiority. The skies offered a chance to strike the Reich directly. The Royal Air Force's victory in the Battle of Britain kept England in the war and gave the Allies a giant base from which to launch a bomber offensive. The strategic situation thus favored a rapid expansion of the AAF. By mid-1944, when it was at its peak strength, the AAF claimed one in every three Americans serving in army uniforms. It had nearly eighty thousand planes, including seventeen thousand combat aircraft in overseas theaters.[15]

Well before Pearl Harbor, the aircraft industry had gone to multiple shifts and assembly-line techniques, making more intensive use of less skilled labor. By late 1943, more than two million workers, including housewives, retirees, and moonlighting white-collar workers, were toiling in aircraft factories. Teachers signed on during the summer, working alongside former students who advised them to stay and make more money. Lockheed hired four thousand students still in high school, arranging for them to divide their time between the classroom and factory. The AAF employed another three hundred thousand workers in its air depots, going so far as to hire the blind, the deaf, and the deformed. The nation's suicide rate plunged during the war years. Given a job, a purpose, and a good enemy, even the grievously afflicted were disinclined to kill themselves.[16]

Entire industries shifted roles. Converted to wartime production, car assembly lines provided a stream of aircraft engines and subassemblies. New factories went up, including Ford's cavernous Willow Run facility. Taking in raw materials and subassemblies through its steel-framed maw and disgorging B-24s at the other end, Willow Run reached the capacity of a plane an hour, a remarkable feat for a machine with more than a million parts. "Bring the Germans and Japs to see it," crowed Ford's production manager, Charles Sorensen. "Hell, they'll blow their brains out."[17]

Things were not so simple in practice. The AAF committed its B-24s and other heavy bombers to a campaign of daylight precision bombing. The idea was to take advantage of the specialization and interdependence of modern industrial society by attacking such targets as ball-bearing factories and oil refineries, on which manufacturing and transportation depended. But bad weather, something bomber pilots flying in tight formation dreaded as much as flak, turned out to be a serious limitation. (The name of one notoriously difficult target, the Romanian refining center at Ploesti, means "rainy town.") Long-range missions operated without fighter escort, adding to the losses. In 1943, army statisticians calculated that the average Eighth Air Force bomber completed a little over fourteen missions before being blasted from the skies. AAF aircrews suffered the highest death rate in the military, with the Eighth Air Force alone losing more men than the Marine Corps. Given its high percentage of officers and educated men, AAF losses cost more than the unadorned casualty figures suggest. Aerial combat over Europe in 1942 and 1943 was the nearest equivalent in American history to the casualties sustained by German university students at Ypres or by British volunteers at the Somme. Perhaps that is why it retains such a powerful and poignant place in the national imagination.[18]

Maintaining morale and combat efficiency (the subject of *Twelve O'Clock High,* a war movie that enjoyed a second career as a staple of management seminars and officer-training schools) proved a constant challenge. As in World War I, airmen endured a stressful cycle of boredom, terror, and alcoholic release. "The worst part was being awakened for briefing, sullenly eating the breakfast, going to briefing, and awaiting the moment when the blue curtain was pulled back, revealing our target and the route to it," William Ryan remembered. "When it was France or the Lowlands, instant relief occurred. When the target was deep in Germany, utter terror. I will never forget how I felt on the morning of 17 August 1943 when the curtain was drawn and we saw the long, long red line to Schweinfurt." On such occasions men broke into cold sweats, became nauseated, and surrendered their breakfasts.[19]

Well after their tours were over, the memories stayed with them. When the crew of the *Memphis Belle* returned to the United States after twenty-five missions, the men agreed to improvise dialogue for William Wyler's documentary of the same name. It would be a bit of Hollywood sport, they thought. But when they saw the unedited combat footage shot from B-17s, they found themselves back in the skies over Germany, fighting down feelings of horror

Allied bombers and aircrew paid a high price for their raids over Nazi territory. *Above:* An A-20 Havoc after a direct flak hit. *Below:* A B-17 after a flak burst tore off a propeller and cowling and wounded the radio operator. The pilot, 1st Lt. Albert Rehn, inspects the damage.

and helplessness worse than those they had experienced in battle. Sitting in their soundproofed dubbing booths, they had no operational tasks to engage their attention, nothing to distract them from the images of chattering guns and falling planes.[20]

Had the war ended when the *Memphis Belle* flew her last mission in May 1943, few would have pronounced daylight strategic bombing anything other than a costly failure. The situation changed in early 1944, with the arrival of long-range escort planes. The best of these was the P-51 Mustang. Its supercharged, 12-cylinder Merlin engine (a British design mass produced by Packard) and huge four-bladed propeller gave it superior speed; the addition of larger internal fuel tanks and wing-mounted drop tanks gave it the ability to accompany heavy-bomber formations deep into Germany. The raids drew the *Luftwaffe* away from the fighting fronts and destroyed it through attrition, the bombers acting as unignorable bait for the outclassed German fighters. Where the Germans had once held the initiative, attacking at will and then returning to their bases, the fighter escorts now pursued them, picking off battle-damaged cripples. Pilots in intact planes fared little better. Teenagers with 60 hours of flying time pitted their ME-109s against P-51 pilots who had logged 300 hours before entering combat. The Germans flew with inferior, low-octane fuel and sometimes took off with mismatched wheels. Spare parts were scarce. Albert Speer had dispersed German industry to avoid the escalating bombing attacks, even stashing aircraft machine tools in a five-mile stretch of the Paris Metro. But, in so doing, he had created serious problems of coordination and supply.

Those problems worsened as Allied air raids cratered oil refineries and marshaling yards, fouling transportation. Fast troop movements became impossible. Roving fighter-bombers, unchecked by the *Luftwaffe,* destroyed everything with wheels, down to horse carts. German attempts to cut Allied supply lines became increasingly futile, as aircraft equipped with high-frequency radar hunted down their surfaced U-boats. "Complete air superiority . . . altogether decided the war," *Generaloberst* Alfred Jodl told Allied interrogators in 1945. "I would go so far as to say that our power on the land was numerically and, from the point of armament, sufficiently strong, if not to win, at least to hold our own on all fronts, if our own air force had kept up on the same level."[21]

Defeated in carrier duels at Midway in June 1942, and the Philippine Sea in June 1944, the Japanese paid a still heavier price for losing control of the air. Even kamikaze attacks failed to stop America's multiplying carrier task forces, the decisive weapon of the Pacific war. Guided by radar, screened by cruisers and destroyers, with battleships providing anti-aircraft platforms and

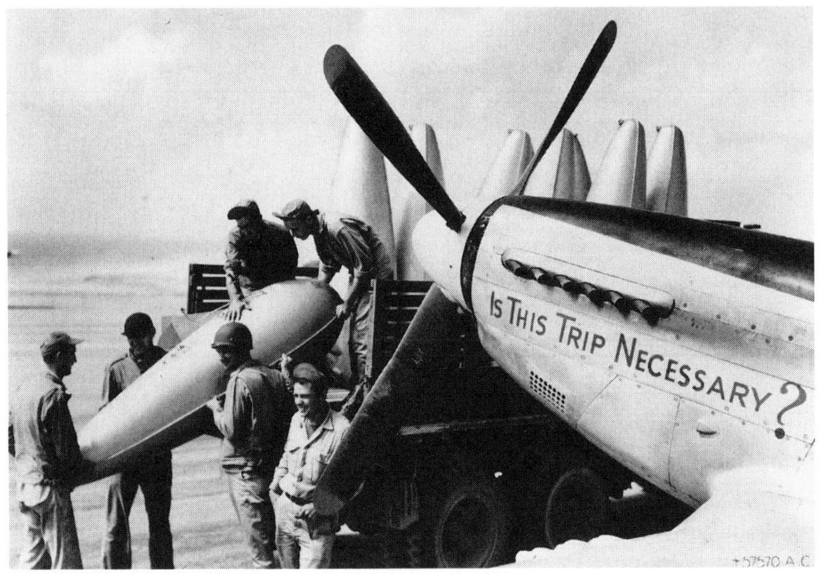

Fighter planes, whose wings were crammed with guns and ammunition, lacked the fuel to accompany AAF bombers past the Rhine. Auxiliary fuel tanks, including two mounted under the wings, gave them the necessary range. Known for their decisive role in Europe—Goering credited them for the success of the Allied air offensive—long-range fighters also saw action in the Pacific. Here, men of the 72nd Fighter Squadron prepare a P-51 on Iwo Jima, an island captured, at great cost, to facilitate B-29 raids. The name, beneath the exhaust ports of its Merlin engine, satirizes propaganda to conserve fuel.

fire support for amphibious landings, the navy's fast carriers ranged freely through the Central and South Pacific, assuring local air superiority for marine and army operations. Aviation engineers transformed the islands they seized, grading runways and laying down steel mats before the last sniper had been cleared. Island-based fighter-bombers, like the P-38 Lightnings and F4U Corsairs Lindbergh flew, attacked Japanese bases and supply ships, isolating and starving entire garrisons. Fighter missions whittled away the slender stick of Japanese air power. "The Jap weakness, and our real hope for victory, is in the air," General George C. Kenney wrote to Hap Arnold in early 1943. "His fleet and his army can hold their own in any league, but he simply cannot train airmen to compare with ours in a hurry. His original highly trained crews were superb, but they are dead."[22]

The capture of bases in the Marianas in the summer of 1944 brought the Japanese home islands within the range of B-29s. Curtis LeMay, given charge of strategic bombing, discovered that he could inflict more damage by low-altitude nighttime area bombing than by the high-altitude daylight precision bombing. Logging 120 hours a month in the air, scattering napalm over Japan's combustible cities, flying low enough that they gagged on the stench of charred flesh, LeMay's crews burned out the heart of industrial Japan. Entire districts of working-class housing vanished. Dazed survivors fashioned lean-tos from scorched tin roofing, the only housing material that survived the inferno. Workplace absenteeism rose to 50 percent. Aerial mining of the Shimonoseki Strait choked off food shipments from Korea and China. The B-29s also blocked harbors: Hiroshima was mined before it was bombed.[23]

Hap Arnold sensed the end approaching. By July 1945, he was making bets with other Allied brass—five dollars with Chief of Staff George C. Marshall, dinner with Air Chief Marshall Sir Charles F. Portal—that the Pacific war would soon be over. "Atomic bomb or no atomic bomb, the Japanese were already on the verge of collapse," he wrote in his memoirs. LeMay drew the obvious corollary. "If you love America," he told a New York audience, "do everything you can to make sure that what happened to Germany and Japan will never happen to our country."[24]

That sentiment was universal among AAF generals after the war. They knew that the Allies had prevailed by holding on until American production gave them an insurmountable advantage. Stalin's 1941 prediction, "this war will be won by the side that has an overwhelming preponderance in engine production," had been right on the money. Soviet troops had towed their artillery behind Studebaker trucks and fought in tanks armored with Lend-Lease steel borne to Russia in oil-fired Liberty ships. But the extraordinary development of offensive air power, epitomized by rockets, jets, long-range bombers, and nuclear weapons, ruled out the possibility of lengthy industrial buildups in future wars. Striking across polar air routes, potential aggressors could inflict immediate catastrophic damage, leaving no opportunity to mobilize. The next Pearl Harbor might come at midnight. Radar could locate targets in darkness, and bombers could hit them with supersonic speed. The engines of the future, Arnold warned Americans, would bear such unfamiliar names as turbojet and ram-jet.

The only antidote to air power was air power itself. For Arnold, that meant four things: a strong air force operating from overseas and domestic bases; healthy airlines prepared for wartime backup; government support for a technologically advanced aircraft industry; and "progressive and interlocked efforts of our scientists and our military technicians"—in short, a military-industrial complex. Though there would be many disputes over funding and priorities during the next two decades, no one in the government seriously challenged these assumptions. Even Dwight Eisenhower, who named the military-industrial complex and warned of its dangers, conceded in the same famous 1961 speech that "we can no longer risk emergency improvisation of national defense" and that "we have been compelled to create a permanent armaments industry of vast proportions."[25]

Eisenhower's passive voice—"we have been compelled"—may have reflected the realities of superpower tension, but it also concealed the degree to which the aviation industry shaped the postwar demand for military aircraft. The manufacturers dreaded a repeat of 1918, when contract cancellations wrecked the industry. Postwar commercial sales would not save them, given the availability of war surplus observation and transport planes. A sympathetic Arnold wanted to melt his victorious fleet into ingots, but more conservative minds prevailed. The government removed the morphine from the first-aid kits and sold off the rest of the equipment. American and United bought up C-54s by the lot and installed upholstered seats, galleys, toilets, and other amenities of civilian flying.[26]

In 1943, anticipating just such a bleak economic situation, the aircraft manufacturers' trade organization hired Hill and Knowlton, the country's leading public relations firm. Hill and Knowlton's job was to increase public support for air power, which would translate into federal spending on research and development and military procurement. With "Air Power is Peace Power" as its theme, Hill and Knowlton prepared radio programs, polished congressional testimony, and sent mass mailings to the 800,000-member American Legion. It made sure air power stories got to journalists, who found growing room on their front and editorial pages.

None of this mattered much in the short run, when pressures to cut defense spending, shift to civilian production, and "bring daddy home" were overwhelming. Even prostitutes were demobilizing, flying home from Honolulu. After V-J Day the government canceled $9 billion in aircraft contracts, and the ink in aircraft manufacturers' ledgers turned red. But the public relations campaign, which continued through the 1940s, forestalled deeper cuts. It united air power advocates and kept the issue before a favorably disposed public. At decade's end, the seeds of cold war militarization—Berlin's blockade and dramatic airlift, Mao's triumph and Stalin's bomb, North Korea's invasion of the South—fell on well-prepared soil. The major airframe makers saw their sales rise from a half billion dollars in 1946 to $1.4 billion in 1950 to $5.2 billion in 1955. "The Air Force came back to Lockheed with orders such as could scarcely have been dreamed," said chief engineer Hal

Hibbard. "You can't get away from the enormous importance of the military in aviation."[27]

The airlines shared the cold war wealth. Private carriers, notably Pan American, flew one hundred thousand personnel and well over half of the total air tonnage to the Korean combat zone. Military Air Transport Service (MATS) planes concentrated on bazooka rockets and other critical cargos. After Korea wound down, the military, wary of negotiating future contracts on an emergency basis, created the Civil Reserve Air Fleet (CRAF). CRAF aircraft, four-engine civilian airliners and cargo planes earmarked for military conversion within forty-eight hours, could provide 40 percent of anticipated wartime airlift requirements. They permitted the Pentagon to spend less on MATS, which already had more equipment than any airline in the world. As Arnold had foreseen, and as subsequent conflicts in Vietnam and the Persian Gulf would demonstrate, American civil and military air transport capabilities had merged into a single interlocking crisis-response system, a *via atmospherica* capable of projecting American power into any part of a troubled world.[28]

The Postwar Airlines

The airlines' main business, however, remained nonmilitary passengers. Prospects looked excellent at the end of the war. The army was disposing of surplus airfields, many suitable for conversion to municipal airports. Two of them, in Pittsburgh and Chicago, would grow into international hubs. With three million veterans returning from the army and navy air services, the airlines had a bottomless pool from which to draw their mechanics, controllers, and pilots. The trick, as one airline medical director put it, was to reverse the military formula: forget the ones who rode motorcycles and select the "normal human beings."[29]

During the war millions of GIs had taken their first plane ride, an experience American's C. R. Smith thought crucial. Unspoken fear and high cost had held the industry back. Those who bought tickets before the war "had damn good reason to travel. Their son fell off a horse, or they had to go to Mayo, that kind of thing. . . . Then we had 10 to 15 million men under arms—and *they* had good reason to travel. Masses of them moved by air, and this was the reason for the big difference in attitudes thereafter."[30]

The experience of wartime aviation changed the way Americans saw the world. André Priester, Pan American's chief engineer, described the new geography in a confidential 1943 letter to Juan Trippe. After the war, he wrote, Pan Am could run a truly international airline from a single, economically

Crewmen aboard the escort carrier USS *Tulagi,* bound for the invasion of southern France. Millions of ordinary Americans who had never touched a plane got hands-on experience during the war. In the postwar economy, their knowledge of maintenance, repair, and aircraft operation and control provided airlines with a virtually unlimited pool of skilled labor, while the first-time flying experience of many military personnel gave airlines an expanded passenger market.

efficient center of operations in New York. From there its planes could radiate across the world, connecting New York with London; New York with Paris, Ankara, and New Delhi; or with any of dozens of other trading centers that lay along great circle routes. People and goods would travel east or west by curving north and then south through unobstructed skies. Some nations, of course, would deny free air passage, forcing planes to skirt their boundaries. But even with political detours, great-circle air routes promised more speed and fewer zigzags than any competing form of surface transportation. Analysts at rivals like TWA and Northwest saw the same thing. They were not about to surrender the market to Pan Am. It was as if they had blood in their mouths, said one executive, "their appetites for international routes whetted by the taste of wartime crossings."[31]

If the means of international air travel were at hand, so was the demand. "The war developed the airplane, released its capabilities, demonstrated that it could fly across oceans and go to far places," Bob Buck observed. "The GIs wanted to show their families where they had waged war, and the heretofore provincial American public learned it was easy to go to Paris, Rome, London, and other places." Airlines jumped on the theme. A 1946 ad, "All Mother Earth's Children Live on the *Same* Street," showed a featureless globe, centered on the eastern United States, labeled only with the names of cities. All political and topographical barriers had vanished. The atmosphere had become indivisible. Americans could go anywhere. They *should* go anywhere. Juan Trippe talked as though international tourism was the sole guarantor of world peace. Pan Am would do good while doing well.[32]

A glance at passenger volume shows just how well Trippe and his competitors did. In 1933, the year American carriers got their first modern, twin-

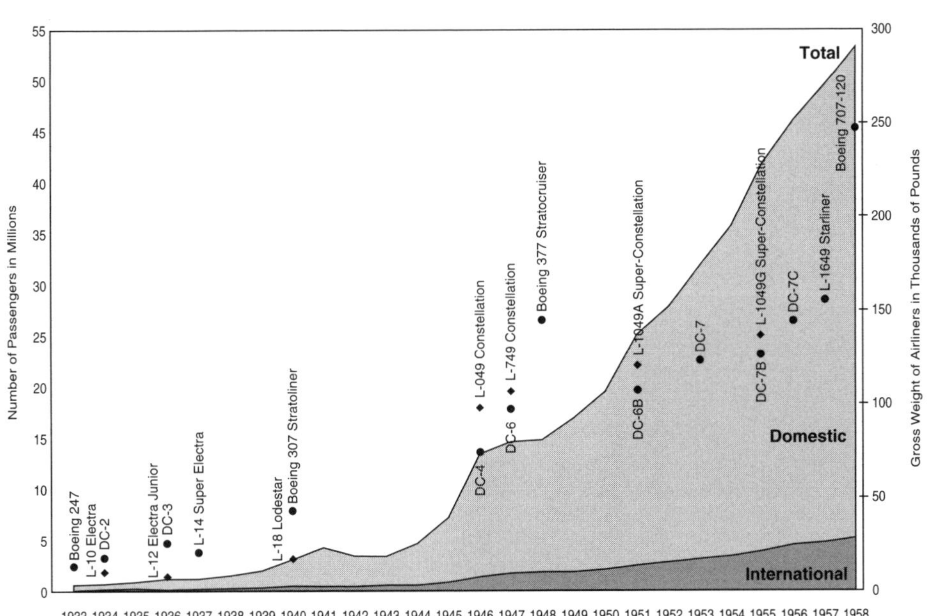

Revenue Passengers Enplaned on U.S. Scheduled Airlines, 1933–1958, with Gross Weights of Airliners by Year of First Commercial Use engine planes, they carried 576,000 passengers. In 1958, the year they got their first jets, they flew close to one hundred times that number. The big rise came after the war, and put the country in a class by itself. In 1947, with 6 percent of the world's population, the United States accounted for 28 percent of the world's international scheduled air mileage and 85 percent of its domestic. Its customer base was broadening: women were buying every third ticket by the decade's end. And that was just for the scheduled carriers. Hundreds of nonscheduled air services added to the American lead. The "nonskeds," mostly veterans flying war surplus equipment, waited until their planes filled with cut-rate passengers and then took off, banking on full cabins to clear a profit.[33]

The nonskeds found a niche because scheduled flying was still pricey. In 1945, a one-way, cross-country fare on United cost $120—down from $150 before the war, but still three weeks net pay for most workers. The scheduled airlines had to chip away at costs. Larger equipment offered one means. Though the leading manufacturers occasionally built small, feeder-route models like the L-12 "Electra Junior" (the plane Ingrid Bergman and Paul Henreid boarded at the end of *Casablanca*), they concentrated on bigger planes with more powerful engines. It made more sense to pay unionized pilots to haul 99 passengers on a 360 mph DC-7 than to poke along with 40 passengers on a 205 mph DC-4. Gains in speed acted as a seat multiplier, making it possible for passenger volume to increase even faster than aircraft size.

By the late 1950s, designers had pushed piston-engine technology to its limits. Intricate turbo-compound engines diverted exhaust gas through spinning turbines, connected to their crankshafts through fluid couplings. The boost in horsepower enabled planes to fly six times as far, with three times as many passengers, and twice as fast as the first DC-3s. The ride was more comfortable, too. This last point was of particular importance to women and children. They came down with more cases of airsickness than adult male passengers, though whether from inexperience, anxiety, or biological difference is hard to say. Smoother rides in bigger planes encouraged passenger diversity. The quality of transportation shaped the population characteristics of a maturing frontier zone, just as it had after the westward expansion of the railroads.[34]

Put more broadly, local social characteristics vary according to latitude, altitude, and depth. "Extreme" activities such as polar exploration, mountaineering, deep-shaft mining, and undersea operations are dominated by men in their prime. The higher, deeper, or farther north or south you go, the more likely you are to encounter mainly adult males—if you encounter anyone at all. Harsh conditions both thin and skew populations. But when technological innovation alleviates the conditions, the population begins to normalize. Then the type-II frontier zone "moves farther out." In the case of aviation, it moved to the more rarefied atmosphere above the altitude at which pressurized commercial flights operated.

Technology seldom advances without exacting a price. Adding more planes and then bigger planes overtaxed ground facilities. Every day thousands squeezed into airports designed to accommodate hundreds. Standing on gum-blackened linoleum amidst piles of baggage, waiting their turn at pay phones to report delays, and lining up outside filthy restrooms, passengers thought bus terminals looked good by comparison. Lines formed in the skies, too. In bad weather passengers found themselves stacked up for hours, tired, anxious, and sick of listening to the one crying baby on the plane. They passed the time by telling airline jokes, like the one about the deadheading airline official who spots a stewardess hunting under all the seats. "What are you looking for?" he asks. "For some of the glamour I was told I'd find on airplanes," she says.[35]

Airports tried to alleviate the delays through expansion. TWA's Harold Blackburn said that, to the best of his knowledge, he had never landed at a completed airport. "They were tearing up LaGuardia the first time I flew in there [in] November 1939 and they still were at it . . . the last time in 1951." Randall Kirk, head of ground operations for Pan Am's Atlantic Division, resigned himself to the situation. Bracing for the impact of the even bigger jets in 1958, he warned public relations staff that they would just have to live with "inadequate" airports. Ground facilities always lagged behind aircraft development.[36]

Big planes confronted the airlines with another public relations problem, one that took the form of a cruel paradox. Though the per mile risk of air travel declined after 1947 (an unusually bad year), the toll of any given accident went up. More seats meant more fatalities. The worst accident occurred in 1956, when a United DC-7 inexplicably collided with a TWA Super Constellation over the Grand Canyon. It took helicopters and Swiss mountain climbers to reach the wreckage and reclaim the 128 bodies. Airline executives could do little about the sensational coverage such disasters generated.[37]

They also had to worry about the planes' price tags. The first DC-6s sold for close to $600,000 apiece. The first postwar Constellations—delivered to TWA in Las Vegas to avoid California's sales tax—cost $690,000. By the time American placed its order for Douglas's new DC-7s in late 1951, the going price was $1.6 million. Airlines borrowed heavily, adding interest payments to their payrolls, maintenance bills, and other fixed costs. The investment would pay off if they could keep most of the new seats full. But ticket demand fluctuated with the economy, seasons, weather, recency of disasters, and a dozen other variables. The war's high tide had long since run out. Average load factors, in the upper 80 percent range during the war, trailed off below 60 percent in the late 1940s.[38]

The obvious strategy was to discount a portion of the seats, creating a class system like that on trains and ships. Discounting permitted the airlines to hold their own against the cut-rate nonskeds and siphon more business from the railroads. Capital Airlines inaugurated coach service in 1948, offering a New York–Chicago fare cheaper than Pullman rates and only slightly more expensive than rail coach. (The catch: Capital's plane departed at 1:00 A.M.) The Big Four soon added their own coach flights. "We called 'em cattle class," TWA Capt. Russell Bowen remembered. "We would just line them in—two double rows, stem to stern. Utilization on those aircraft was tremendous—better than ever before or since." Coach fares drew twice as many first-timers as regular fares. Cattle class may not have been luxurious, but it got people past the fear-of-the-unknown barrier and built the airlines' customer base.[39]

In 1946 and 1947, Pan American tried luring vacationers with 20 percent cuts on Latin American flights. Then, in 1948, it went after a very different clientele with seventy-five dollar flights from San Juan to New York City. What Pan Am liked to call "the first overseas air tourist service" was in fact air steerage. Still, a packed DC-4 beat five days on a converted troop ship. Two-thirds of the five million Puerto Ricans who came to the United States after the war did so on one of Pan Am's San Juan–New York flights. It was, wrote Carl Solberg, "the world's first migration by air."

Trippe saw that discounting paid. He introduced tourist-class service on South American and Bermuda flights and then convinced the International Air Transport Association (IATA), the international airline cartel, to permit the same service on transatlantic flights. Passengers willing to put up with thirty-four-inch seat pitch, less baggage, and plainer food got a huge break in price. On May 1, 1952, Pan Am dropped its round-trip New York–London fare from $711 to $486. Volume soared. In 1954, Pan Am introduced "Fly Now, Pay Later," a credit gimmick catchy enough to win a place in the language. By 1956, more people traveled westbound across the Atlantic in planes than in ships. By 1958, lower-cost fares provided two-thirds of Pan Am's North Atlantic business. Most of those flying "tourist" were making their first trip on a plane. Having experienced long-distance air travel at first hand, they were perfect candidates for the jet revolution that Trippe and Boeing had waiting in the wings.

Trippe boasted that the introduction of discount fares, which permitted "the ordinary man" to fly, was the third most important landmark in the history of the airlines, following Lindbergh's flight and the coming of the jets. There was some truth in this. Price was the last barrier to democratization, as deregulation would prove. Women, who did most of the family travel and vacation planning, were quick to take advantage of the new fares. By the end of the decade, 46 percent of Pan Am's transatlantic passengers and 54 percent of its Bermuda passengers were women. Two decades before, when the only substantial discounts Pan Am gave were to marines, women had bought just 22 percent of Pan Am's tickets.[40]

But social class was another matter. In 1955, the airlines did three-quarters of their business with the wealthiest quarter of the population. Coach fares on domestic routes fluctuated between 60 and 75 percent of first-class fares, still a lot to pay for working people. Installment plans were common. And someone paying $486 for airfare to Europe was hardly ordinary in terms of education and income. Postwar social trends—more disposable income, more leisure, more education—promised to enlarge the market. Twice as many Americans had high school or college degrees in 1956 than in 1940, and the art history survey was plainly Pan Am's friend. For the time being, though, ad executives ran their copy in the tonier newspapers, reservation agents dealt with high-end customers, and passengers dressed up to fly.[41]

If postwar passengers were not yet ordinary in a social sense, the *experience* of flying was becoming ordinary, in the sense of predictable and routine. Like the stewardess in the joke, first-timers might look about the cabin for imagined glamour. The veterans settled in and stuck their noses in their papers. Save for the speed of their transit, they might as well have been on a train—exactly what aircraft designers, airline executives, and advertisers had in mind. They knew that the more automatic, anodyne, and invisible flying became, the more likely it was to become a mass phenomenon.

No danger, no mystique.

—ROBERT WOHL, "REPUBLIC OF THE AIR"

CHAPTER 8

Routine Stuff

Most historians describe commercial aviation's postwar progress as evolutionary and continuous, a steady climb along the course marked out during the golden age of the late 1920s and 1930s. Before commercial jets roared into the picture, the war's principal legacies were bigger, faster, and higher-flying prop planes; improved navigational and landing aids; and additional, if still inadequate, airports. Build them better and more will come.

Another way to think about aviation's mid-century progress is as a process of cultural development—specifically, the creation, formalization, and mechanical expression of a frontier culture. Movement into unfamiliar regions poses challenges to safety and comfort, forcing rapid adaptation. Space, for example, negates the assumptions of gravity. The "6" seen by a weightless astronaut may be an upside-down "9," and ordinary activity no longer keeps bones strong. To master new environments people develop new techniques and new rules of appropriate behavior. Or they have to acquire them elsewhere. Necessity has as often been the mother of liberal borrowing as of invention.[1]

Those who settled along America's midland backwoods frontier borrowed from Finnish immigrants. The Finns had migrated to New Sweden, in the Delaware Valley, in the mid-seventeenth century. As it happened, they knew a lot about surviving in dense, bear-infested woods. They had developed techniques of axmanship, slash-and-burn agriculture, rifle hunting, and open-range herding in the Scandinavian forests well suited to colonizing the American woodlands. What the Finns did not know they picked up from the Indians, adding skills like corn and squash cultivation. The Scotch-Irish, whose later migration provided the weight of numbers, adopted this "blended" culture. They added a few tricks of their own, such as the distillation of grain into whiskey for easier transportation to distant markets. The result was a new culture, a syncretic whole greater than the sum of its parts, ideally suited for rapid forest colonization.[2]

The Sources of Aviation Culture

Aviation's pioneering culture likewise drew from many different sources. Birds had long inspired glider experimenters. Otto Lilienthal called his 1889 treatise *Birdflight as the Basis for Aviation.* The Wright brothers, impressed by birds' ability to sustain flight without flapping, saw no reason why humans could not do the same with cambered wings. Observing birds taught them the most efficient way to regain balance during a roll. Birds tilted one wingtip up and the other down, then reversed the process to roll back in the other direction. Pulling on control wires to helically twist a canvas wing would have the same aerodynamic effect. "Here," Wilbur later claimed, "was the silent birth of all that underlies human flight."[3]

"All" was too strong a word. The Wrights and other aviation pioneers also drew on nautical principles to navigate the ocean of air. Moving a rudder turned the nose of a plane in the same way that it moved the bow of a ship, by creating a sideways force on the tail or stern. Rudders solved the problem of yaw control. Elevators—horizontal rudders, like those on early submarines—solved the problem of pitch control, enabling the pilot to turn the plane's nose up or down.

It is striking how much of the language of the air derived from the language of the sea. Pilots flew with the help of propellers, used beacons to maintain a safe course between airports, and measured their progress in nautical miles. On longer flights they used sextants to fix their positions, or estimated them by dead reckoning, using charts and compass bearings. Airliners had captains and navigators in cockpits. Stewards and stewardesses on the flight deck checked passenger lists and prepared food in a galley tucked away in the hull. We refer to planes (and space shuttles) in the feminine, another nautical tradition.

The arrangement of chairs on either side of the aisle followed railroad practice, as did the introduction of upholstered, reclining seats. Sleeper transports copied features of the Pullman cars with which they competed. Aviation enthusiasts experimented with steel-tubed hooks for aerial mail pickups, a variation of the railroad mail-car hooks that snagged mailbags from station platforms. Airport procedures—tickets, baggage claims, tipping the redcaps—derived from railroad practice. From the passenger's point of view, an airport terminal in the 1940s differed from a train station primarily in terms of its size, squalor, and proneness to weather delay.[4]

Airplanes also incorporated automotive technology. "In all the development of aviation," Henry Ford pointed out in 1930, "there has never been a real airplane engine." Even engines of radial design worked the same way as gasoline car engines, with spark plugs and pistons and rods and crankshafts. Ford said he looked forward to the day when some clever lad—he recalled his own youthful turn from steam to internal combustion—would discover that gas engines were not the best means of aerial propulsion. Five years after that prophecy a young Royal Air Force officer named Frank Whittle set up a research company. He called it Power Jets, Ltd.[5]

Whittle's work on turbojets was not wholly original, for his engine shared many features with the turbines that drove fast naval vessels. But it did show that aviation could take technology in surprising new directions. The same was true of piloting. Experience gave aviators new insights into the art and science of flying, insights unconnected with any other transportation culture. They passed these on as rules of thumb or aphorisms:

- The higher the field, the thinner the air, the faster the landing.
- Runway behind and altitude above are useless.
- A downwind turn close to the ground is dangerous.
- If you are faced with a forced landing, fly as far into the crash as possible.
- The only time an aircraft has too much fuel on board is when it is on fire.
- Steer your parachute away from trees. If you can't, better keep your legs together.

Veteran fliers shared their hard-won wisdom with students who perched attentively on broken-down hangar couches. They told them how they had gotten out of a spin, or stopped a sideslip by ruddering into it, or a hundred other useful things. Unconsciously, they passed on the culture's lingo and lore. "Zero-zero" meant no ceiling and no visibility, "Parker time" phony hours penned into a log, a "grease job" a perfect landing, and "ground flying"—well, that was what they were doing.

When the airlines arrived, the co-pilot system provided advanced training. Green co-pilots absorbed the wisdom of veteran pilots and then applied it under their watchful eyes. They learned when three-quarters flaps worked better than full, which DC-3 takeoff rattles could be safely ignored, and how to protect the passengers from pressure change by descending no faster than 500 feet per minute. How the pilots smiled when Frank Lloyd Wright proposed his mile-high skyscraper with high-speed elevators. They warned him that fast drops of thousands of feet would play havoc with the riders' inner ears.[6]

An experience-based culture developed in the cabin, too. Flight attendants advised passengers on etiquette, safety, and comfort. Please do not throw cigars out the window. Keep your seat belts fastened in rough air. If the pressure change hurts your ears, try this stick of gum. (One woman took it, chewed it, and put the wad in her ears.) Stewardesses answered a thousand questions, everything from what kept the plane in the air to why tailwinds sped eastbound flights. The answers were rehearsed but prompt and courteous. The more people knew about flying, the more likely they were to return to the air.[7]

Formalizing the Culture

By the late 1920s, aviation had evolved a complex culture that blended knowledge and procedures from older transportation systems with the steady accumulation of new insights into the art and science of flying. That culture made possible the growing human presence in the sky. But the more complex the culture became, the more difficult it was for those who ran the airlines and regulated the airways to be sure that aircrews knew everything necessary for safe operation. The pilots' oral culture, the old-timers talking to kids chewing grass stalks down by the south hangar, was all well and good. But it was no longer sufficient.

So they began writing everything down. In 1929, André Priester prepared the first Pan Am operations manual. Army pilots Bill Ocker and Carl Crane distilled instrument flying into *Blind Flight in Theory and Practice* (1932), a book that became a bible for aspiring pilots. In 1937, Fred Fagg, a former bomber pilot and law professor, codified civil air regulations, simplifying access to the proliferating rules. "I will feel better . . . if no complaint arrives from the CAA within the next few days," Lindbergh confessed in 1942, after flying a Ford VIP over a baseball diamond. "Dropping baseballs to start games used to be all right in the early days of aviation, but for some years past it has been strictly against regulations."[8]

To make sure their pilots knew what was kosher, the airlines incorporated federal regulations into their own hefty operations manuals. To please their passengers, they gave flight attendants instructions very nearly as detailed. Carry gum and ammonia capsules. Keep a railroad timetable handy in case the plane is grounded. Watch passengers headed for the lavatory to be sure they do not blunder out the emergency door. Stewardesses on Douglas sleeper transports had to work through a 1,177-item preflight equipment checklist, specifying everything from checker boards to electric shavers. Piled outside the hangared plane, the gear resembled the contents of a "modern drug store."[9]

Training became more formal. By the 1940s, "air colleges" required stewardess trainees to take courses in fifteen different subject areas, from meteorology to charm. Mechanics, air traffic controllers, and pilots wrestled with their own textbooks. Flying students spent more time in hooded Link trainers. The Air Corps bought them in bulk after the 1934 air mail fiasco revealed how poorly its pilots performed on instruments. By 1958, some two million aviators, including 500,000 military pilots trained during World War II, had learned instrument flying in Edwin Link's eponymous simulator.[10]

Bob Buck, reflecting on a life in aviation, picked the movement toward formal instruction as one of its most conspicuous trends. He himself did a stint training TWA co-pilots. They learned to use standard commands, simple phrases like "gear up" or "gear down," chosen for their lack of ambiguity. By standardizing language, the airline could shift personnel without running the risk that someone would misinterpret an unfamiliar command. Otherwise a pilot might say, "Well, let's have the rollers," and his new co-pilot, in charge of operating the landing gear, would not know what he was talking about. Standardized procedures, Buck admitted, took a while to impose. "The opposition of the individualists was strong, never completely overcome with some old-timers."[11]

Here was another problem. Instructors could teach pilots rules of safe operation, but they did not invariably follow them. Failure to do so might reflect defiance, or lack of discipline, or poor training. But most often it was simply a matter of forgetting to apply the rule in a complex situation in which the pilot had his mind on other things. A thousand things could cause a crash, and they were not the same thousand things for every airplane. The P-39 Airacobra carried a 37-mm cannon in its nose. Flying without the heavy ammunition, the manuals warned, required ballast in the nose section, otherwise the plane would become unbalanced. But nose ballast was an easy thing for pilots and ground crews to overlook. Pilots died while flying noncombat missions, contributing to the plane's poor reputation. The B-29's weakness was flap operation. Unless pilots remembered to retract their flaps slowly, the giant bomber would suddenly lose lift on takeoff and crash, killing all on board.

Risks like this drove engineers crazy. Why, one wondered, should anyone *tell* B-29 pilots to retract their flaps slowly when simply "changing the angle of a bell crank" would force them to do so, the way a pneumatic door-closer automatically slowed the door's final closing? Or why warn busy stewardesses to keep an eye on passengers who might mistake the emergency exit for the lavatory door? Better to design an emergency exit with an appearance, position, and operation that would make it impervious to the Three Stooges. Much of the history of modern aircraft development has involved the mechanical re-expression of aviation culture's rules of safety and comfort in airframe, engine, and control design. Trust the equipment to do a better job than the humans who operate it. If rudder movement can stress a jet tail fin, then simply add a mechanism to limit the pilot's ability to move the rudder at high speed—a standard feature of jet design.[12]

The B-47 Stratojet gave the U.S. Air Force its first 600 mph bomber and Boeing the key to its 700-series airliners: jet nacelles slung forward and below flexible, swept wings. The design's one drawback was Dutch Roll. This tail-wagging yaw could induce airsickness or even loss of pilot control. The solution, typical of the drive to engineer safety, was to install an automatic yaw damper. Every time the device, "Little Herbie," detected the onset of Dutch Roll, it moved the rudder to correct it without the pilot's assistance or knowledge. Engineers built variations of Little Herbie into all swept-wing jets.

Mechanical, hydraulic, and, later, electronic devices relieved much of the tedium of routine flight. Gyroscopic autopilots, "Metal Mikes," kept planes stable along all three axes of rotation (roll, pitch, and yaw) without manual assistance, permitting pilots to concentrate on the weather, engine manifold pressure, and other concerns. Wiley Post used one of the first autopilots on his solo round-the-world flight in 1933. B-17 navigators making star shoots asked pilots to switch to autopilot, knowing it held the ship steadier than any human hand. (The pilot's feelings were a little hurt, remembered one navigator, but he said "Okay.") The B-17's Norden bombsight was tied in to the autopilot. As he approached the target, the pilot relinquished control of the plane to the bombardier, who made final adjustments while peering through his crosshairs. At the climax of the mission pilots became nervous spectators, watching the flak bursts and praying that the bombardier, fiddling with his knobs, would not steer them into another plane.[13]

A social historian of technology might describe the cumulative effects of aeronautical engineering advances as "deskilling" pilots, much as the numerical control of machine tools rendered their operators less skilled and more tractable. Judging from the pilots' own testimony, "involuntary reskilling" would be a better label. Piloting remained a demanding, highly trained, and remunerative profession—so remunerative that ALPA, the Air Line Pilots Association, offered insurance to aging pilots afraid of flunking their physicals. But the nature of the job changed radically between the mid-1920s and the mid-1940s. To use a medical analogy, pilots went from performing as surgeons of flight, their hands constantly in motion, giving commands, attending every detail of a procedure, to performing as anesthesiologists, watchfully scanning their instruments, sitting quietly when things proceeded normally, but swinging into action if something went wrong. Piloting became less an experience of the senses and more an experience of the mind, less an experience of controlling present motion than of anticipating future problems. "The airplane flies by itself," pointed out one Pan Am official. What he wanted was a thoughtful monitor, not some hotshot sporting a neck scarf.[14]

This shift accounts for the strong current of nostalgia running through the memoirs of Charles Lindbergh, Beryl Markham, Dean Smith, Basil Rowe, and others who learned to fly in the days before instruments ruled. It may be possible to make surgeons into decent anesthesiologists, but that does not mean they will identify with the job. Ray Little was a mail pilot who went to work for the airlines. When he saw the new breed of pilots—men who wore business suits, rode in heated cabins, and spent their time talking to controllers on radiophones—he said he felt like a cowman watching a dude in polo pants on a slick horse. "Well, the Forty-niners and the cowboys had their day, and it looks like we air vets have about had ours. . . . There is now little more adventure in flying a transport plane than there is in running a street car."[15]

Though the nostalgia is most intense in the writings of the pioneer fliers, who used words like "love" and "wonder" and "joy" to describe their experience of the sky, it is present to some degree in all pilots' memoirs. No matter when pilots entered the historical stream of the profession, the current of progress bore them steadily in the direction of more automation, more regimentation, and more external control. Transport pilots who came up thinking it was all right to make a detour over an interesting geological feature thought otherwise when on-board barometers recorded their altitude and radar detected every course change. If you shut off your autopilot and started drifting off course, TWA's Mo Bowen remembered, the radar boys would call you up. "When it is a thunderstorm that you say you are veering to avoid, they say OK. But they want to keep you within five miles of your track." Air traffic control put an end to days when, as Dean Smith put it, a flier's tracks in the sky were as individualized as his signature.[16]

The pilots fought a few rearguard actions. Their most successful was the postwar campaign against radar-based Ground Controlled Approach (GCA). Developed during the war, GCA permitted controllers to locate, track, and "talk down" planes approaching airports in foul weather. During the Berlin Airlift, GCA permitted coal- and flour-laden C-54s to barrel into Tempelhof Airport three minutes apart, despite the clinging fogs of the north German winter. Back in the United States airline pilots and their union resisted GCA, preferring the CAA's Instrument Landing System (ILS). A radio glidepath and runway alignment system, ILS gave the pilots more control over their final approach and landing. Pilots welcomed radar in their own planes, where they could use it to avoid storms and obstructions. But they remained wary of groundlings staring at screens and telling them what to do.

Still, the tide of rationalization was running against them. A series of highspeed midair collisions, beginning with the 1956 Grand Canyon disaster, and the imminent arrival of bigger and faster jets, led civilian and military authorities to accelerate plans for long-range radar. They also extended "positive control" over more of the nation's airspace. Pilots in positive control areas operated under instrument, rather than visual, flight rules. They flew on instruments in good weather or bad, whether they thought it necessary or not. If their aircraft lacked the appropriate instruments, the Federal Aviation Agency (FAA, successor to the CAA) barred them from certain airways altogether.[17]

Pilots still had occasion for heroic action. Had flying been perfectly routinized, novelists like Ernest K. Gann and Arthur Hailey would have been hard pressed for plots. But drama was confined to unusual situations. Pilots spent most of their time anticipating and preventing trouble, though they were trained to act decisively in an emergency. "The most dangerous pilot was a scared one," wrote Horace Brock, who trained crews for Pan Am. "I wanted pilots who were not afraid of anything *because* they had confidence in their ability to handle it." Brock simulated every emergency he could think of, even dense smoke from a baggage-compartment fire.[18]

Cabin attendants practiced their own safety routines. One stewardess, National's Mary Frances Housley, put hers into practice when a DC-4 skidded on an icy Philadelphia runway, smashed through a fence, and began to burn. "Just be calm," she told her screaming passengers. "Take it easy, and everybody will get out." What Housley did next became legendary. One by one, she escorted ten passengers, some with their clothes on fire, to the cabin door, pushing them through to an eight-foot drop and safety. She could have jumped herself, but she returned to the burning cabin an eleventh time, looking for four women and two babies still inside. She died on the way back out, cradling a four-month-old infant in her arms.[19]

The Cultivated Banality of Flying

If the airlines selected and trained their aircrews for exemplary conduct in emergencies, their advertisers wanted passengers to think as little of emergencies as possible. Speed sold air travel. Fear discouraged it. The trick was to advertise flying's safety, but without calling undue attention to the issue. Pan American resorted to euphemism, calling itself "the world's most experienced airline." TWA billed its postwar transatlantic flights as "routine stuff." International passengers did not even have to change airlines—a dig at rival Pan Am, handicapped by its lack of domestic feeder routes. They simply stayed on TWA planes, flown by crews as familiar with overseas operations as they were with domestic ones. Howard Hughes underscored the point by changing his airline's name. Transcontinental and Western Air became Trans World Airline.[20]

Considerable thought went into these campaigns. Mid-century publicity photos and advertisements generally showed airliners in level or near-level flight. "Look, let's agree right now never to show airborne planes at a cock-eye angle," insisted one ad executive. "It looks either like a model at best or, at worst, like a giant plane out of control." Pan Am sales reps were asked to pass on information about unusually young or old passengers. The public relations department could then work up human interest stories calculated to assuage the fears of the nervous and the elderly.[21]

The on-board experience was important, too. In Tom Wolfe's version of aviation history, the "right stuff" voice emanating from the cockpit was a

What's odd about this picture? The pilot has turned off three engines and feathered their props. The Chicago and Southern Airlines' news bureau released the photo to prove its new Lockheed Constellation could fly on just one of its Wright Cyclone engines. The show of redundancy—heightened by the cropping, which drew attention to the engines by eliminating the empennage—was calculated to appeal to anxious passengers.

subcultural emulation of legendary test pilot Chuck Yeager's no-sweat, top-of-the-status-sphere drawl. In fact, airlines gave pilots speaking lessons. In addition to being competent pilots, they had to sound like competent pilots. Stewardesses also practiced reassuring passengers, playing back their taped voices to make sure they were gentle and soothing. They were taught to ask for individual names at the beginning of the flight. That way each passenger could hear their assured, professional voices and relax.[22]

No issue involving aircrew conduct touched a deeper nerve than that of sobriety. Like most masculine frontier cultures, that of the original pilots was hard-drinking. Sometimes things got out of hand. Drunken pilots stole bread trucks, pounded on doors at 4:00 A.M., tried to force their way into stewardesses' hotel rooms. Pan Am's burly Steve Bancroft, a favorite of Hemingway, lost his job after he broke down a Moana Hotel door. The military culture with which the airline pilot culture overlapped was, if anything, even wetter. ALPA, the pilots' union, put veterans of too many late nights at the officers club on notice. Alcohol abuse was the number one destroyer of public confidence, and there could be "no room in the Association for this type of conduct." Pilots developed tricks, like alternate weeks of abstinence, to keep their drinking in bounds. Those who did not got fired, or, in later years, quietly referred to the airlines' in-house employee assistance programs.[23]

The object of all this was to get reluctant passengers on planes, where flying worked its own persuasive magic. First-timers glued their noses to their windows, experiencing the same transformative view of the earth that had thrilled Lindbergh on his first flight. Hank Henry, a young marine returning home from the war, used $80 of his $300 severance pay to buy a ticket to Kansas City. The great thing about the DC-3, he remembered, was that it was not pressurized—he had a "close-up" view of the Rocky Mountains. Soon, however, familiarity inured air travelers to the charms of the landscape. W. G. Weisbecker, a self-described "air greenhorn" enjoying his first flight in 1938, noted that the veteran commuters around him ignored everything but their cigarettes and their newspapers.[24]

As time passed, even those inclined to enjoy the view had less to see. Before pressurization, windows were comparatively large. (One of those who escaped the flaming DC-4 in Philadelphia, a quick-witted sailor, squeezed through a window.) After pressurization, cabin fenestration took the form of vestigial portholes. Planes flew so high that passengers peering through them could make out little detail. On overcast days, they could not see anything at all. Writer Bernard De Voto called it "the dullest mode of travel." He spent his time correcting galleys; Lindbergh passed his writing letters, struggling to keep up with his correspondents.[25]

Airlines sought ways to alleviate the boredom of their less industrious passengers. Faster equipment meant less tedium, a big selling point for the early jets. Boredom was also known to be solvent in alcohol. Emerging from the shadow of Prohibition, and operating in a culture in which drinking remained controversial, American carriers did not push alcohol as enthusiastically as European rivals like KLM, which reportedly offered "free drinks and cigarettes . . . after every revolution of the propellers." The reluctance owed much to decorum. Drunken passengers were known to push their way into cockpits, urinate on bulkheads, or take off their clothes. One naked actress found herself tied to a palm tree when the plane took off again after a brief layover. Pilots subdued the obstreperous drunks by adding altitude, knowing the thin air would put them to sleep—a bit of improvised culture that disappeared with pressurization. Despite these episodes, customer service executives pressed for in-flight liquor. Passengers who could not get their martinis might patronize a rival airline. The beverage cart was a profit center, especially when stocked with tanker-car gin. Money won. By the mid-1950s the major U.S. carriers had relaxed their strictures. Passengers could purchase alcohol on domestic as well as international flights. Pan Am's 707s became flying bars, so well (or carelessly) stocked that every year thieves made off with between $200,000 and $300,000 in stolen liquor.[26]

In-flight movies offered another way of diverting passengers and lightening their wallets. Carefully selected to avoid offensive material or plots involving air disasters—nobody wanted to run near-thing movies like *The High and the Mighty* through the cabin projector—films reassured nervous first-timers and alleviated the boredom of experienced travelers. Or such was the thinking in TWA's marketing department, which pushed movies hard in the early 1960s. Rivals devised their own entertainment packages. American Airlines installed a customized "Astrocolor" system. Four hours of film could wind its way silently through the cabin, passing through fourteen projectors mounted in front of fourteen separate screens. The windows, coated with a sunlight-reactive material, darkened automatically, further obscuring the now-irrelevant view.

Airlines generally rented out the movie headphones, and a few enterprising stewardesses let themselves in on the business. They gathered the headsets abandoned by deplaning passengers, resealed them in plastic bags with a hot iron, and pocketed the fees. Passengers on the next flight got recycled headphones. If they were disinclined to submit to *Tammy Tell Me True* or *Guys and Dolls*, they could tune in to classical, jazz, pop, or "mood music." The latter was Pan Am's euphemism for the stringy schmaltz its customers usually encountered in elevators between the thirtieth and thirty-fifth floors.[27]

Which, for all intents and purposes, was where they were.

Pan American World

Ernie Gann once remarked that, as commercial aviation matured it also died, having lost its sense of adventure. But this spiritual death, at the hands of the executives, bureaucrats, and engineers who rationalized, formalized, and reified its early frontier culture, was a necessary prelude to flying's economic resurrection. Hence the price-of-progress realism that tempers the nostalgia of aviation memoirs.

There is a marketing paradox inside this story of tradeoffs. Airline executives and advertising experts knew that improved safety and efficiency had broadened their market. But they also knew that rationalization had eliminated much of flying's mystique. Dusty Rhoades said his trimotor passengers tolerated the din and cold fried chicken so they could tell their friends they had flown into town. "There was prestige in flying," he remembered. "It was fairly expensive, a macho sort of thing to do." Clair Maxwell, the man who sold *Life* to Henry Luce, caught the mood:

> We called ourselves 'fliers,' although few of us had ever sat in a cockpit. Some of us kept it a secret, not only from wives, but from creditors as well. But every one of us was proud to make a business appointment in a distant city, saying that we would fly to keep it. *It gave us prestige.* Of

As flying became routine, airline advertisers replaced images of planes with enticing destinations. The illustrator Henry Syverson reduced the formula to its essentials: "fun in the sun." By 1970, the Pan Am logo, here in the guise of a beach umbrella, had become one of the world's most widely recognized corporate symbols.

> course, air lines did not operate then with the same degree of regularity as now, but no matter how much we may have kicked about the service, we liked flying, wanted more of it, and boosted it to beat the band to non-flyers.

That spirit departed after the war, and the sense of exclusivity faded with the arrival of coach fares. The problem facing marketing experts was whether they could find something better than Astrocolor to restore the lost sense of excitement.[28]

The something else turned out to be the destination. As early as the 1930s, images of airplanes began to figure less prominently in airline publicity, disappearing altogether in some postwar ads. The selling point became the destination, rather than flying. If the public was unenthusiastic about the destination—well, that could be addressed too. The same techniques of marketing, design, and engineering that transformed flying transformed many of the places to which airplanes flew.[29]

Pan Am, the leading international carrier, had the biggest overseas stake. It also stood to lose the most should its efforts to promote tourism founder. Pan Am's president, Juan Trippe, had bet the company on high-capacity jets. Convinced that jet technology had ripened to the point of commercial feasibility, he had approached both Douglas and Boeing, promising large orders if they developed planes to his specifications. Douglas was the world's leading commercial aircraft manufacturer. But Boeing had a head start, thanks to its experience with swept-wing, podded-jet bombers. Trippe wound up ordering planes from both; twenty Boeing 707s and twenty-five Douglas DC-8s. He committed $269 million, prompting an industry-wide, follow-the-leader jet buying spree.

In 1958, Pan Am got its first Boeing jets. The next year the long-range version of the plane, the 707-320, began offering nonstop service between New York and Europe's capital cities. Pan Am took full advantage. Captain James Fleming crossed the Atlantic one hundred times in the first ten months of jet operations. He became so exhausted that he fell asleep over the table in a Rome restaurant. At first there were not enough seats to go around. The Hungarian-born British physicist Dennis Gabor tried three times running to book jet passage from New York to London, confirming his reservations in advance. Each time he arrived at the airport he was bumped to a prop plane. Bait-and-switch overbooking, a common practice at Idlewild, showed how hot a ticket a seat on a transatlantic jet had become. Soon everyone was in the game. By the 1960 summer tourist season, almost every transatlantic carrier had switched to jets. Late-model Constellations and DC-7Cs, so recently the queens of the sky, were relegated to charter service.[30]

Trippe shed no tears over their passing. The Henry Ford of international air transport, he had an unlimited faith in advancing technology and a determination to extend its blessings. Jets offered a realistic chance of achieving his dream, the swift, safe, and economical movement of ordinary people throughout an aerialized world. The 707s and DC-8s marked only the beginning. Trippe wanted a still-faster jet, the supersonic transport (SST), and, in the interim, a larger, subsonic jet. "If you build it, I'll buy it," he told Boeing's Bill Allen during a 1965 fishing trip. Allen did, very nearly bankrupting Boeing in the process. But the wide-bodied plane Boeing produced, the 747, proved to be the most efficient means of aerial transport yet invented. Later models of the plane achieved a seat/mile cost a third less than that of the 707.[31]

In January 1970, the 747s entered Pan Am's Atlantic service. By 1977, they carried about 90 percent of the airline's traffic. Unfortunately, the price of the plane matched its size. Pan Am's initial order for twenty-five planes, placed in April 1966, came to $525 million, increasing the company's total debt to nearly a billion dollars. That would have been tolerable if traffic kept growing at 15 percent a year, as Trippe projected. If it did not, the big jets posed the risk of fatal overcapacity. Pan Am might turn away the Dennis Gabors of the world in the early days of jet travel, but the sellers' market could not last. In fact, Pan Am's North Atlantic load factor had already slipped to 51 percent by 1961, down from 64 percent in 1960. Analysts attributed the drop to all the new jet seats.[32]

Executives at the J. Walter Thompson (JWT) advertising agency, which handled the Pan Am account, thought they had a solution. "If Pan American's business is to grow and profit, we must develop large numbers of air passengers," they concluded during a late 1961 account review. "We cannot rely on 'conquest' sales of existing air travel customers and prospects. Competitors are increasing, as is total jet capacity, which is the real threat to the share of the market which Pan American enjoys." Instead, they would "blend 'transportation' advertising of service, speed, frequency, and dependability with a balance of 'destination' ingredient—lure and mood. These will combine to convince more people to travel Pan American to the many wonderful places in the Pan American World."[33]

Enticing more American passengers to fly to Europe, or European passengers to fly to the United States, was easy. London, Paris, and New York abounded with cultural attractions and tourist amenities. But Pan American was a global airline, with extensive and far-flung routes, particularly in the Caribbean and Latin America. Hemispheric tourism would sell more seats on Pan American and Panagra, the Latin American subsidiary of which it owned a half share.

The problem was Latin America's unsavory reputation. Americans traveling there in the 1940s and 1950s complained of bad food, filthy toilets, springless cars, feckless staff, lost laundry, and heat so intense it popped the strings of Yehudi Menuhin's violin. Chicks suffocated in cargo crates, dogs burned their feet, and Managua steamed like "the middle kettle of hell." "Most of what our prospects . . . know is bad," summed up a confidential JWT review of South American travel: "Revolutions, bad political situations, abject poverty, dirt, earthquakes and the 'Manana' attitude of the people they have to depend on for help and service." Of the continent's customs, languages, and geography they knew nothing. "Most people think of it as a big blob down there below the Panama canal."[34]

Latin America did offer a few well-known destinations. The Mexican government had developed Acapulco as a world-class resort. Fulgencio Batista had made Havana a Caribbean Las Vegas, complete with casinos, mafia, race tracks, and luxury hotels. But within a year of Fidel Castro's revolution the Cuban tourist industry had succumbed to the uncertainties of the new regime. Even the Tropicana was moribund. Havana was out. Alternative jet destinations would have to be found.[35]

Henry Syverson drew more than fifteen hundred cartoons for airline ads. In the first sketch, a Pan Am captain confidently leads a rookie tourist on his big adventure. Syverson then played with the concept, cloning the Everyman tourist. It is an arresting image, both suggesting and satirizing homogenization as the key to success.

Part of this process involved an advertising makeover, an upgrading of the region's image from one of "squalor and mediocrity to one of variety and sophistication," making it "'smart' to have 'done Latin America.'" Those who had shopped, dined, explored, hunted, and climbed mountains elsewhere might be attracted by off-the-beaten-path opportunities, like a fishing excursion in the Andes. "When you sell ideas of this kind," advised JWT's James Young, "just forget your DC-8 talk and other unrelated items. Keep your 'fishing' story first: make the feature a famous fisherman, a kind of Hemingway type."

Hemingway, not a man who had much luck with airplanes, nevertheless popped up in other Pan Am promotional schemes, often in cryptic Madison Avenue shorthand: "Arouse latent desire—Secret Places—Live life—'Hemingway.'" Of course, the airline's prospects were not as multilingual and adaptable as the genuine Papa article. Vacationers wanted Hemingway lite: packaged adventures offering unusual experiences—say, skiing in Chile in July—in English-speaking tour groups occupying American-style hotels. If Pan Am was to sell seats, it had to make sure its passengers were bound for accommodations as safe, comfortable, and predictable as its plane ride. It had to make world travel a seamless experience.[36]

Pan Am was in a good position to integrate the travel experience because it owned hotels as well as airplanes. In 1946, the airline had, with the help of a $25 million dollar loan from the Export-Import Bank, established the Intercontinental Hotel Corporation (IHC). The plan was to boost local economies while offering accommodations that combined "American efficiency with local individuality." That meant ice, air conditioning, waiters who washed their hands, and "an American supplemental menu" to accompany indigenous appointments, costumes, and cuisine. One of Pan Am's few consistent moneymakers, IHC turned the airline into a total travel company. Its agents and advertisers could tie jet transportation, in-house tours, and IHC rooms in an attractive package, with discount fares, refrigerated bottles, disposable diapers, and hotel childcare thrown in for those traveling with infants and small children.[37]

Pan Am's hotel network grew rapidly, from sixteen hotels in 1959 to sixty-three in 1972. Company officials knew, however, that Pan Am could not build or own all of the estimated two to three hundred new hotels needed worldwide. Into this breach stepped Hilton, Hyatt, Sheraton, Resorts International, and other chains. They poured millions into formulaic resort complexes with pools, golf courses, tennis courts, and expensive watering holes featuring fruity drinks with little parasols. Trippe let himself into the game, selling Pan Am stock to acquire Bermudan and Bahamian properties. A million tourists visited the Bahamas in 1968, an all-time record. Hotel operators could not build rooms fast enough.[38]

The Bahamian government encouraged the boom, as did officials in many developing nations. "Jumbo jets carry charter groups from Europe to the beaches of Thailand," South Vietnam's economic minister Pham Kim Ngoc told reporters in 1973. "We also offer sun and sand, so why not Vietnam?" In a few years, "provided the truce does not get any uneasier," Pham visualized turning Con Son Island—the prison colony equipped with human tiger cages—into "a resort area catering to tourists where they could enjoy miles of palm-fringed beaches that are not mainly occupied by giant turtles." As bizarre as that scheme was, it was no less remarkable than the Communist government's turnabout in the 1990s, when Vietnam belatedly claimed a share of the $4.4 trillion world tourism industry with its own historic, scenic, and ecological excursions.[39]

All of this came too late to do Pan Am any good. Just as it got its jumbo jets and expanded hotel chain, the company entered into a two-decade death spiral. It was brought on by heavy debt, rising interest rates, high labor costs, stagflation, oil shocks, ineffectual management, declining service, a too-late and too-expensive acquisition of domestic routes, and a run of horrific luck, culminating in the 1988 bombing of Flight 103 over Lockerbie. If Pan Am went into the funeral business, the joke went, people would stop dying.

But the idea Pan Am pioneered—efficient jet travel to heavily promoted destinations with amenities befitting American standards and tastes—lived on. In the eyes of its critics, it literally transformed the world. Instead of the usual influx of poor migrants into the metropolitan centers, air tourism created an acculturating outflow of prosperous city folk to a neo-colonial "pleasure periphery." The new "golden horde"—537 million arrivals in 1994, up from 69 million in 1960—stayed in an expanding "cocoon of packaged environments" in poor, socially divided countries where beefed-up security quelled dissent and protected the tourist industry. Journalist Anthony Sampson thought jet tourism had brought Lindbergh's nightmare of global cultural leveling a long step closer to reality. People all over the world boarded 747s, listened to the same safety instructions, watched the same second-run movies, whitened their coffee with the same creamer, landed at indistinguishable airports, walked past duty-free shops stocked with identical perfume and liquor, and headed for enclave resorts where they tanned themselves amidst their countrymen. Trippe, Sampson concluded, had it backwards. Jet travel did not broaden people. It narrowed their range of experience and reinforced their stereotypes.[40]

As criticisms go, this one was a bit precious. Pan Am's planes bore their millions to museums and shrines as well as to beachfront tourist mills. The jobs the airline provided were good ones: people who had never seen a plane before the war ended up working in airports and travel agencies.[41] Still, surprisingly few writers have had kind words for Trippe, who has entered the pages of aviation history as an erratic and overreaching visionary. He was right about one thing, though. Trippe thought the future of commercial aviation, both international and domestic, belonged to ordinary people. What happened in the two decades after his death, in 1981, would validate that prophecy beyond the frail old man's wildest dreams.

To me, they're all just marginal costs with wings.

—CAB CHAIRMAN ALFRED KAHN,
WASHINGTON POST, APRIL 12, 1978

CHAPTER 9

Marginal Costs with Wings

On January 25, 1955, TWA hosted a discussion on the future of air travel at New York City's Hayden Planetarium. Each of the invited experts had ten minutes to predict what air travel would look like in thirty years. Wernher von Braun, the aristocratic German rocket pioneer who had transferred his allegiance to the U.S. Army, spoke first. By 1985, he said, needle-nosed airliners protected by heat-resistant alloys would fly more than 2,000 mph at altitudes approaching 80,000 feet. Passengers who had breakfasted in New York would take their midmorning coffee in Los Angeles. For shorter trips, helicopters would compete with cars. Families would enjoy vacations in "helicopter house trailers." Space travel would be a reality, with orbiting stations serving as portals to deep space.

J. Geoffrey Notman, president of Canadair, the leading Canadian aircraft manufacturer, took his turn at the console. The next thirty years, he said, would see airline volume increase fifteen- to twenty-fold. The masses would ride in a mixed subsonic fleet, some jets, some turboprops. Airliners would average about twice the seating capacity and half again the speed of existing equipment. "Finally, a personal wish," Notman told his audience. "I hope that the 1985 airline passenger does not have to walk through rain and snow to go on board the aircraft, and that he will get his baggage without delay after disembarking."

Apart from baggage delay, apparently an irreducible aspect of the human condition, Notman's prophecies held up much better than von Braun's. In 1985, the world's lone SST, the needle-nosed Concorde, survived more as a status symbol than as a practical airliner. One critic likened it to a Batmobile in a market dominated by buses. Police and military pilots, rather than vacationers, operated most of the helicopters. Permanent space stations remained an unrealized dream, sixteen years after the triumph of Apollo.

Von Braun's mistake had been to confuse the technologically possible with the economically feasible. The Concorde failed because it required a ton of fuel for every transatlantic passenger. Helicopters—tricky beasts—were too expensive for ordinary people to maintain and operate. NASA's dwindling resources and the high cost of its shuttle operations squeezed out the space station. Notman had put his money on ideas known to *lower* costs, namely, faster subsonic planes with more seats. Even his hoped-for jetway had the virtue of getting people on and off planes faster, as well as keeping them dry. Beyond picking the innovations with the biggest practical payoffs, Notman enjoyed a bit of luck. As it turned out, the political, economic, and social trends of the next thirty years all favored the democratization of commercial aviation.[1]

Flying the Numbers

Technological advances, particularly in jet propulsion and electronics, continued to make air travel cheaper and safer. By the mid-1960s, airline pilots paid the same life insurance rates as their passengers, who, if so inclined, could buy cheap supplemental insurance from terminal vending machines. Yet fears persisted. As late as 1987, 10 percent of men and 25 percent of women who had flown during the last year said they were frightened either all or most of the time. Engineers could not do much more to help them, for they had already achieved most of the easy gains in safety by the time turbofans came along. Further progress would be expensive and incremental, measured in fractions of a single death per one hundred million miles. The increased number of crashes caused by the global surge in air travel obscured even this statistical progress. The solemn television commentary over mountainside crash footage trumped the latest figures on airline safety. Aviation's mean world had not disappeared. It had migrated to CNN.[2]

At least there was no ambiguity about costs. They were headed down, and fast. Using 1978 prices as a benchmark, passengers paid just eight cents for every mile they flew in 1978, compared to thirteen cents in 1958. Prices had dropped more than a third even before deregulation officially began. Most of the savings came after the mid-1960s. That may seem odd, given that jets entered service in the 1950s. But there were in fact two jet breakthroughs, and it was the second that achieved the greatest savings.[3]

The first jet airliners got their thrust from turbojets, propulsion tubes that burned compressed air and fuel. Before shooting out the back of the tube, the exhaust gases spun a turbine, connected by a shaft to air compressors in the front of the engine. (Adding a second turbine, shaft, gears, and a propeller made the engine a turboprop, or turbine-propeller combination.) Turbojets were easier to maintain than piston engines. C. R. Smith listed their advantages: fewer spare parts, fewer overhauls, "outstanding reliability." Compound piston engines were prone to failure. One Stratocruiser pilot had to return to Seattle twice before making it out of town in a third plane. Idling during ground delays fouled spark plugs. Passengers already running late watched helplessly as their planes taxied out of flight lines to have their plugs changed. Turbojets promised to end all this frustration. But they had two drawbacks. They burned a lot of fuel, and they created too much noise near urban airports.[4]

The turbofan, another military engine development, solved both problems. The turbofan was a turboprop with its propeller, in the form of a giant, multi-bladed titanium fan, located inside the nacelle. The fast-spinning blades shot compressed air through the engine core and a second stream of air around it. The "bypass" stream, channeled by the fan's housing, provided an independent source of thrust and shrouded the hot core engine and its fast-moving exhaust gases with a blanket of denser, slower-moving air. The result was less noise, more power, and better fuel efficiency. Turbofans stretched aircraft range, lowered costs, and made possible a new generation of wide-bodied planes. Under development since the 1950s, turbofans came along just in time to avoid the noise and fuel-cost concerns that bedeviled the SST. Turbofans kept gaining in power and reliability, so much so that in 1985 the FAA modified a piston-era rule and permitted certain twinjets to fly on Atlantic routes. It would take a billion hours of operation, one expert calculated, before both turbofans failed, causing an ocean ditching.[5]

That better engines produced better planes surprised no one. The Wrights themselves had said that engine power and reliability were the keys to aeronautical progress. The big postwar surprise turned out to be the growing importance of electronic circuitry. People ceased flying in airplanes and began going aloft in electromechanical systems designed, built, and managed by computers. Computer Assisted Design (CAD) streamlined drafting. No longer did the weight of the paper equal the weight of the

The first Boeing 747s entered service in 1970. Two-and-a-half times as large as the 707, the giant plane could seat up to 550 passengers. Fuel economy eventually reached sixty miles per gallon per passenger, at speeds ten times those of cars and twenty times those of ships. The airlines' problem—evident as the flight attendant clears trays—was how to keep the seats full. The solution, discounting prices, helped to democratize air travel.

prototype before metal-cutting began. Automatic riveting machines under numerical control assembled wings, rather like robot welders on car assembly lines. Computers fed weather data excelled human dispatchers in selecting the best long-distance flight paths. The combination of transponders (electronic airplane dog tags, another World War II innovation), clutter-free radar displays, enlarged mainframes, and the most complex software yet devised made possible new systems of regional and municipal air traffic control. Controllers tracked planes using alphanumeric codes inching across their screens. When a plane passed from one sector to another, the code began blinking, signaling the next controller to assume responsibility for the flight.[6]

Computers found their way on board planes. "Fly-by-wire," an electronic flight-control system demonstrated by NASA in 1972, replaced mechanical controls. Programmable computers directed, translated, and automatically corrected the pilot's actions. Here was the ultimate means of formalizing aviation's culture. Rules about when or how far to move control surfaces became so much binary code, executed by machines that performed more reliably, consistently, and quickly than humans. Fly-by-wire dispensed with control cables, rods, and pulleys, thereby saving weight, eliminating breaks and snags, and simplifying maintenance. Engineers began designing oddly configured aircraft, such as stealth fighters, confident that onboard computers' near-instantaneous adjustments would compensate for the airframes' inherent instability. They built avionics into commercial airliners, ultimately producing a plane, the 275-passenger Boeing 777 twinjet, that flew with all-electronic controls. (The first 747s, by contrast, had four sets of hydraulic control systems.) Fly-by-wire devices offered a smoother ride and superior fuel economy. More than ever, professional pilots found themselves "flying the numbers," relying on digitized instruments for takeoff, cruising, and landing.[7]

Computers revolutionized airline reservations and marketing. Well into the 1960s, booking an airplane seat was a paper and pencil operation. At United, clerks cradling phones on their shoulders spun a big lazy Susan, hunting for mounted flight reservation sheets matching their customers' travel plans. There had to be a better way. In 1970, the airlines began planning a single electronic reservation system to link their offices with travel agents around the country. The Justice Department threatened antitrust prosecution—a curious action, given the industry's status as a regulated cartel. So the leading airlines, notably American and United, developed their own systems. Travel agents, who handled three-quarters of the plane tickets sold in the United States by the mid-1980s, loved the electronic convenience. Airlines without their own systems could use the service, but only if they paid a booking fee of so many dollars per flight. Computer reservation systems thus emerged as an independent profit center.

They also gave airlines a tool for managing "yield," or per-mile revenue. Airlines sold a time-sensitive product. Imagine, said a Boeing executive, "a vast Christmas tree lot" with billions tied up in inventory. The trees would not be worth anything after Christmas, just as empty seats would not be worth anything after takeoff. So haggling went on as the weeks, days, and hours ticked away. The person willing to pay just two hundred dollars for a seat, who wound up sitting next to someone who had paid eight hundred, was, in this sense, a successful haggler. The airline benefitted as well. The two hundred dollar fare was better than nothing.

But haggling was simpler in theory than in practice. The deadline that came but once a year for tree lots fell every day for the airlines. No human could manage the calculations necessary to optimally price thousands of seats on scores of routes affected by scheduling changes, seasonal load fluctuations, competitors' discounts, and the like. It took American Airlines' programmers, economists, and marketing experts a decade to perfect a computer system that ensured that "no passenger paid any less than exactly what it would take to get him on the plane." When American's president, Bob Crandall, deployed the system in 1985, launching the Ultimate Super Saver era, he had a formidable weapon at hand.[8]

The Deregulation Era

Crandall needed that weapon to survive in the new era of deregulation. Low-cost airlines like People Express were challenging full-service carriers like American by offering cut-rate fares. Upstart price competition was a familiar aspect of the business, dating back to the postwar nonskeds and the Freddie Laker charter wars of the 1970s. Like most cartels, the airline industry had to fend off party crashers, small operators using novel tactics to circumvent regulatory barriers. But the conflict had taken on new dimensions, and had vastly larger consequences, as a result of the 1978 Airline Deregulation Act.

At first glance, the Airline Deregulation Act seems like a political oddity. Americans looked favorably on the airline industry during the 1970s. Despite debt and overcapacity problems, the public felt no sense of crisis. The airlines, with one or two exceptions, preferred the regulatory status quo. So did their creditors and unionized workers. Airlines passed on wage increases through CAB-approved fare hikes on routes offering little or no competition. Business travelers with expense vouchers did not mind. They preferred to stretch out on half-filled planes, untroubled by the hoi polloi. The Democratic party, which recaptured the White House in 1977, had historically accommodated unions. It had favored the regulation of interstate carriers. Why, then, did the bill pass?

The best short answer is that the consumer movement became a potent political force during the 1970s. Key Democrats, notably Edward Kennedy, Howard Cannon, and Jimmy Carter, saw deregulation as a popular, pro-consumer measure. Evidence from California and Texas, where intrastate carriers had a freer hand, showed that competition by low-cost airlines increased volume and reduced prices. The General Accounting Office estimated that the lack of competition on interstate routes cost passengers upwards of $2 billion between 1969 and 1974. The American Conservative Union and Common Cause, groups that did not often pull at the same oar, came out in favor of deregulation. So did the economist Alfred Kahn, whom Carter named to head the CAB in 1977.

Kahn, a determined, acerbic man with a gift for one-liners, wanted the airlines to compete wherever they chose, to set their own prices, and to stop bothering the CAB every time they wanted to try some promotion. If they felt like guaranteeing refunds for ski trips spoiled by lack of snow, fine. "No one could blow his nose without getting my permission," Kahn complained. "It was insane." Even before the 1978 legislation phased out federal control of routes and fares, Kahn expedited airline requests to operate on new routes at competitive prices. John Robson, Kahn's immediate predecessor, had already set the process in motion. Robson's board had approved such novelties as "peanuts fares," Texas International's half-price tickets on its least popular runs. "We'd never carried three people and a dog between here and Salt Lake City and all of a sudden planes were full," recalled Don Burr, one of the Houston-based airline's Young Turks. Kahn pushed the CAB to move faster toward liberalization. The early results were encouraging. By June 1978, five months before Carter signed the deregulation bill, revenues and profits were already running 16 percent above 1977.[9]

Kahn and his allies assumed that air transport was not a natural monopoly, like a municipal subway system, where competition would be wasteful. Perhaps the airlines had needed government subsidy and protection in their early days, but with a mature technology and airports everywhere, restraint on competition smelled of special interest anachronism. Deregulation phased out route controls by the end of 1981 and fare controls by the end of 1982. The CAB itself disappeared at the end of 1984. No one foresaw, however, just how turbulent the industry would become after the competitive barriers fell.

New entrants like People Express, which Kahn called "the archetypal deregulation success story and the most spectacular of my babies," prospered for a time. By offering no-frills service, making nonunion employees stakeholders, and keeping overhead low, the airline charged prices that rivaled interstate bus lines. Newark to Buffalo cost twenty-three dollars, with no Thruway tolls. Search committees at budget-strapped universities hinted strongly that assistant professor candidates should avail themselves of People's reasonable fares. Cross-country flights ran as low as ninety-nine dollars.[10]

The full-service carriers fought back. They offered frequent-flier programs, charged more for their computer reservation systems, lowered prices on selected routes to ruin their rivals, and then jacked prices back up until the next competitor came along. But the key was controlling costs. Rather than

National Airlines television ad, 1971. Prior to deregulation, interstate air carriers competed on the basis of service, offering meals, movies, and sex appeal to their mostly male passengers. Continental's stewardesses promised to "really move our tails for you." National introduced themselves on TV with such double-entendres as "I'm Cheryl, Fly Me!" (Flight attendants at a rival airline wore buttons that said "Fly Yourself!") Deregulation did not end the hype, though it did make it secondary, as airlines came to depend on price competition to attract increasingly diverse customers.

flying passengers nonstop from point to point, airlines routed them through hub airports like Dallas-Fort Worth. Hubs antedated deregulation, but passengers had often used them to transfer from one airline to another. Now that airlines could run as many "spoke" routes as they pleased into their hubs, they could keep the passengers on their own planes. By timing their flights to arrive and depart during peak intervals, they could expedite connections, generate higher load factors, and achieve greater productivity. While the number of passengers in a given hub increased exponentially, the number of ground workers needed to service them increased only arithmetically. By the end of the 1980s, the airlines were routing two-thirds of their domestic traffic through their busy hubs. The passengers got cheaper fares, though with more connections, longer trips, and increased likelihood of delay.

Other means of economy presented themselves. American famously saved $40,000 a year by serving olive-free salads. The biggest olives, though, were the ones in the cockpit. In the early 1980s, Continental pilots averaged 131 flying days a year and earned $90,000. Salaries like these gave a huge advantage to new entrants, which hired pilots, mechanics, and flight attendants for far less. Executives at the established airlines trimmed labor costs where they could, renegotiating contracts, laying off workers, and underfunding pension plans. Frank Lorenzo became so notorious for using bankruptcy threats to wring concessions from the unions of his newly acquired airlines that his name ended up on the Berlin Wall with a slash mark through it.

By the early 1990s, the industry was beset with massive losses, embittered labor-management relations, and a string of bankruptcies. It had become, in Bob Crandall's words, "a nasty, rotten business." Just how rotten, Crandall himself demonstrated back in 1982, when Braniff's president, Howard Putnam, taped one of his phone calls:

> Crandall: I think it's dumb as hell for Christ's sake, all right, to sit here and pound the shit out of each other and neither one of us making a fucking dime.
>
> Putnam: Well—
>
> Crandall: I mean, you know, goddamn, what the fuck is the point of it?
>
> Putnam: Nobody asked American to serve Harlingen. Nobody asked American to serve Kansas City, and there were low fares in there, you know, before. So—
>
> Crandall: You better believe it, Howard. But . . . we can both live here [in Dallas-Fort Worth] and there ain't no room for Delta. But there's, ah, no reason that I can see, all right, to put both companies out of business.

Putnam: But if you're going to overlay every route of American's on top of . . . every route that Braniff has—I can't just sit here and allow you to bury us without giving our best effort.

Crandall: Oh sure, but Eastern and Delta do the same thing in Atlanta and have for years.

Putnam: Do you have a suggestion for me?

Crandall: Yes. I have a suggestion for you. Raise your goddamn fares 20 percent. I'll raise mine the next morning.

Putnam: Robert, we—

Crandall: You'll make more money and I will too.

Putnam: We can't talk about pricing.

Crandall: Oh bullshit, Howard. We can talk about any goddamn thing we want to talk about.

Presented with this kind of material, aviation writers gleefully turned from the cockpits, where graying pilots sat in takeoff lines worrying about their pensions, to the boardrooms, where the real action was to be found. "Crando" and his ilk had become the new barnstormers, corporate swashbucklers who cracked up billion-dollar corporations rather than mere planes. Enter Frank Lorenzo, exit Eastern Airlines.

Walter Folger Brown had been right after all. Unrestrained competition in a capital-intensive transportation industry had brought chaos and ruin. But the deregulators had been right, too. Prices kept declining, from 8.29 cents per seat mile in 1978 to the inflation-adjusted equivalent of 4.57 cents in 2001. In 1978, U.S. airlines carried 275 million passengers. In 2000, they carried a record 666 million, then slipped back to 622 million in terror- and recession-plagued 2001. Whether the gains were worth the losses depended, sometimes literally, upon where one sat. "Deregulation was a massive exercise in the redistribution of wealth," wrote Thomas Petzinger Jr., "a zero-sum game in which not billions but trillions of dollars in money, assets, time, convenience, service, and pure human toil shifted among many groups of people, from one economic sector to another." Kahn conceded as much. "While I adore Southwest, and think they're half my justification before God," he said in 2002, "I hate standing in those long lines."[11]

When Alfred Kahn stands before God, his Creator may choose to remind him of many things. One is that airline expansion involved more than deregulation. The operating costs of new planes, manufactured with lightweight composite materials and equipped with the latest in engines, avionics, and wing designs, continued to drop. Winglets alone extended jet cruising range by up to 7 percent. Meanwhile the demand for airline services kept growing, and for reasons that had nothing to do with cost-cutting moves by academic deregulators.[12]

For starters, there were more Americans and they had more money. The U.S. population grew 21 percent during the century's last two, prosperous decades, while average household income, subtracting taxes and inflation, rose more than 30 percent. Most Americans had acquired a familiarity with airplanes, the habit of long-distance travel for family visits and vacations, and higher levels of education. In 1940, just one in twenty Americans age twenty-five or older had graduated from a four-year college. Only one in four had graduated from high school. By 1990, one in five had finished college, and three in four had finished high school. Education increased demand independent of income. One study found that a college-educated person was between three and eight times more likely to make a non-business air trip than a grammar school–educated person of comparable financial means.[13]

Air travel was thus bound to increase after 1978, regardless of whether the government phased out fare and route restrictions. Deregulation, with hard-boiled CEOs slashing costs and prices, made for a good story. But impersonal forces also bore on the industry's fate. Recessions aside, the tide was running toward stronger and broader demand. In the late 1970s, rising demand met the declining prices caused by deregulation and aeronautical refinement. The fast growth that resulted set the stage for the near-gridlock crisis at century's end.

Democratization

The same combination of factors—more efficient jets, deregulated fares, growing affluence and interest in travel—affected who flew, as well as how many. Just as the frontier populations gradually took on the characteristics of the more settled communities, Americans in the air became more like those on the ground. Though they never matched up perfectly, the cabin of a late-century commercial jet mirrored American society more closely than an equivalent flight in a mid-century airliner.

One source of changing passenger mix was the society-wide shift in gender roles, which increased women's professional flying. In 1977, women accounted for one in every eight business trips on airplanes. In 1998, they accounted for one in every three. Women also made up a slight majority (53 percent) of leisure travelers, those on vacation or visiting friends and family. Leisure travelers had smaller average incomes and less education than business travelers, yet their share of the market grew much more rapidly. Between 1971 and 1984, the percentage of the U.S. adult population that had flown on business during the previous year rose just one point, from 8 to 9 percent. But leisure flying jumped from 16 to 22 percent. Only three in ten of the leisure trips were taken by passengers with family incomes above forty thousand dollars, compared to six in ten of those traveling on business. Cheaper fares had increased the relative size of the most diverse group.[14]

Low-cost personal travel also meant more older and younger passengers. Business people did their flying after college and before retirement. Leisure travelers might be of any age. As a practical matter, few retirees could afford to fly before the mid-1960s. Then federal spending on the elderly accelerated. The number of people over sixty-five who lived in poverty fell from one in three in 1960 to one in eight in 1987. Armed with COLA-protected Social Security checks, private pensions, and senior-citizen discounts, retirees took advantage of the declining air fares to travel abroad, attend Elder hostels, and visit their far-flung children and grandchildren. Or their grandchildren came to them. Airlines arranged for parents to hand off children to flight attendants, who saw to it that they reached the right party at journey's end. With discounted seats and no need for adult escorts, the savings were considerable.[15]

In the early 1970s, airlines went after student travelers. When Southwest experimented with a special ten dollar in-state Texas fare, college students lined up at the departure gate, standing next to old people and families. One official said he expected to see "a chicken coop on top of the airplane." Overseas charter operators went after students with transatlantic fares as low as $120. "Hell, you see hippies get across the water by plane and walk the rest of the way," growled C. R. Smith. But the scheduled carriers cut their own fares and offered special amenities. Pan Am put on a Tuesday flight to Amsterdam featuring rock and roll, beer, and sangria. The jet lag scarce bears contemplation. KLM, competing on the same route, gave young passengers who filled out a questionnaire a disguised rebate of fifty dollars—a tidy sum for backpackers in those days. Even after the inflationary wave of the late 1970s, transatlantic air fares remained within reach of students, thanks to discounting by low-cost carriers. People Express offered nonstop jet service from San Francisco to Brussels for ninety-nine dollars.[16]

A 1998 Gallup survey highlighted the effects of two decades of deregulation. The pollsters asked two key questions: Have you ever flown on a commercial airline? Have you done so during the previous twelve months? Four out of five said they had flown at least once, up from about one in two in 1971. The experience of commercial flying had become something most Americans had in common. Active flying was another matter. Those who had flown during the past year had more income and education. Current college students, shuttling between home and campus, were even more likely to have flown than college graduates.

1998 GALLUP AIR TRAVEL SURVEY OF U.S. ADULTS, AGE 18 AND OLDER

Population Characteristic	*Percent ever flown on a commercial airline*	*Percent flown on a commercial airline in previous 12 months*
Males	82	42
Females	81	37
Age 18–34	77	37
Age 35–54	87	46
Age 55+	78	31
Income under $20,000	62	18
Income $20,000–$39,999	81	29
Income $40,000–$59,999	85	41
Income $60,000 or more	96	68
Northeastern Residence	81	37
South-Central Residence	76	6
North-Central Residence	79	33
Western Residence	92	53
High School or Less	68	24
Some College	88	31
College Graduate	96	45
Currently a Student		47
White		40
African American		29
Hispanic		39
Asian		34
Native American		66

Source: Student and racial data are available only for the previous twelve months (March 1997–March 1998). From *Air Travel Survey, 1998* (Washington, D.C.: Air Transport Association, 1998).

Only about three in ten African Americans had flown during the previous year, unsurprising given that higher-income groups bought most of the tickets. Even so, the situation had changed dramatically since 1962, a year in which only three in every hundred African Americans had flown. The black absence from the sky in the 1960s had been de facto rather than de jure. Airplanes (though not airports) had escaped Jim Crow laws, and stewardesses lavished attention on black celebrities like Duke Ellington. Royalty was royalty. But ordinary blacks lacked the income, expense accounts, and means of getting to the airport that affluent whites enjoyed. The gains scored by middle-class blacks after the civil rights movement eliminated some of these economic barriers. Their economic progress, plus low-cost fares, explains the ten-fold increase in African American flying.[17]

If flying was a function of income, then why did Native Americans fly more than any other racial group? This may be a statistical anomaly, caused by their small number in the sample. But it may also reflect their western residence. Westerners have long led the country in flying, both as passengers and plane owners. Western predominance in the air was itself a legacy of land frontier development. The region's settlers had tended to cluster together in boomtowns. As early as 1880, westerners were the most urbanized people in the country. But their communities were isolated, separated from each other and from eastern cities by vast stretches of inhospitable terrain. Interurban passenger service, where it existed, was primitive. Travelers went mad riding cramped, jolting stagecoaches through scorching days and freezing nights. Some leapt from the coach and wandered into the desert, never to return. Even rail travel could be excruciatingly slow. When Dean Smith left Oregon for boarding school in St. Louis shortly before World War I, he passed five days and five nights on the train. He remained in St. Louis for the entire academic year. The length of travel ruled out any vacations other than summer recess. No wonder westerners embraced air transport. Planes annihilated the cruel, arid distance.[18]

Commercial flying thus retained distinctive biases. At century's end the typical passenger was a white male between thirty-five and fifty-four years of age who earned sixty thousand dollars or more a year and who lived in the western United States. Compared to his mid-century counterpart, however, he would have traveled in much more diverse company. Above all, he would have found himself with more female passengers, 47 percent on an average flight. Commercial flying had achieved rough gender balance, though not yet full social democratization.[19]

Many writers have used the concept of democratization to loosely describe passengers' appearance and behavior, rather than their annual earnings and educational careers. Henry Bech, John Updike's alter ego,

> could remember when getting on a plane was an adventure for the elite, dressed in suits and cocktail dresses, the chic of it intensified by the air of danger as they bounced around among silvery, Art-Deco thunderheads, an air to which free champagne and duck or steak dinners served on real china added a *Titanic*esque elegance. But now the sort of people swarmed aboard who used to go by bus. They wore shorts and blue

Roscoe Turner and actress Bebe Daniels christen one of Nevada Airlines' four Lockheed Vegas, 1929. Promotions for the airline stressed the time advantage: L.A. to Reno in three hours instead of twenty-two. The promise of fast travel appealed strongly to westerners, who became America's most frequent air travelers.

jeans and even what appeared to be their pajamas, a scrum of sweaty bodies taking a thousand-mile hop as casually as a drive to the 7-Eleven. Flight was no more a miracle to them than their daily bread. They crammed their duffel bags and scuffed laptops into the overhead bins and didn't even bother to look out the windows from six death-defying miles up.

It is easy, as Updike does here, to overlook the less glamorous aspects of mid-century flying. Passengers and crews rode to the airport in rattletrap limos stale with smoke. Weather could delay them for hours. Airborne vibration, noise, stress, dehydration, and anoxia exacted a steady toll. Pilots suffered from depression and exhaustion. Dusty Rhoades, who collapsed after a 1943 New Delhi-Brisbane trip, thought he would never feel rested again. Even pressurized flights could be an ordeal. One passenger likened sixteen hours on a Stratocruiser to slow torture. He—anyone—would have been better off in the coach section of a swift, quiet, and steady jet. The simplest way to measure progress in air transport, as Gene Vidal once put it, was to count the unused air-sickness containers.[20]

Still, we know what Updike meant. Commercial flying long ago ceased to be *recherché,* or even particularly civilized. Aerial decorum has changed since the young Jack Kennedy dined aboard the Pan Am Clipper en-route from England to Boston for his fall Harvard classes. Stewardess Claudette Bradish recalled one man who, his mouth stuffed full of food, signaled his urgent need for more butter by sticking her in the rear with a plastic fork. Pan Am's Aimée Bratt saw a woman breast-feeding her cat. "The man in 15H asked me to turn off the light so he could make love to his wife . . . ," another flight attendant wrote, describing a 1996 Chicago-to-Paris flight. The wife objected, and a screaming row ensued—this in the first-class section. Patricians yearned for the days of proper dress and manners. One of them happened to be a former student of Alfred Kahn. He wrote a letter to his famous professor complaining that he had to sit next to a hippie, a man who had not shaved and did not smell good. What had deregulation wrought? "Well," Kahn replied, "I'm waiting to hear whether there are any complaints coming from the hippie."[21]

Status Enclaves and Frontier Niches

Routinization and democratization—the loss of a sense of adventure in commercial aviation, followed by the loss of social exclusivity—occurred first in the United States, the world's leader in air transport. By the turn of the century, however, discount carriers like Ryanair or Virgin Express served a vari-

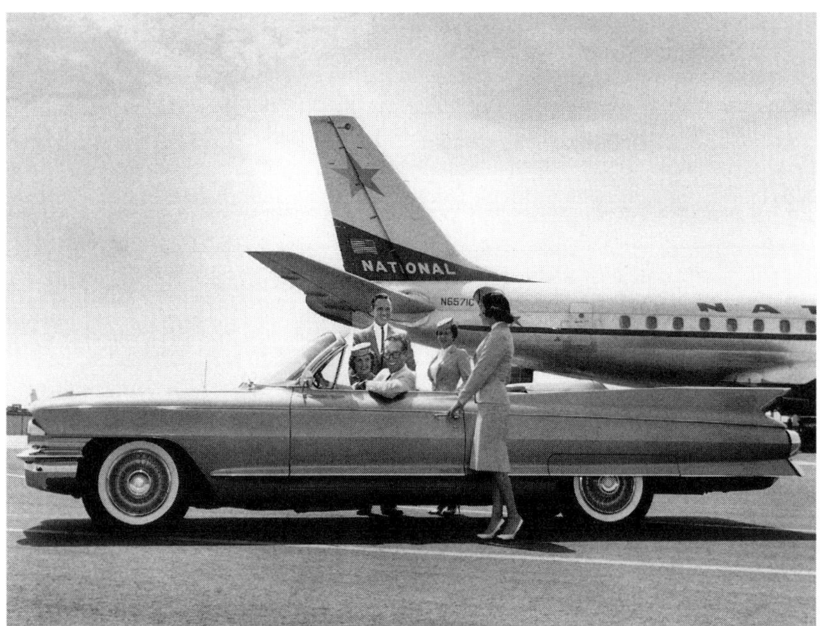

Though by the late 1950s commercial flying had ceased to be adventurous, it retained vestiges of glamor, as emphasized in this National Airlines publicity photograph. The driver of the 1959 Coupe de Ville is Robert Q. Lewis, actor and sometime guest panelist on *What's My Line?* The intended message, that one flashy empennage deserved another, soon became dated. During the 1960s and 1970s, commercial aviation completed its transition from a class to a mass business, with commercial jets serving as workaday vehicles rather than celebrity chariots.

ety of international markets. British drinkers went pub-crawling in Prague, where cheap liquor more than offset the cost of a twenty-five dollar ticket. In 2002, one-way fares from Heathrow to Dublin sold for as little as thirteen dollars, less than a train ticket from central London to the airport. (With a quality of service—minimal—to match.) Commercial passengers, as historian Kenneth Hudson put it, had become "walking freight." The Internet, to extend the analogy, became their global inventory and reservation system. It also constrained fare increases, because consumers could shop around. During the 1990s, booking a cheap seat became as easy as a trip to the nearest Internet café.[22]

Some types of flying retained their social exclusivity. The Concorde, with its bone china, vintage champagnes, and one-way transatlantic fares starting at five thousand dollars, was an obvious exception. Concorde prices, like those of high fashion, guaranteed exclusivity rather than practical utility. After the 2000 Air France disaster turned the plane from the world's safest to most dangerous jet airliner in a single fiery crash, supersonic travel acquired the risky feeling of the old trimotor days. One way to think about the history of commercial aviation is that, in the 1920s, every passenger flew on the social and actuarial equivalent of the Concorde. By century's end the only scheduled airline equivalent of the Concorde was the Concorde itself. Even that self-exception did not last. In April 2003, British Airways and Air France announced the retirement of the remaining supersonic transports, too often flying half full.[23]

Corporate aircraft also carried an exclusive clientele. Private business flying had its roots in the 1920s, when oil companies and other corporations with far-flung operations began buying planes. Wartime restrictions limited corporate flying, though it revived after the war and then flourished with the arrival of small business jets in the 1960s. In 1968, business aircraft accounted for 38 percent of general aviation air mileage. By 1995, they accounted for 70 percent. They also carried 130 million passengers, or nearly a quarter as many as flew on the scheduled airlines. That was another reason commercial flying became more socially diversified: the business elite forsook it for the flexibility and prestige of corporate jets. A few individuals—presidents in Air Force One, Hugh Hefner in his DC-9, CEOs in their Boeing Business Jets—had their own customized airliners. But they represented the extremes of power and wealth. Few mortals could afford cabin upholstery of Himalayan goatskin.[24]

Still, private plane ownership of any sort remained a mark of social distinction, and private recreational flying remained confined to the affluent. Early on, aircraft salesmen had learned to size up a prospect by observing the make of his car. Some hoped that a mass market might emerge after World War II. Ex-military and CPTP pilots would want to keep on flying. Veterans could use the GI Bill for flight training. Light aircraft manufacturers had plenty of capacity. In 1946, general aviation sales hit 31,000 planes. But the boom did not last. Sales fell to around 3,000 planes a year in the early 1950s. Most people could not afford a car and plane. Some pilots economized by buying war surplus aircraft, or building their own from kits. But they still had to worry about maintenance, repair, insurance, fuel, and renting hangar or tie-down space. If a boat was a proverbial money hole in the water, a plane was its equivalent in the air. Doctors might be able to swing weekend trips to the Bahamas in their own planes, but most people's leisure-trip flying remained confined to commercial airliners, whose unadorned seats kept declining in price.[25]

General aviation's routine commercial operations, such as crop dusting, conferred no particular status. But a few activities still promised adventure. "Tanker gypsies" in aging Neptunes dumped chemicals on raging forest fires. Smugglers skimmed moonlit waters in cocaine-stuffed Cessnas. Alaskan bush pilots maneuvered their ski planes to rescue stranded mountain climbers. There were still a few frontier niches, risky operations that forced pilots to use all their wits.

The biggest frontier niche was piloting hot military aircraft, and it retained the classic hallmarks of masculinity, uncertainty, and heightened mortality. Military aircraft designers, aiming for high performance, expressed aeronautical technology in riskier forms than commercial designers. The danger was most acute in the early 1950s, when military pilots struggled to make the transition from propeller planes to faster and less forgiving jets. Between January 1, 1950, and June 30, 1952, the air force lost 429 men in 1,833 jet accidents. The situation in the navy was equally grim. Navy pilots had about a one-in-four-chance of dying in an accident during a twenty-year career, and a better than even chance of having to explosively eject from an out-of-control plane. Ejecting at supersonic speed could rip the skin off a man's face.[26]

Military pilots unwound with alcohol. The Tailhook Association, which gave its name to the 1991–92 scandal, began life in 1957 as a naval aviators' drinking club. Though it took on the trappings of a professional organization—admirals and defense contractors dutifully attended its annual Las Vegas meeting—Tailhook never shed its reputation for drunken debauchery, driven by a can-you-top-this mentality. In 1991, Lt. Paula Coughlin, an admiral's aide returning to her hotel, had to fight her way through a gauntlet of pie-faced fighter pilots. She was "practically gang-banged," she told her unsympathetic boss the next morning. It turned out that she was one of the scores of women assaulted that night.[27]

Tailhook catalyzed feminist resistance to the jet pilots' macho culture of excess and helped open combat aviation billets (and hence opportunities for faster promotion) to female pilots. But scandal was not the only force operating in the 1990s to rationalize military aviation. Engineers continued to undermine the heart of the subculture—risk—by using advanced avionics. New generations of jets were more stable and survivable. Ultimately, electronic control reached the point where the pilot's presence became superfluous. During the Afghanistan campaign, the air force reassigned fighter pilots to "fly" unmanned aerial vehicles (UAVs) by means of keyboards, computer joysticks, throttle buttons, and brake pedals. Fighter pilots hated the remotely controlled planes, "unmanned" in every sense of the word. But politicians loved them. "They are cheaper than manned aircraft," a *Wall Street*

Journal reporter commented, "and Americans don't get killed flying them." The imperatives of safety and efficiency, having triumphed in commercial aviation, were reshaping military aviation as well.[28]

Within the fraternity of those who flew military jets, one group, the test pilots, formed an elite within the elite. Jackie Cochran as a rare female exception, test pilots were ambitious, highly disciplined men who combined deep aeronautical knowledge with superb flying skills. Their knowledge helped them to collaborate with the test engineers, who formed a parallel aeronautical elite; their skills kept them alive, at least for the time being. "I could be president of Sikorski for six months before they found me out," the test pilot Dick Faull reportedly said, "but the president would only have my job for six seconds before he'd kill himself."[29]

At President Eisenhower's insistence, NASA chose its first astronauts from the ranks of military test pilots. This elite within an elite within an elite emerged from a gauntlet of physical and psychological tests, everything from ice-water endurance to writing twenty answers to the question, "Who am I?" The right answer, it turned out, was Charles Lindbergh. Psychologist

Rocket-plane pilots, who operated at the extremes of speed and altitude, enjoyed special status within the test-pilot priesthood. On April 30, 1962, NASA pilot Joseph A. Walker separated from his B-52 mothership, started his rocket engine, accelerated to near Mach 5, and set an altitude record of forty-seven miles. On August 22, 1963, he did it again, reaching sixty-seven miles, a record for winged space flight that stood until the shuttle era.

Robert Voas explained that the Mercury evaluators wanted men who displayed "intelligence without genius, knowledge without inflexibility, a high degree of skill without overtraining, fear but not cowardice, bravery without foolhardiness, self-confidence without egotism, physical fitness without being muscle-bound, participatory sports preference over spectator sports, frankness without blabbermouthing, enjoyment of life without excess, humor without disproportion, fast reflexes without panic in a crisis."[30]

They also wanted, and got, men who had the utmost respect of their peers. When evaluators had winnowed the pool of 110 qualified test pilots to just 18 survivors, and they were trying to settle on the final group of Mercury astronauts, they paid particular attention to one question, "Whom would you assign to the mission if you could not go yourself?" Though later groups of astronauts included both civilian and military test pilots, they all remained acutely aware of their reputations. Asked on a questionnaire if he had any suppressed desires, Edwin "Buzz" Aldrin wrote "respect by contemporaries." It would be hard to find a more succinct statement of the emotional imperative at the heart of aviation's hot-pilot subculture—a subculture that stretched all the way back to the Curtiss and Wright exhibition fliers.[31]

The idea that the aviation frontier never disappeared, that risk-taking pioneers had merely pushed it beyond the atmosphere, had wide currency in NASA's heyday. Politicians and pundits praised the astronauts as "frontiersmen," "scouts," "explorers," and "adventurers" whose efforts were again extending the nation's reach. A decade after the moon landing, Jimmy Carter, the president who signed the deregulation bill into law, said the lunar footprints of American astronauts symbolized "the pioneer spirit that built our great country." Two decades later, in 1999, Robert Zubrin was still extolling the space frontier, calling for a renewed commitment to its expansion by refocusing the space program on planetary colonization. Frontier as metaphor remained alive and well in space.[32]

Meanwhile frontier talk, exceptions like bush pilots noted, had disappeared from the realm of commercial flying. Out of earshot, pilots and flight attendants might casually refer to their passengers as dogs or sheep. But none in that fiercely competitive industry would have described the masses crowding aboard their airliners, paying as little as possible for the privilege, as pioneers of flight. Alfred Kahn had been closer to the mark. What they really represented was yield, borne aloft on marginal costs with wings.

T+40	*There's Mach one.*
T+58	*Throttle up.*
T+60	*Feel that mother go. Woooohoooo.*
T+1:13	*Uhoh.*

—*CHALLENGER* PILOT MICHAEL J. SMITH

CHAPTER 10

Space as Frontier

The concept of an expanding space frontier, at the peak of its influence in the 1950s and 1960s, proved to be the greatest political omnibus since the GI Bill of Rights. It gave cold warriors a chance to sound their tocsin, space visionaries a means to fund their dreams, aerospace contractors a gusher of dollars, graduate school tuition to scientists and engineers, and NASA administrators the opportunity to turn an obscure research agency into the darling of the federal bureaucracy. With as much as 4 percent of the federal budget at its disposal, NASA spending provided income for a million workers and their families in the mid-1960s. As a source of pork, space was unrivaled. Lyndon Johnson once summoned a NASA official to his suite in Houston's Rice Hotel at 7:30 in the morning. Johnson introduced him to a young lady, said, "Give this girl a job; she is a mother," and recited (the detail makes the story entirely credible) a poem about motherhood. She got a GS-2 spot.[1]

Combining aspirations of progress, patriotism, and security, America's advance into the space frontier appealed to ordinary citizens. Some sent contributions to NASA. "I don't care whether getting to the moon is practical or even important," wrote a Wisconsin housewife. "I'm tired of taking a back seat to the Russians." Wernher von Braun's fan mail filled twenty-six boxes. Walter Cronkite, the CBS news anchor who covered the moon landings, thought space one of the few things holding the country together during the tumult of the late 1960s. "The great thing about the space program in those days," he said, "was that it kept us dreaming about the future, which had a very salutary effect in maintaining national sanity."[2]

When Apollo had run its course, what next? On January 5, 1972, Pres. Richard Nixon announced plans for a new space transportation system. It would, he said, "transform the space frontier of the 1970s into familiar territory, easily accessible for human endeavor in the 1980s and 1990s. The system will center on a vehicle that can shuttle repeatedly from earth to orbit and back. It will revolutionize transportation into near space, by routinizing it." NASA officials had assured the White House, Congress, and press that the shuttle would provide cheap, dependable, flexible, and frequent access to low-earth orbit. Von Braun foresaw payload costs dipping below fifty dollars a pound, weekly launches, and passenger rides smoother than an airliner's. Space flight would repeat—no, best—the history of atmospheric flight. Round-the-world airfare cost fifteen hundred dollars, NASA Administrator Thomas Paine told an interviewer in late 1968. "In the '80s we'll be able to travel to space for that."[3]

Time was no kinder to these prophecies than to von Braun's hopes for vacations in the family helicopter. Three decades after Nixon's decision, shuttle missions remained infrequent, delay-prone, risky, and expensive, running about a half billion dollars apiece. Having abandoned manned missions to the moon and planets, NASA failed even to provide cheap access to low-earth orbit. As Apollo launch towers rusted away in the Kennedy Space Center's bone yard, the very phrase "space age" came to signify a receding past rather than an imminent future. "None of us thought that America would turn into a nation of quitters and lose its will to lead an outward-bound manned exploration of our solar system," wrote an embittered Chris Kraft, whose name had once been synonymous with Mission Control. "That just wasn't possible." But it was possible. It did happen. The question is why.[4]

Hell of a Win

The first, most commonly given answer is that America's manned space program grew out of a transient superpower rivalry. The development of military rocketry, economic growth sufficient to sustain billions in discretionary spending, and the offerings of space writers and illustrators had helped convince Americans that something as complex, expensive, and novel as space exploration was feasible. Rocket ships were blasting off from every drugstore magazine rack in the country. Then, on October 4, 1957, something happened to convince Americans that they needed to turn fiction into fact, and quickly. The Soviet Union had launched the world's first artificial satellite.[5]

Weighing 184 pounds and carrying nothing more threatening than two beeping radio transmitters, *Sputnik* ("fellow traveler") created a sensation. America's free-world leadership, as historian Walter McDougall pointed out, rested on two premises. The first was that the nation's system of democratic capitalism offered the best hope of prosperity as well as freedom. The second was that the nation's technological lead made it, and its allies, impervious to aggression. By erasing the impression of Soviet economic backwardness and technological ineptitude, *Sputnik* undercut both assumptions. It raised the specter of Soviet control of space, whence future Pearl Harbors might be visited on the defenseless American homeland. "Space superiority" was about to replace "air superiority," von Braun warned after the Russian coup.[6]

Von Braun understood, as he had when he made his Faustian pact with the *Luftwaffe,* that military imperative offered the only realistic hope for funding his dream of space flight. (Conveniently, a meddling Heinrich Himmler had once ordered his arrest on charges of putting space travel ahead of weapons development. Von Braun later parlayed the episode into the image of an apolitical rocket scientist unlucky in his choice of patron.) Seizing on the new crisis, von Braun called for a coordinated program covering all aspects of human space flight. His long-considered plan (the "von Braun paradigm") called for stepwise advances. Satellites launched from expendable rockets would be followed by human orbital flights, then reusable spacecraft for achieving earth orbit. These spacecraft would build and service a manned space station, from which exploratory missions to the moon and Mars would be launched.[7]

Eisenhower's response was a good deal less ambitious. Denying that *Sputnik* had compromised the nation's security, and wary of competing to score propaganda points, he favored the methodical development of missiles for strategic deterrence and satellites for gathering intelligence. The Soviets, in fact, had done the United States a favor. They had set a precedent for the free passage of satellites, and hence spy cameras, above sovereign nations. Outer space could wait. Eisenhower's science advisors assigned human orbital flights, lunar exploration, and interplanetary exploration the desultory priorities of "later," "still later," and "much later still." Eisenhower himself always believed that space spectacles were a costly blunder. Interviewed in retirement, he grew so angry at the mention of Apollo that he pounded his desk. Three times.[8]

Eisenhower's position, that America should compete only for limited objectives of real strategic value, was perfectly reasonable. But, with the intense anxiety surrounding *Sputnik* and the ensuing succession of Soviet space "firsts," Senate Democrats knew he was vulnerable. Haunted by McCarthyism and sensing an opportunity to turn the tables, they pounced on "Who lost space?" as the equivalent of "Who lost China?" "The Roman Empire controlled the world because it could build roads," Senate Majority Leader Lyndon Johnson told an Austin audience. "Later—when men moved to the sea—the British Empire was dominant because it had ships. In the air age we were powerful"—note the past tense—"because we had airplanes. Now the Communists have established a foothold in outer space." Talk of launching a better satellite ("perhaps it will even have chrome trim and automatic windshield wipers," Johnson sneered) was not enough.[9]

Of all the 1960 Democratic presidential hopefuls, Sen. John F. Kennedy exploited space most skillfully. The United States, he charged, had fallen behind in the one contest that mattered: the cold war. The failure to keep abreast of the Russians in space, along with a supposed missile gap, lagging scientific education, and slower economic growth, had embarrassed the nation before the world. If Americans rededicated themselves to expanding the century's new frontiers, space prominent among them, they could recover their lost leadership and prevail in the struggle against liberty's totalitarian foes.[10]

When Kennedy took office, he knew he had to move on space. But he was not yet sure where to put his chips. Events forced a quick decision. On April 12, 1961, the Soviet Union launched Yuri Gagarin into orbit, a triumph magnified a week later by the collapse of the CIA-backed Bay of Pigs invasion. Kennedy asked Vice Pres. Lyndon Johnson to conduct an urgent, high-level policy review. Which space projects offered both drama and a reasonable chance of American priority? After consulting with von Braun and other experts, Johnson reported that the United States "could conceivably be first" in manned lunar circumnavigation and landing. Kennedy worried, with reason, that such feats would wreck the budget. NASA Administrator James Webb and Secretary of Defense Robert McNamara eased his conscience. They assured him that the struggle for prestige and technological leadership justified space feats, even those of uncertain commercial, scientific, or military value. Lunar exploration was "part of the battle along the fluid front of the cold war."

With a consensus forming behind the possibility of a U.S. lunar first, with the Mercury astronauts dominating the pages of *Life*, and with Alan Shepard having just completed America's first suborbital flight, Kennedy made his move. On May 25, 1961, he told a joint session of Congress, "I believe that this nation should commit itself to achieving the goal, before this decade is out, of landing a man on the moon and returning him safely to earth." Von Braun's conference room, where his rocket team had gathered to listen, erupted in cheers. "No single space project in this period will be more impressive to mankind as it makes its judgement of whether the world is free," Kennedy said, adding that "none will be so difficult or expensive to accomplish." He asked Congress to make a half-billion dollar down payment on what ultimately turned out to be a $24 billion bill.[11]

A tape of a November 1962 meeting, held one month after the Cuban Missile Crisis, reveals exactly what the president wanted for the taxpayers' money. "We hope to beat them to demonstrate that, starting behind, as we did by a couple of years, by God we passed them," Kennedy said. "I think it would [be a] hell of a win for us." Webb had protested that the moon was *one* of the top priority NASA programs, and that the United States should aim broadly at preeminence in space. No, Kennedy said, beating the Russians to the moon was *the* top priority. "Otherwise, we shouldn't be spending this kind of money, because I'm not that interested in space."[12]

Webb, a garrulous politician, did manage to hang a fair amount of science, and much else, on Apollo. But he could not escape the fact that his one big program rested on the shifting sands of political calculation. The pioneers of aviation had built on firmer foundations. Though they too had depended on the support of the federal government, Glenn Curtiss and Juan Trippe and Bill Boeing knew in their bones that the airplane had a tremendous future. Their vision of the continuous refinement and widening scope of this remarkable invention had a clarity, concreteness, and practical appeal that the manned space program never matched. Lindbergh achieved nonstop transcontinental flight for $13,500. Investors understood the significance of that, and bought aviation stocks. The moon at $24 billion was a harder sell.

Apollo prevailed because Kennedy's end-of-decade goal gave it urgency and focus. Had the program advanced at a more leisurely pace, the political will and funding might not have held together. They did, just. The Gemini crews honed the techniques necessary for lunar-orbit rendezvous. The Apollo project managers confronted, and corrected the weaknesses revealed by, a 1967 testing accident that asphyxiated three astronauts trapped in a burning capsule. Then, in 1968, Apollo 8 made its historic Christmas eve broadcast from lunar orbit. "My impression," astronaut Frank Borman said of the moon, "is that it's a vast, lonely, forbidding-type existence, or expanse of nothing." He might as well have been looking at Antarctica. Practically speaking, he

In September 1961, President Kennedy gave a space policy speech at Rice University. Kennedy embroidered his moon objective with impossible-dream rhetoric: "Why climb the highest mountain?" he asked. "Why—35 years ago—fly the Atlantic? Why does Rice play Texas?" The last analogy proved more apt than he knew. Overmatched Rice eventually joined another conference and quit playing Texas. Budget constraints in the late 1960s and early 1970s forced the U.S. space program into a comparable reordering of priorities. The man who would reluctantly order the first big cuts, Lyndon Johnson (in sunglasses), looks on.

was, given the economic artificiality of the lunar enterprise. Frontiers ordinarily focus attention outward, toward new horizons. Apollo's lasting achievement was to shift attention *homeward*, toward the dappled blue oasis of earthrise. "The vast loneliness up here at the moon is awe-inspiring," said Borman's compatriot, Jim Lovell, "and it makes you realize just what you have got back there on earth."[13]

The earthlings were duly impressed. The astronauts made so many postflight tours abroad that the State Department complained about their wives' hairdressing bills. Before Apollo 11 went up in July 1969, NASA flacks gave each journalist working the moon story a 250-page press kit. (Put it aboard the lunar lander, suggested one. That way anyone visiting the site in the future would be sure Americans had been there.) The world watched the moon landing live, save in the Soviet Union. Former Vice Pres. Hubert Humphrey, visiting Moscow at the time, nevertheless sensed a deep impact. The Soviet leaders, he told an interviewer, knew the United States "was not a country to be underestimated, or fooled with."[14]

So the intended point was made. It would go on being made through Apollo 17, which departed Cape Canaveral in a spectacular night launch on December 7, 1972. NASA's problem, apparent even before the success of the lunar landings, was how to define, articulate, and fund its post-Apollo mission. If space was a frontier, NASA was its boom town, its mostly young workers haunted by a sense of impermanence. (In 1969, the average age of the operations staff at the Manned Space Flight Center was twenty-six years.) The last, unpropitious years of the Johnson administration hinted at how short the boom would be. As Vietnam and the Great Society pushed up taxes and inflation, Budget Director Charles Schultze looked for cuts in discretionary spending. He made space his primary target. Johnson spared Apollo, but little else. In July 1967, Webb had to shut down the Saturn V rocket production line, eliminating heavy-lift boosters beyond those necessary to complete Apollo. That move killed any hope for extended lunar exploration or a permanent space station during the 1970s. The same summer Congress eliminated $2 billion for a robot probe to Mars. Frustrated by the budget defeats, Webb left NASA the following year.[15]

His successors faced other challenges. Despite Vietnam, and to some degree because of it, both the Johnson and Nixon administrations wanted to manage the U.S.-Soviet rivalry in a less dangerous and costly way. That meant limiting nuclear arms and decelerating the space race. One initiative, the 1967 Outer Space Treaty, forbade signatories from claiming sovereignty over space, or placing weapons in it. The deal removed strategic incentives for aggressive exploration. Some space enthusiasts read this as a stab in the back, the State Department robbing NASA of its cold-war energy. But that is to confuse the straw of a single agreement with the wind of détente, blowing from an unfavorable quarter. Superpower cooperation on civilian space projects, rather than competition, became the diplomatic watchword.[16]

The late 1960s' zeitgeist of anti–anti-communism, disenchantment with technology, and social liberalism spelled more trouble, evident in the growing criticism of NASA in the bellwether *New York Times.* ("They are trying to discredit me through you," Lyndon Johnson confided to Webb. "Those Hebrews are trying to get me.") Apollo suffered guilt by political and technological association with Vietnam, which tarnished its achievement. Environmentalism, which Lindbergh judged "far more important" than space exploration, looked like the next big thing. With the SST going down to congressional defeat in 1971, with Sen. William Proxmire on the boondoggle warpath, and with President Kennedy's last surviving brother, Edward, prominent among the Senate's space critics, NASA administrators faced at least temporary retreat along the space frontier.[17]

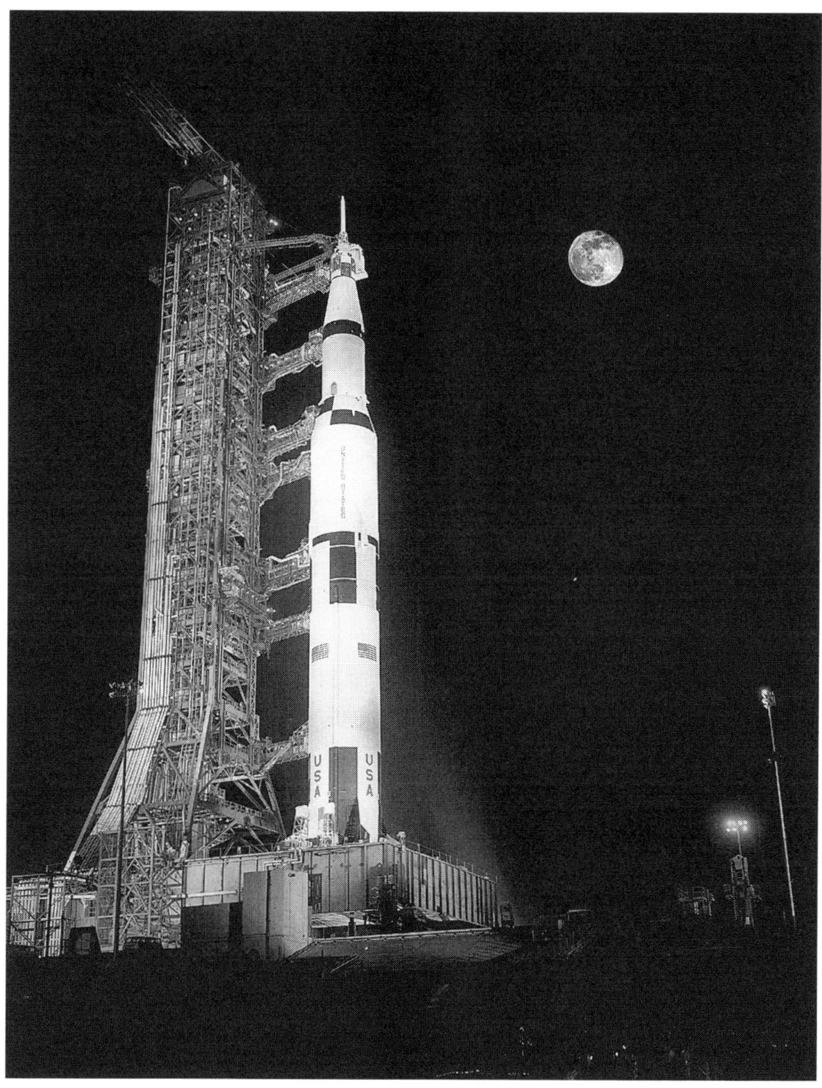

Poised for launch at the Kennedy Space Center's Pad 39A, Apollo 17 lifted off shortly after midnight on December 7, 1972. The three astronauts on board, Eugene Cernan, Ronald Evans, and Harrison "Jack" Schmitt, were the last three humans to travel beyond earth orbit during the twentieth century. Budget cuts killed Apollo missions 18 through 20. Only Skylab, an experimental, one-hundred-ton space station assembled from leftover Apollo hardware, remained in NASA's pipeline.

They could not even depend upon the strong ratings space broadcasts had once generated. Viewers had grown tired of the moon missions and their seemingly predetermined success. (Apollo 13's lost-in-space drama was the exception that proved the rule.) NASA's own employees became jaded. When they went off duty at Mission Control during Apollo 17, they quit watching the live feed from the moon and went out into the lobby to catch the Jets and Raiders on Monday Night Football. With Joe Namath and Daryle Lamonica at quarterback, anything could happen. (That night, it did.) Few Americans felt the same way about Gene Cernan and Jack Schmitt gathering geological samples in their lunar rover. No contingency, no interest.[18]

"'Countdown' at Cape Kennedy is not from *ten* to *one*," wrote R. Buckminster Fuller. "It is from *ten million* to *one*." It took a myriad of tasks accomplished by each of hundreds of thousands of people over many years to assure success. Therein lay Apollo's last and most paradoxical legacy. Its program managers, with their simulations and redundancies and quality assurance tests, had succeeded, in the eyes of the public, in routinizing space travel. But, at upwards of a half billion dollars per Saturn launch, they never succeeded in making it truly and usefully routine.[19]

Taxi to Nowhere

President Nixon gave NASA another chance. Nixon liked the space program, regarded the astronauts as heroes, and thought the country was in space to stay. A champion of the supersonic transport program, he had, in adviser John Ehrlichman's words, "died very hard on the SST." (The idea that a French president could arrive at an international conference in supersonic splendor particularly galled him.) Not a man to take reverses lightly, Nixon welcomed a new project that would boost the beleaguered aerospace industry and sustain America's technological edge. But his political strategy—to build a centrist majority by blending conservative and patriotic rhetoric with a selective expansion of reformed social welfare programs—left no room for NASA's full agenda. Like a meteorite reduced to a cinder, the von Braun paradigm burned up in the atmosphere of Nixonian political calculation. By the time the administration completed its lengthy review of NASA's manned operations, all that remained was a pared-down shuttle.[20]

Even that was a near thing. Analysts in the Department of Defense and the Office of Management and Budget (OMB) derided the shuttle as a "taxi to nowhere" and characterized early projections of its cost and performance as "absurd." Some wanted to scrub Apollo missions 16 and 17 as well as the shuttle. Their political elders overruled them. NASA had a good track record,

By 1970, Wernher von Braun had grown discouraged about the future of the space program. "These goddam Apollo guys had their day in court, they had all the fun, but now that we have landed on the moon, let's quit," was how he summed up the situation. He nevertheless accepted an associate administrator's job at NASA headquarters and tried to lobby the Nixon administration, the stern Santa of this NASA in-house cartoon.

OMB Deputy Director Caspar Weinberger pointed out in an August 12, 1971, memo to the president. True, its spending was discretionary and therefore cuttable. But future NASA projects would offer work for otherwise hard-to-employ scientists and technicians. Their labors would yield civilian spinoffs as well as space access. Abandoning space would convey to the nation and the world "that our best years are behind us, that we are turning inward, reducing our defense commitments, and voluntarily starting to give up our superpower status, and our desire to maintain world superiority. America should be able to afford something besides increased welfare, programs to repair our cities, or Appalachian relief and the like."

Weinberger had perfect political pitch. His boss, OMB director George Schultz, wrote "I agree with Cap" on the first page. Nixon himself wrote "OK" next to Weinberger's proposal to fund shuttle development. Not least of Nixon's considerations was the employment crisis in the aerospace industry, which had slipped into a deep recession after the 1960s boom. The shuttle program, even when trimmed to fit the budget, offered a lifeline to aerospace workers in battleground states like California. Like much else in late twentieth-century American history, the future of space hinged on tactical considerations for the 1972 election.[21]

Thus politics, pork, and prestige, the same combination that had inspired Apollo (and the Concorde, Charles de Gaulle's preferred means of challenging "America's colonization of the skies") got the shuttle project going. In public, however, NASA officials made their case on utilitarian grounds. A "reusable system like an airplane which can fly to and from earth orbit," ran a typical memo to a typically skeptical senator, would slash the costs of launching, recovering, and repairing satellites. The shuttle would be the C-47 of low-earth orbit, a winged space truck. Or perhaps dump truck: Nixon thought it might rid the earth of nuclear waste. "We should realize," he told NASA's James Fletcher and George Low, "that it will open up entirely new fields when we actually have the capability the shuttle will provide."[22]

Therein lay, so far as NASA was concerned, the amorphous beauty of the project. The shuttle not only kept the manned space program alive, it kept open the door to the moon and Mars. The shuttle itself could not travel beyond earth orbit. But, should funds become available, its crews could assemble a space station. Blasting off from the earth's surface was what made space flight so expensive. Orbiting above it, the space station could serve as a jumping-off point for affordable missions to deeper space.

In hindsight, it was a clever political strategy. The ascendant Republicans were space-friendly. The Reagan administration (1981–89) breathed life back into the space station, and the senior Bush administration (1989–93) flirted with a Mars mission. Had the agency actually devised the means of cheap and dependable orbital access by the time these opportunities presented themselves, the space program—and by extension, the space frontier—would have looked quite different in the 1980s and 1990s.

But NASA did not, and neither did the Soviets. The shuttle *Buran* ("snowstorm on the steppes") made a single unmanned flight in 1988 and ended up in Gorky Park. NASA's shuttles were always more experimental than operational vehicles. The crucial error was the assumption, in the face of serious budgetary constraints, that the agency's engineers and contractors could devise the thermal protection, reusable rocket engines, automated checkout system, and other technological innovations necessary for routine and efficient operation. Historically, aerospace engineering had advanced in evolutionary fashion. The B-52 had grown out of the B-47, Apollo out of Gemini. The shuttle was a forced revolution, comparable to jumping from the Douglas transports of the mid-1930s directly to the jet airliners of the late 1950s.[23]

NASA's sternest critics, among them rocket engineer Robert Truax, rejected the shuttle concept itself. Truax's case, set out in a prescient 1970 article, was that complex vehicles weighed down with wings and landing gear defied common sense. Like Lindbergh contemplating the Atlantic, Truax realized that simplicity was the key. Simplest of all was a liquid-fueled rocket that could be recovered as its spent stages dropped into the ocean. "Make it big, make it simple, make it reusable," Truax said. "Don't push the state of the art, and don't make it any more reliable than it has to be. And *never* mix people and cargo, because the reliability requirements are worlds apart. For people you can have a very small vehicle on which you lavish all your attention; everything else is cargo, and for this all you need is a Big Dumb Booster."[24]

To the question of why NASA had insisted on pushing the state of the art, rather than refining existing rocket technology, Truax gave two subtle answers. For the engineers, the shuttle proved irresistibly sexy. Why would anyone, particularly contractors working on a cost-plus basis, want to build better, cheaper rockets when it was possible to use public money to build a next-generation system? Leapfrogging offered more excitement, jobs, profits, patronage, and high-tech spinoffs. Then there were the airplane pilots, astronauts included, who held key posts at NASA. Still wedded to wings and wheels, they saw the shuttle as a means of solving the "spam in a can" problem. Pilots could fly the shuttle, have some fun. With other people's money at stake, fun won. The market discipline that had advanced airliner and general aviation designs along evolutionary lines, and which would have dictated post-Apollo rocket development in a private industry milieu, never came into play.[25]

Rank heresies in the NASA-can-do climate of the early 1970s, such criticisms gained credence as time passed. Turbine blades cracked, nozzles broke, and fires erupted when engineers tested the orbiter's main engines. Installing, checking, and replacing the 30,759 ceramic tiles to protect against the furnace-like reentry heat was an ordeal. Technicians managed just 1.3 tiles per person per week. Each of the numbered tiles had a unique shape and, as the test launches demonstrated, a disquieting tendency to pop off the orbiter's aluminum frame. OMB officials urged President Carter (1977–81) to cancel the delay-prone program. He spared it, though he refused to approve a fifth orbiter. NASA would have to make do with a fleet of four shuttles.

The first of these, the *Columbia,* lifted off from the expensively reconfigured Saturn V launch facilities at Kennedy Space Center in April 1981. It was the first of four test flights that ended, amidst patriotic hoopla, on July 4, 1982. With its space transport system officially operational, with its aura of technological leadership restored, with the United States again in possession of "a significant and highly visible instrument of foreign policy," and with the Reagan administration committed to using the shuttle to launch all government payloads, NASA's manned space program entered a brief silver age. All that remained was to commence launching on a regular basis. One rule governed shuttle economics. With high development and overhead costs, the more often it flew, the lower the average cost per flight.

That was where the program foundered. With refurbishing and inspection requiring more than a million separate procedures, NASA measured shuttle turnaround time in months rather than days. Anticipating forty-eight launches per year, the most the agency ever achieved, in 1985, was nine. Scientists and air force officers, whose experiments and satellites were hostage to the delayed cargo manifest, grew impatient. Then, on January 28, 1986, disaster struck. It took the form of a hot gas leak from the right booster rocket that detonated the *Challenger*'s main liquid fuel tank. The explosion broke up the orbiter and plunged its crew compartment into the ocean 65,000 feet below. Still living, though perhaps mercifully unconscious, the astronauts hit the water with a force equivalent to 200 Gs.[26]

The dream of a flourishing shuttle program died with them. The air force bailed out, reverting to expendable launch vehicles. (Ironically, one of the reasons for the shuttle's design had been the air force's desire for "cross-range capability." Because of the earth's rotation, polar orbits—i.e., missions over the Soviet Union—necessitated maneuvering some 1,265 miles back to the original base, hence the delta wing to provide adequate lift at hypersonic reentry speeds. When the air force withdrew, the delta-wing design became even more pointless.) NASA canceled further missions until 1988, then settled into a cautious regime of a few launches per year. Officially, safety remained the top priority. One more disaster and "we're dead," Administrator Sean O'Keefe warned NASA employees shortly after his 2002 appointment. For Truax, the real disaster lay in the concept itself. "The Space Shuttle represents a truly marvelous implementation of an absolutely absurd idea," he said in 1999, fuming over NASA's refusal to kill the program. "Its development and use have cost some $20 billion–$40 billion, and it has set back economical access to space about 35 years."[27]

The loss of the *Columbia* in February 2003 added an exclamation point to Truax's case. The shuttle failed at its most unnecessary point, the wing, dooming the entire crew. Had any of NASA's efforts to develop a new generation of reusable vehicles borne fruit, the agency might then have phased out its shuttle fleet. What the industry calls "blood priority" had ended the careers of the Fokker F10 Trimotor, the De Havilland DH-106 Comet, and other failure-prone designs. Better planes took their place. But the failure or cancellation of reusable launcher experiments had left nothing to fill the shuttle void. Modifying and inspecting, let alone replacing, the aging shuttles had strained the agency's budget, down 13 percent in real terms from 1993 to 2002. The broken engineering tail was wagging the starving science dog. "If you're looking strictly for science bang for the buck," said Paul Ronney, an engineer whose experiment fell to pieces with the *Columbia,* "then I think you would just have unmanned vehicles."[28]

President George W. Bush's response to the crisis, announced in January 2004, was to publicly reaffirm the future of human spaceflight. Evoking the spirit of Lewis and Clark, he called for Americans to return to the moon as early as 2015 and then to prepare for an even more ambitious Mars mission. He said the shuttles would be retired in 2010, following the anticipated completion of the International Space Station. The task of "extending a human presence across our solar system," he continued, would fall to an unspecified new generation of spacecraft, whose way would be prepared by unmanned lunar and Martian probes. But this was 2004, not 1962, and Bush's words evoked as much skepticism as excitement. "Basically, they looked at piloted space and said, 'Let's shut it down and let's have a hedge against the possibility that the Chinese will go to the Moon,'" said defense analyst John Pike. "That's it. There's nothing to replace shuttle and station except artwork."[29]

In hindsight, the cost of the shuttle went beyond the billions spent on a flawed design. The way NASA managed the program also hurt private space enterprise. Its worst mistake was to contract aggressively for commercial payloads, even having space-walking astronauts pose with "for sale" signs above the shuttle's open cargo bay. It was as if, in 1925, the post office, instead of making plans to privatize air mail, had planned to carry all cargoes in one novel type of government plane. Inconsistent as well as unwise, NASA's policy ran contrary to the Reagan administration's stated goal of encouraging the private launch industry. But NASA needed to pile up missions in order to justify the shuttle's overhead and bring down its per launch costs. With the air force's nervous acquiescence, NASA officials canceled future orders for Delta, Atlas, and Titan rockets. The manufacturers shut down their production lines. With these launch options foreclosed, commercial customers had to choose between the shuttle and the European Space Agency's Ariane rocket.

NASA's launch business, with forty-four commercial and foreign satellites in its clogged pipeline, went down with the *Challenger.* In 1986, Reagan forbade NASA from launching commercial payloads, save those that actually required the shuttle, and announced a policy of reviving the domestic launch industry. That took time. American boosters did not again lift commercial satellites into orbit until 1989. Ariane retained the lion's share of the business, having gained a huge advantage in the *Challenger* aftermath. Any complete accounting of the shuttle's legacy must include the lost years of domestic booster production and development.[30]

To be fair, aerospace industry complacency compounded the effects of NASA's clumsy attempt at monopoly. Cost-plus contracting discouraged innovation. Aerospace firms were notorious for preferring assured government profits over the risk of their own capital. Daniel S. Goldin, an aggressive administrator put in charge of NASA in 1992, did not hesitate to point his finger at contractors. In 1996 he publicly challenged the Space Transportation Association to quit relying on "Uncle Sugar" to underwrite risks and to "get rich and open the space frontier" with cost-efficient launch vehicles. "I didn't come to NASA to watch the shuttle go up and down," he said. "I came to NASA to help us open the space frontier, and together we're going to do it." But these brave words brought no appreciable change. When Goldin left NASA in 2001, the shuttle was still making its infrequent rounds. The industry's attitude remained, if NASA or the air force wants a better launch vehicle, let them front the money for it.[31]

Stuck Watching

Space transportation, like commercial aviation, has two sides: supply and demand. As with aviation, supply has received most of the attention. But it is also worth looking at demand. Did NASA and other space-access providers overlook sources of revenue that would have defrayed their costs and funded innovations?

Many observers have pointed to the neglect of the "space tourism industry," though a better phrase would be the experiential market, exemplified by airplane rides. Apart from military and cargo operations, aviation demand progressed through three stages: watching, experiencing, and traveling. The first customers paid to observe other people, daring young pilots, perform in planes. When they grew tired of watching, the more adventurous sought to experience flying for themselves. Barnstormers scratched their itch with war surplus planes. Then, as commercial aircraft became increasingly safe and economical, well-heeled travelers began flying to save time. From that point on, the story was one of increasing volume and broadening social base.

Space flight got stuck in the watching stage. Tax dollars gave citizens space spectacles, but no chance to experience space flight. Yet volunteers had offered to go up in Von Braun's V-2s almost from the moment he moved his rocket team to the United States. Following Stanley Kubrick's *2001: A Space Odyssey* (1968) and the Apollo moon missions, the waiting list for Pan Am's "as yet unscheduled" lunar service swelled to more than 93,000 names. Ronald Reagan, Barry Goldwater, and *Star Trek*'s William Shatner all made reservations. The shuttle's flush times, from 1982 to early 1986, brought another flood of would-be passengers. One man applied to NASA forty times. Pregnant women offered to have their babies in space. "Ready and counting," said Ken Kesey, one of many writers who volunteered. With passengers experiencing only 3 Gs during launch, astronaut fitness standards did not apply. All passengers needed to know, Chuck Yeager said, "was how to go to the bathroom and eat their food in space." Asked if he would like to go up, Yeager allowed that "it would be fun to fly the thing, but I wouldn't particularly care about laying in the back amongst mission specialists." The masses were less choosy. Forty-five percent who responded to a *USA Today* poll said they would like to ride the shuttle.[32]

The great difficulty in meeting such demand was the intrinsic expense and risk of rocket-powered vehicles. Several entrepreneurs floated commercial passenger schemes. Truax called his the "Volksrocket," but he had no better luck than anyone else. In 1996, the X Prize Foundation sweetened the pot by offering $10 million to anyone who could launch a reusable private spaceship. The vehicle had to carry at least one person with payload capacity for two others, reach one hundred kilometers, return safely, and go up again within two weeks. By May 1998, fourteen teams, including one financed by technophilic novelist Tom Clancy ("It's cool, it's fun, it's exciting"), had entered the competition. None enjoyed immediate success. As the twenty-first century began, the only experiential offerings were "edge of space" rides in high-performance aircraft like the MiG-25 Foxbat.[33]

That left, by default, the U.S. and Russian space programs. The latter, desperate for cash, ventured into the tourist market in 2001, sending businessman Dennis Tito on a $20 million orbital vacation. Internet entrepreneur Mark Shuttlesworth, the first South African in space, ponied up $20 million the following year. NASA, with post-Apollo budget woes of its own, opposed all such schemes. Why not, space boosters wondered, conduct lotteries for shuttle seats, raising hundreds of millions for the space program? Or outfit one of the shuttles to carry paying passengers? Or charge to orbit cremated remains?

NASA declined to sell shuttle space to nonessential passengers in any state of compaction. The agency's attitude, dating back to Project Mercury, was that space belonged to NASA and the astronauts, and a certain kind of astronaut at that. The old guard had opened the door to space, slowly and grudgingly, to nonmilitary test pilots, then scientist astronauts, then payload specialists. Female astronauts did not go up until 1983, two decades after the

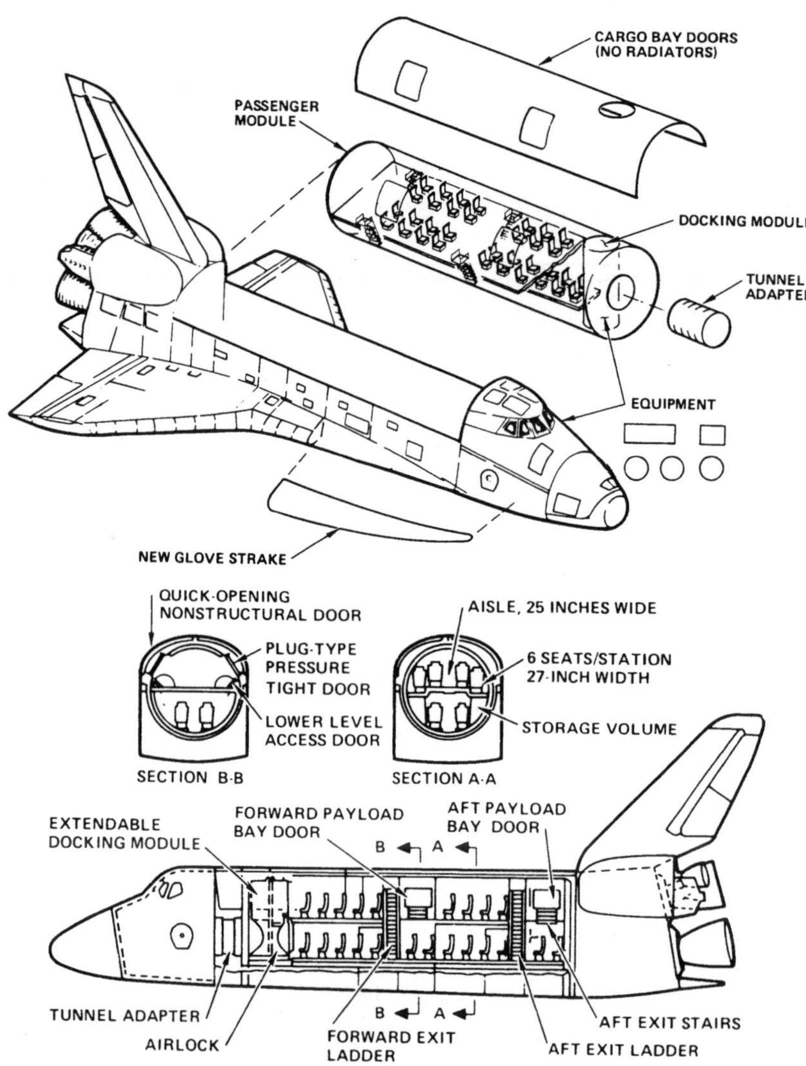

To illustrate how the shuttle could carry space-construction workers, Rockwell International drew up plans showing a reconfigured orbiter with seventy-four passenger seats, sixty-eight in the payload bay and six on the lower flight deck. The modification cost, including additional toilets, came to $220 million in 1979 dollars. Space boosters pointed out that such a design could carry paying tourists as well as technicians. NASA was not interested. It made one token gesture, the Space Flight Participants program, the means by which teacher Christa McAuliffe found her way aboard the ill-fated *Challenger.*

Soviets put the first woman in space. The agency's sometimes conflicting priorities—aerospace engineering, science, and national security—precluded selling space to rich dilettanti. (Or to stamp dealers, as the crew of Apollo 15 discovered when they were caught peddling lunar philately.) Had the shuttle performed as advertised—that is, often—the agency might have unbent with time. Meanwhile the only entrepreneurs NASA welcomed were those with satellites and small science experiments, dubbed "Getaway Specials." Anything else was infra dig.

Budgetary realities reinforced NASA's aversion to tapping the experiential market. Had the agency raised money through such means as passenger lotteries, Congress might simply have subtracted a like sum from its appropriation. Every dollar coming into the agency was discretionary and fungible. Civilian shuttle rides (save for key congressmen like Sen. Jake Garn and Rep. Bill Nelson) could waste resources without yielding budgetary gain. Here again bureaucratic calculations impeded the space frontier's natural economic development.

NASA officials knew, however, that they could not ignore private citizens altogether. A few nonpaying passengers would add drama and symbolically deliver on the pledge of space access. The Reagan administration wanted the first to be a teacher. Christa McAuliffe, selected from among more than eleven thousand applicants, got the nod for shuttle mission 51-L. She was to have—in a way, did—broadcast two live lessons: "The Ultimate Field Trip" and "Where We've Been, Where We're Going, Why?" The seven-person crew included another woman, Judith Resnik, an African American, Ronald McNair, and an Asian American, Ellison Onizuka. NASA had finally assembled a crew that looked like America, and then lost every one of them in history's worst launch accident.[34]

In the safety first, limited-launch regime that followed, the agency put "average citizens" on the remotest of back burners. Civilians could go up only if qualified and fully trained as astronauts or mission specialists. Otherwise, warned Clinton science adviser John Gibbons, the public would misunderstand the risks and fail to respect the crews' "hard work and bravery"—as if this had anything to do with the original point of the program. The "shuttle," a name implying both regular operation and public access, had become a multibillion-dollar misnomer.[35]

With citizen passengers as well as most commercial and military satellites struck from its manifest, the shuttle's post-*Challenger* future was tied to that of the space station. Introduced early in the Reagan administration, Space Station Freedom (later and more diplomatically called the International Space Station) proved to be the most controversial, contested, and oft-reconfigured program in the agency's history. One thing everyone could agree on: a permanently occupied station would give the shuttle a destination and a mission. But critics attacked every other premise on which the project rested. Better to launch the space station like Skylab, with one big booster. Or better not to launch at all, the station being a scientifically useless aerospace boondoggle that offered no prospect of advancing the space frontier. "NASA's manned program remains frozen in the headlights of von Braun's old plan," complained Timothy Ferris, an advocate of direct interplanetary missions. "The space station we're about to start building will be of almost no use in getting to Mars, the Moon or anywhere else—except into debt."[36]

The most persistent criticism was cost. Between them, the space station and the shuttle threatened to devour NASA's budget and vaporize tens of billions of federal tax dollars. Getting rid of one, the station, would make it possible to get rid of the other, the shuttle, a misbegotten political program that had never paid its own way. "The way to get truly big savings out of NASA," the *New York Times* editorialized in 1995, "would be to eliminate the entire manned space program and the shuttle flights."[37]

Unmanned *vs.* Manned

That a liberal newspaper in a city with homeless people sleeping in its subways should advocate such cuts was unremarkable. So was the tendency of newspapers in space-industry towns to defend the same programs. More interesting was the long-held view of many scientists, within and without NASA, that manned exploration wasted resources. Apollo was about transportation, not exploration, fumed lunar geologist Eugene Shoemaker. Probes and robots could have done the same job years earlier and "at one fifth the cost."[38]

Echoing Eisenhower, military analysts and earth scientists worried that manned space initiatives might draw resources from the satellite network upon which the nation's security and progress depended. The big payoffs were in communication, navigation, intelligence gathering, terrain mapping, and weather and crop forecasting. Even scientists who believed NASA's gaze should remain fixed outward favored unmanned probes. The Viking, Pioneer, and Voyager spacecraft, all launched in the 1970s, bore them out. They collectively visited every planet save Pluto, provided years of scientific data, and made surprising discoveries, among them "rings around Jupiter, volcanoes on Io, geysers on Triton, . . . [and] new moons around Uranus and Neptune." Riccardo Giacconi's rocket-launched X-ray telescopes garnered the first Nobel Prize for research with significant NASA funding. Not every mission was a prizewinner. In 1999, an orbiter, a polar lander, and two basketball–sized probes all failed to send back data from Mars. But these failures followed a string of other, successful Mars missions. More important, no one got killed. The commonsense rule, wrote astronomer Thomas Gold, was never send up a person when an instrument would do—a point underscored when the 2003 *Columbia* breakup dismembered another family-of-man crew.[39]

When it came to missions outside the solar system, people plainly would not do at all. The time and power requirements—forty years and thousands of gigawatts—needed to reach the nearest star, Proxima Centauri, would be prohibitive even for an exotic spacecraft equipped with laser-light sails, propelled by an array of lasers based in our solar system. The only realistic alternative, Ferris has argued, would be self-replicating, nanotechnology-based, "grapefruit-sized probes" capable of planting the seed of life on "hospitable but lifeless planets." Or we could content ourselves with using radio and optical telescopes to search for extraterrestrial intelligence (SETI) while broadcasting signals of our own. A "monologue-dominated interstellar network" (with many thousand-year lags between messages!) may be the only hope of distant contact, given inescapable difficulties of voyaging to other stars.[40]

Ferris's argument raises an interesting question. Is it possible to have a frontier without a living presence? Recall the definition of a frontier as a zone of interaction between populations. Historically, that has meant interactions between living creatures, human, animal, and microbial. Even pilots in the "empty" sky had their share of run-ins with birds, insects, and unfamiliar germs. It may be, however, that space-time constraints limit any space-frontier interactions to robotic and electronic exchanges. The effects of such exchanges would still be revolutionary for human history and consciousness. That being so, why not get on with the business of exploring the space frontier with the cheapest and most practical means at hand, giving up the project of human travel beyond—perhaps even within—the solar system?

The criticism of NASA's fixation on human space flight has provoked two broad lines of response. One is that, like it or not, machines are no substitute for astronauts. "In the eyes of the people, the thing that really counts is the guy who puts his life on the line," said Robert Gilruth, who directed Houston's Manned Spacecraft Center. Hubert Humphrey thought unmanned missions would have been as exciting as Columbus's ships without crews. "Exploration requires emotional commitment," wrote Chris Kraft. "Intellectual commitment is not enough to inspire a president, propel a Congress, or draw intense support from a diverse public." Robot rovers were all well and good, but until he saw men and women live from Mars, Kraft said, his heart would not race again.[41]

The emotional commitment problem has never gone away. What is cost-effective in space is not necessarily budget-effective. Without human "scouting" expeditions, interest wanes, as NASA learned during the "faster, better, cheaper" probe regime of the 1990s. With the increasing use of UAVs (unmanned aerial vehicles), the air force discovered a human-presence problem of its own. In 1997, Capt. Greg Harbin won the Aerial Achievement Medal for guiding a malfunctioning UAV to a safe landing at Mostar Air Base in Bosnia-Herzegovina. Result: crisis in the status sphere. The "pilot mafia" raised a stink, and, in 1998, acting Air Force Secretary F. Whitten Peters directed that the medal would henceforth go only to those "onboard an aircraft while participating in aerial flight." Though the next secretary, James Roche, reversed the ruling (after UAVs drew praise in Afghanistan), the snafu revealed a deep political truth. Risk paid dividends. Minimizing risk entailed loss of status. NASA's version of the dilemma was less attention and fewer resources if it jettisoned its astronauts—who, as it happened, qualified for special consideration when they appeared before air force promotion boards.[42]

The second response to criticism of manned flights stressed the historical prematurity of the space frontier. Motivated by an untimely superpower rivalry, the United States and the Soviet Union failed to develop cheap and dependable human access to space because they tried too soon. It was as if they had embarked upon a crash program to achieve powered flight before the invention of the internal combustion engine. Developments since Apollo, such as lightweight composite materials and compact computers, promise to reduce vehicle weight. Experiments with rotary and aerospike engines have pointed the way to more efficient rockets. Eventually, some combination of magnetically levitated track launches, nuclear or pulse engines, microwave beam vehicles, and "space elevators" (long tethers lifting humans from the atmosphere to a geostationary terminal), may reduce costs even further. "Automobiles and aircraft have progressed from fragile, dangerous contraptions to relatively robust, comfortable machines in which lives are entrusted daily," point out Roger Launius and Howard McCurdy, two of space travel's guarded optimists. The principal challenge for the future will be the development of equivalent machines, "safe, reliable, low-cost vehicles operating between the surface of the Earth and the edge of the space frontier."[43]

If time proves the optimists correct, if overdetermined technological progress produces affordable vehicles, then space enterprise will move into its second, participatory stage of development. People have grown tired of spectacles. Rich adventurers want to experience space's vastness for themselves. Ultimately, some will want to make it the means of interplanetary travel. The success of that ambition, and its cost, will determine whether the history of the space frontier fully and finally recapitulates that of the sky.

Part III

The Significance of Air and Space in American History

The people of the United States have taken their tone from the incessant expansion which has not only been open but which has even been forced upon them. He would be a rash prophet who should assert that the expansive character of American life has now entirely ceased.

—FREDERICK JACKSON TURNER, "THE SIGNIFICANCE OF THE FRONTIER IN AMERICAN HISTORY," 1893

CHAPTER 11

Winners and Losers

The question of why Americans failed to develop cheap and dependable access to space has yet another answer. It is that, in a broader sense, they did not fail at all. Whatever its defects, the space program more than returned its investment by generating spinoffs. NASA claimed paternity of digital body imaging, waste purification, solar energy, cordless appliances, laser surgery, liquid crystal displays, epoxy adhesives, portable computers, parallel processing, and dozens of other breakthroughs. Unexpected gains, von Braun pointed out in 1950, followed great explorations. Columbus and Marco Polo opened new economic worlds. So had the Wright brothers. Space would do the same. This time history proved him right.[1]

But at what price? Critics scoffed at the spinoffs argument and the related claim that every dollar invested in space returned seven dollars to the nation's gross income. These same products might, after all, have been developed independently and at less cost through focused research. And why should the United States provide technological benefits, along with scientific data, to free-riding European and Asian competitors?[2]

The arguments about spinoffs' benefits are unresolvable, given the welter of counterfactuals at their core. Who really knows when, or whether, engineers would have devised programmable heart pacemakers without NASA's work on two-way telemetry? Yet the idea behind the contested details, that aerospace developments affect society in important and unexpected ways, is attractive and plausible. Turner studied land frontier expansion because he wanted to understand how it had shaped the nation's character and development. It is possible to do the same thing for sky frontier expansion, defined broadly as the growing activity in and above the atmosphere, including unmanned vehicles and their electronic systems. Some of the effects, such as Sunbelt growth, have been mentioned in passing. Now it is time to look more carefully at the economy and the armed forces, the twin foundations of national power. No gain came without loss. Some losses were borne by human actors, though the heaviest burden fell, as Lindbergh had foreseen, on the environment itself.

Commercial Integration

The most basic problem in U.S. history has been one of integration: how to tie together people, markets, and governments (including a few that doubted the wisdom of union) in a large and diverse nation that outgrew its modest coastal beginnings. Politically, the knitting-together process began in the late eighteenth century. Physically, it commenced in earnest in the nineteenth century, when improved roads, canals, steamboats, railroads, and telegraphs linked "island communities" within and without the distended continental nation. These linkages had their disruptive side, particularly for small farmers and merchants exposed to the shocks of distant competition. But they also yielded big gains for the increasingly interdependent national economy. Interregional trade prospered. Fast-growing cities such as Chicago served as shipping points and, later, as manufacturing centers.

Airways connected the industrial cities to one another and to their hinterlands. Planes sped vital cargos, such as machine replacement parts to keep a cannery operating during the salmon run. Planes carried deposits to earn interest, serums to combat epidemics, news photos to fill front pages, and movies to entertain waiting audiences. "They are sending all the finished pictures by air express now," Will Rogers joked in 1928. "If we are wrecked, look what the world will miss seeing." The film distribution problem—production concentrated on one coast, consumption on the other, with industry players shuttling between—had its equivalents in other businesses. The solution was fast, long-distance transport planes. Visionaries like Howard Hughes and engineers like Kelly Johnson provided them, burying the European commercial competition.[3]

Planes connected business operations throughout the country. Since the late nineteenth century, mergers within industries and strategic acquisitions of companies necessary for materials and distribution had produced giant, bureaucratically organized corporations with large spheres of operation. With ownership separated from daily management, and with daily management complicated by branch offices and remote factories, transportation became critical. Trains were fine for bulk shipments, but they ran slowly and on fixed routes. That was no help for Standard Oil when it needed to rush drill bits into remote corners of the oil patch. The same principle applied to key personnel. In 1927, the directors of Standard Oil of Indiana logged thirty-seven thousand air miles. Often flying in their own corporate aircraft, oil executives and geologists briefly made Tulsa the world's busiest airport.[4]

Corporate needs explain the skewed demography of early air transport. Airlines catered to executives who needed to be in three places at once. (The alternative, long-distance telephone calls, were still very expensive during the airlines' formative years.) Sixty percent of United's passengers in 1933 were corporate officers; another 20 percent represented their firms in such capacities as sales officials or engineers. Commercial fliers, and the aircrew who served them, formed a distinctive aerial elite that learned to measure distances in hours rather than miles. As the economy expanded and fares came down, the number of frequent business fliers grew. But non-business flying grew even faster, hence the relative democratization after coach fares, fanjets, and deregulation changed aviation from a class to a mass enterprise.[5]

Eddie Rickenbacker once observed that flying had effectively shrunk the United States to the size of Pennsylvania. The shrinkage both integrated national businesses and expanded local ones. Flower growers, farmers, and fishermen could tap markets once closed by time and distance. Before Easter, Horace Brock remembered, every spare bit of space on Pan Am's Bermuda-to-New York flights was filled with lilies. After World War II, veterans snapped up military surplus cargo planes and began shipping perishable products all over the country. Fish iced in Boston arrived in Nashville the next morning, while rail delivery might take as long as six days. The word "landlocked" disappeared from common usage because flying voided it of practical meaning. College presidents—and their coaches—recruited widely, turning regional schools like Michigan or Stanford into national institutions. Also international institutions: eight students studied abroad in 1978 for every one who did so in 1950. Missionaries widened their horizons. Every Monday, Pan Am's William Seawell pointed out in 1978, one hundred Mormons left Salt Lake City in search of converts. They created a new world religion.[6]

Professional sports' major leagues, called "National" and "American," did not earn their names until flying became routine. Road trips were just that, trips made on paved roads or railroads. Play was confined to the Northeast and Upper Midwest. Fast, four-engine planes opened up the western and southern sports markets. New Yorkers bade farewell to the Giants and the Dodgers, air-shy players to their jobs. "There was always something about a plane I wanted to protect myself from," admitted Jackie Jensen, one-time American League MVP for the Boston Red Sox. "I gave up playing baseball so I wouldn't have to fly." John Madden, football coach turned sportscaster, found a better way to cope. He traveled from game to game in a customized motor coach, outfitted with a full kitchen.[7]

For those who could not afford such amenities, the fear of flying proved a serious handicap. By the 1950s, flying was an assumed feature of successful professional careers. By the 1970s, it was an assumed feature of "commuter marriages" among job-separated professional couples. Holdouts who refused to fly had all but renounced, in Adam Goodheart's phrase, "their citizenship in the commonwealth of flight." Others swallowed hard and clutched their armrests. "I guess I'm not an air person," said Andy Warhol, "but I'm on an air schedule, so I have to live an air life."[8]

The air life meant international as well as domestic flying—the premise on which Trippe had built his imperial airline. While the Big Four knit together the home markets, the "chosen instrument" of Pan Am sped abroad American personnel, products, and ideas, in the form of fresh editions of the *Herald Tribune*. "Pan American drove steadily southward," Trippe boasted in 1940:

> First went young American engineers to blaze the trail, to carve airports out of the jungle, to clear sites for weather stations in lonely mountain passes. Their aides were Indians who had no idea of what an automobile might be and who had never heard of a railroad train. Next came builders, to construct hangars, passenger stations, hotels and the 200-odd radio control stations and weather bureaus which today guide the 120 aircraft flying the airways of the Americas. By 1934 the United States was linked with every country and colony in the three Americas.

From there Pan Am turned to the Pacific, building bases on the islands of Oahu, Midway, Wake, Guam, and Luzon to extend America's aerial reach westward from San Francisco to Manila. (And from Manila only 1,150 miles to Shanghai, as Trippe reminded Franklin Roosevelt.) Bermuda and Faial, in the Azores, served as insular stepping stones for Pan Am's transatlantic seaplane service. That service was still in embryonic form in 1940, when the war revolutionized transoceanic flying and gave Americans unprecedented access to every part of the world.[9]

Fear of flying created a dilemma for athletes in an age of global competition. Cassius Clay's trainer, Joe Martin, spent four hours convincing his young charge that no train ran between Louisville and Rome, and, even then, Clay almost skipped the 1960 Olympics. He finally left wearing an army-surplus parachute, which he donned before squatting in the aisle and praying. Here, twelve years later, as Muhammad Ali, he looks less terrified, though still rather stiff and uncertain.

According to one influential school of diplomatic history, the guiding principle of American foreign policy has been "non-colonial imperial expansion." That is, Americans wanted access to overseas markets without the burden, administrative or moral, of running European-style colonies. If that was so—admittedly, a controversial if—then it was ocean-spanning airplanes, rather than Admiral Mahan's vision of secure sea lanes and insular coaling stations, that truly made possible a virtual empire. Journalist Carl Solberg, who covered business and politics as well as aviation, put it this way:

> After 1945, when air power ruled the world, the United States built an empire without annexing any land. Under an aerial nuclear umbrella, the nation established bases in forty-four countries around the globe. These bases Washington managed and largely manned by air. At the same time American businessmen, traveling the same airways, branched overseas and created multinational corporations that enlarged the American presence on every continent. With jets not only businessmen but also millions of tourists found it just as easy to go to Madrid as Miami and vacationed three to six thousand miles from home. And jets ushered in a new diplomacy whereby Presidents, turning up as far away as Peking in a few hours, conducted our foreign relations face-to-face with other chiefs of state.

Overseas privileges extended beyond Air Force One. When Solberg wrote those words, in 1978, the U.S. State Department issued 3.2 million passports a year. Two decades and a deregulation revolution later, the number of new passports had doubled to 6.5 million.[10]

America's air empire was "territorial" in at least one sense, however. Aviation turned Alaska and Hawaii from remote possessions into full-fledged states with close commercial ties to the mainland. Because other means of transport were so cumbersome, flying proved particularly important in Alaska. By 1939, Alaska airline pilots carried, proportionately, twenty-three times as many passengers as their stateside counterparts. Fur trappers, coffee salesmen, prostitutes, politicians—everyone flew. When direct flights from Seattle to Juneau commenced in 1940, the flow of military personnel and workers accelerated. Though some of the influx was seasonal, Alaska's population still tripled between 1940 and 1960. As long-distance land planes replaced island-hopping seaplanes, Alaska gained in military significance. The territory—in 1959, state—went from an irrelevant blob on the margin of the Mercator projection to the center of aviation's polar projection, adjacent to both the Pacific Rim circle routes and the paths of intercontinental bombers and missiles.[11]

Alaska illustrated four of aviation's transformative effects: integration within, expanding connections without, the synergistic development of air and land frontiers, and the reshuffling of economic winners and losers. Just as the railroad had changed the fortunes of cities and regions in the nineteenth century, elevating Chicago over St. Louis and North over South, commercial jet aviation favored the likes of Atlanta and Dallas-Fort Worth over non-hubs like Cleveland and Kansas City. Las Vegas and Reno (originally served by a plane called the *Alimony Special*) could not have blossomed without air travel. Southern California and the Puget Sound area prospered in the 1950s and 1960s, fattening off aerospace contracts and growing overseas orders. Boeing led the way, assembling 747s in a plant so vast that clouds formed in its ten-storey sky.[12]

Aviation's long postwar boom turned American airlines and airports into major employers. By 1998, the airlines had 621,000 people on their payrolls, each averaging $64,000 in compensation—a figure skewed by pilots' salaries. O'Hare Airport alone employed 50,000 people. Its true impact was closer to 160,000 jobs, counting all the service workers whose livelihoods depended on its facilities.[13]

Aviation's benefits extended beyond wages paid, tickets bought, and airplanes sold. By 2000, civil aviation generated—this counts direct, indirect, and induced effects, everything from increased tourism to productivity gains from just-in-time shipping—an estimated $904 billion and 11.2 million jobs for the American economy. Worldwide, 28 million people owed their livelihoods to air transport. More than a few of them were instructors of English, the *lingua franca* of aviation and official language of international air traffic control.[14]

Externalities

These impact data come mainly from industry sources, and so reflect a one-sided accounting. The rise of civil aviation also produced its share of externalities, unanticipated benefits and costs borne by others than those who occasioned them. (Such as displaced instructors of French.) The most obvious losers were those who operated long-distance passenger trains. At first, the airlines were content to target Pullman customers. As air fares came down, they went after rail coach service, simultaneously being battered by cars and highways. (One advantage of driving, which neither trains nor planes could match, was the freedom from rental cars and taxis.) Wartime granted a reprieve to long-distance rail service. Pullman revenue miles jumped between 1941 and 1944. Then inexorable decline set in. Passenger trains had become "evolutionary misfits," Pan Am's Senior Vice President Najeeb Halaby remarked in 1966, so many brontosauruses in "a world of jackrabbits and swallows."[15]

The transatlantic liners, even fast ships like the *France* and the *United States,* fell into the same dinosaurian category. Postprandial naps in deck chairs might appeal to the rich and retired. Flying to stretch limited time made more sense for everyone else. The industry survived, in barely recognizable form, as a cruise service, with smaller, air-conditioned ships running on alcohol and suntan lotion, shuttling among exotic ports. In September 1967, the *Queen Mary* and the *Queen Elizabeth* passed each other in the North Atlantic for the last time. The former was destined for the Sunday brunch crowd in Long Beach, the latter for the Hong Kong scrap heap.[16]

Some externalities were more subtle. Aerial smuggling began as a sideline—barnstormers selling the odd case of Mexican scotch to Texas roughnecks—and evolved into a lucrative business. In a way the 1919 Volstead Act, rather than the 1925 Kelly Bill, provided the first federal subsidy to commercial aviation. Bootleggers, remembered aircraft designer Benny Howard, were the only ones willing to invest real money in planes. At a time when joyriding prices were declining, liquor runs kept pilots in the air. Pan Am's Ed Musick was among the many early airline pilots who honed their flying skills as rum runners. Landing the liquor at Miami's causeway beach, he and a waiting accomplice would load the cases onto a truck. When the truck had vanished and the Coast Guardsmen arrived, Musick would offer them a few bottles and ask if they would "lend a hand in pushing the seaplane into the water."[17]

Gypsy pilots tried other angles, smuggling watches and Chinese immigrants. In the 1940s, Mexican-based traffickers began flying significant amounts of narcotics across the border. As the range and reliability of general aviation aircraft improved, smuggling routes lengthened. Colombian marijuana arrived by air in the 1960s and 1970s, followed by a deluge of Andean cocaine in the late 1970s and 1980s. Traffickers bought, rented, or simply stole private planes. By the mid-1980s, half of airplane thefts were drug- related. Drug pilots got fifty thousand dollars for their trouble and more for bribe money. Nobody worried about FAA rules. "If you've got enough money to pay the landing fee in South America you don't get shot," explained one drug runner. "If you don't pay the landing fee, you get shot."[18]

Heroin traffickers took advantage of the increase in North Atlantic traffic ushered in by the jets. When a "panic" hit New York City in 1966, driving street prices from five dollars to eight dollars for a small amount of adulterated heroin, informants told narcotics agents that the real culprit was the airline strike. Smugglers' tactics varied. They paid off ground crews to steer their baggage away from customs or to secrete drugs between bulkhead walls. They lowered plastic-wrapped packages into toilet tanks, tethering them with a rope attached behind the stainless steel bowl. They put narcotics in condoms and forced them down the numbed throats of hapless couriers, who prayed the latex held. Kennedy International Airport became the major conduit for airborne heroin, Miami International Airport for cocaine. By 1985, the Drug Enforcement Administration estimated, scheduled passenger and cargo flights accounted for 40 percent of the heroin and 25 percent of the cocaine entering the United States.[19]

Airplanes broadcast poisons in another way, through crop dusting. Their first target was the boll weevil. Before airplanes, cotton planters fought the pest with mule-drawn dusting machines. Field hands operated them at night, when the wind had died down and the calcium arsenate stuck best to the dewy foliage. Low-flying aircraft, dispensing positively charged dust that clung to the plants, covered the same acreage in a fraction of the time.

Crop dusting caught on in the mid-1920s and spread quickly. Pilots worked North American fields during the summer, then shipped their planes to South America for the winter growing season. "We offered it for anything that had bugs on it, or fungus, not just cotton but lettuce and tomatoes and the like," remembered Harold Harris, an army flier who went into the business. Over the next two decades researchers developed new insecticides, including DDT, a cheap means of killing mosquitoes and lice. Allied armies and planes carried DDT around the world, even spraying it by accident on Iwo Jima's Japanese garrison. The few surviving defenders said that, at first, they thought the cloud was poison gas.[20]

It was an understandable mistake. One of the striking things about the 1940s was the progress American scientists and engineers made in devising aerial means to kill their human *and* insect enemies, creating a species of total environmental warfare. A boon to malarial and typhus-afflicted populations and commercial farmers, DDT and other insecticides nevertheless fouled water supplies, entered the food chain, accumulated in fatty tissues, killed birds and fish, sickened livestock, and poisoned humans, including the crop dusters themselves, who became so intoxicated by the fumes they lost control of their planes. Another form of aerial poisoning, the dumping of herbicides to deny insurgents cover and food, defoliated 10 percent of the South Vietnamese countryside between 1961 and 1971. Three decades later the residual dioxin exacted a toll of cancer and birth defects. Peasants clearing land met more sudden ends in the form of mines and unexploded five-hundred-pound bombs.[21]

The Environment

The story of aerial spraying limns a larger truth: aviation's deepest consequences were environmental. A 747 dumped as much carbon dioxide into the atmosphere in the course of one transatlantic round trip as eighty gas-guzzling vehicles managed in an entire year. Condensation trails, the ubiquitous, cirrus-like streaks of water vapor frozen around engine exhaust particles, reflected sunlight during the day and prevented heat from escaping at night. After the September 11 attacks, when the North American skies were free of commercial jet contrails for three days, the difference between the daily high and low temperatures increased by two to five degrees Fahrenheit.[22]

Airplanes reshuffled land activities in a hundred ways. Where geodetic survey flights located oil fields, derricks sprouted. Where airborne prospectors noticed ore outcrops, mining companies staked claims. Where flying archeologists spotted ruins, shovels turned soil. Where passengers tossed lit cigarettes—a real worry before pressurization—forests burned. Where planes set down on runways, hitchhiking animals departed. Brown tree snakes, the classic invader species, secreted themselves in cargo holds and wheel wells. Iguanas, monkeys, and parrots, as many as two thousand to a planeload, arrived courtesy of smugglers. By 1995, animal trafficking ranked only behind drugs as an illegal global business. Floridians watched alligators battle escaped Burmese pythons. Seven-foot monitor lizards and other exotic imports multiplied in the Everglades, an ecosystem fast coming to resemble an airborne *Jurassic Park*.[23]

Municipal airports—along with the SST and aerial spraying, the environmentalists' main targets—had a double impact on land use. Consuming thousands of acres for their own facilities, they simultaneously pulled cities toward them, turning access roads, motels, conference centers, and perpetually idling shuttle buses into another smoggy urban node. Diesel fumes, not aviation kerosene, became the defining airport smell. It is interesting that tall buildings, the century's other great skyward-reaching technology, initially had the opposite effect. They drew people toward the central business district, at least until cities like Houston and Los Angeles became polynuclear, with multiple building clusters rising all over town.

Airports added to noise pollution, especially after overnight delivery services proliferated in the 1970s and 1980s. Cargo planes flew at night, while most airliners flew during the day, permitting round-the-clock use of facilities. The price of this efficiency was a "Fedexternality" for anyone in the flight path trying to sleep. Because airports were development magnets, the problem got worse over time. No one complained when Los Angeles International Airport rose in carnation fields outside town. When it was surrounded by houses, airport managers could not make a move without running the risk of noise or other environmental litigation.[24]

No place was unaffected by aviation's progress. Just as the land frontier had created opportunities for hunters—fur trappers, bounty collectors, and day-trippers who potted buffalo from train cars—planes bore men with rifles into ever remoter regions. Hunters paid thirty-three dollars to fly into Idaho's fabled Chamberlain Basin, and four cents a pound for the meat they shipped out. Polar bear hunters flocked to Kotzebue, Alaska, an Inuit village equipped with a small hotel. From there they ranged over the ice packs in light planes. When the pilots spotted a bear they landed the plane, allowing the hunters to finish stalking their quarry on foot.[25]

Not everyone was so sporting. Some hunters (and bored airmail pilots) simply shot animals from the air. Coyotes were a favorite target. Airborne shooters learned to lead them from behind, taking into account the onrushing speed

Airplanes, like railroads, cars, snowmobiles, and two-way radios, increased pressure on game species in remote regions. Outfitters and bush pilots organized expeditions, advertising their services—and guaranteeing kills—in hunting magazines. Here, the holy grail of such quests, a record "Brownie," was taken at Cold Bay on the Alaska Peninsula, in May 1948.

of the plane. Another trick was to buzz the prey, driving the exhausted animals toward hunters waiting on the ground. Others used planes to overtake birds on the wing. By 1929, federal prosecutors had brought thirty-two cases against illegal aerial hunting of migratory waterfowl. Though laws eventually forbade most forms of aerial hunting, no one could prevent accidental collisions. Planes hit condors as high up as seventeen thousand feet. One bald eagle attacked a plane, shearing off its own wing in the process.[26]

At sea, radio-equipped spotters directed coastal fishing fleets toward large shoals of fish, increasing their catch up to thirty fold. Whalers and seal hunters employed ship-launched aircraft for the same end. Yet flying did not always increase pressure on animal populations. Wildlife managers used planes to spot poachers, stock remote lakes, feed starving herds, and conduct censuses. Tanker gypsies battled blazes that threatened animal habitats. The environmental externalities cut two ways—or perhaps three ways, for those who thought fire suppression a long-term mistake.[27]

The lesson of social and environmental history is that aviation's consequences have been more complex and crosscutting than facile summaries of so many billions of dollars or millions of jobs would suggest. Consider infectious disease. Aircraft have been spraying mosquitoes since the mid-1920s, a public health intervention that cumulatively saved millions of lives. Yet they also triggered epidemics by transporting infected mosquitoes and passengers who deplaned before developing symptoms. The incubation periods for airborne viral diseases—several days for some flu strains, up to ten days for SARS, two weeks for measles—allowed ample time for undetected international passage. The longer a virus's incubation period, the greater its potential impact, because more people could be infected before health officials realized what they had on their hands. The "Patient Zero" of the North American AIDS epidemic, a promiscuous Air Canada steward named Gaetan Dugas, broadcast the HIV virus as he jetted around San Francisco, Los Angeles, Vancouver, Toronto, and New York City. (One French researcher called AIDS "the charter disease" because so many of the early European cases contracted the disease after booking cheap transatlantic flights. They had visited the same bathhouses frequented by Dugas and his partners.) Jet-based "sex tourism" played a comparable role in spreading venereal diseases among heterosexual travelers. By 1989, Thailand had three thousand HIV-positive prostitutes. Most were still asymptomatic, and still servicing foreign men. In the age of fast planes, cheap fares, mass tourism, and long-distance migration, no nation was safe from novel infections. Nor, in an age of terrorism and clandestine biological weapons labs, could it be supposed that the prospect of such exposure was entirely accidental.[28]

Cars, Planes, and Oil

When historians describe the consequences of transportation technology in modern America, they usually start with cars. But if motor vehicles were so important—and they were—is it a mistake to emphasize the impact of aerospace development? After all, millions of cars and trucks were moving people and goods, reshaping the environment, and expanding lifestyles (not to mention waistlines) when airplanes still numbered in the thousands. Was not America's real twentieth-century frontier the "crabgrass frontier" of suburbs, highways, and commuters?[29]

Any fair reply would concede the car's preeminent place before World War II. America drove before it flew. Aviation's fast wartime buildup could not have happened without the automobile industry, whose conversion made possible the mass production of engines and airplanes. (That is why 1942 cars are so rare—the February changeover cut short the model year.) The planes pouring out of the factories all depended, as Henry Ford said, on piston powerplants that had evolved from automobile engines.

One thing, however, cars could not do. They could not guarantee the supply of oil upon which they and the nation's postwar prosperity depended. Two distant nations, Saudi Arabia and Kuwait, together held more than a third of the world's proven oil reserves. That oil lay so close to the surface, and so close to the ocean, that it could be produced for almost nothing. It was, in the words of a 1945 State Department report, "a stupendous source of strategic power, and one of the greatest material prizes in world history." Maintaining access to that prize required the United States to project its power halfway around the world. At the outset of the cold war, in 1947, the Truman administration sent carriers to the Eastern Mediterranean and stationed aircraft in Libya, Turkey, and Saudi Arabia. Their mission was to check Soviet ambitions in the region and watch over the tankers sailing from the Persian Gulf.

At first most of the tankers (including those of a rising Greek shipowner named Aristotle Onassis) were bound for European ports. Middle Eastern oil revitalized the western European economies, strengthened the NATO alliance, and enriched American corporations. Carl Solberg judged that between 1950 and 1965, U.S. oil companies siphoned more wealth from the Middle East "than the British took out of their empire in the entire nineteenth century." It may not have been colonialism, he observed, but it was a mighty near thing. American companies got rich selling other people's oil under Washington's strategic umbrella; Washington got economic and political stability in the industrial nations vital to its cold war alliance system; the allies got U.S. forward bases that protected the whole interlocking system.[30]

As time passed, Washington became more concerned with its own oil imports than those of Europe and Japan. Part of the problem was the car itself. Detroit never came up with the equivalent of a jet. Compared to a Ford Model T, an American sedan of the 1950s or 1960s got the same, often less, gas mileage. That was fine as long as there was plenty of oil. But rising demand and stagnating domestic production increased reliance on imports. By 1973, Americans imported more than a third of their oil. By the century's end, they imported more than half, their appetite undiminished by disruptive oil price spikes in 1973, 1979, 1990, and 1999.

All of this made Middle Eastern reserves even more critical to the United States, which used its air assets to protect the oil supply and curry diplomatic favor. The Ford administration sold Sidewinder missiles to Saudi Arabia, the Carter administration F-15 fighters, the Reagan administration AWACS radar planes. If high-tech placation failed, there were other means. During the 1973–74 embargo crisis, Nixon and his advisers seriously considered sending airborne troops to seize oil fields in Saudi Arabia, Kuwait, and Abu Dhabi. The crucial test, however, came in 1990, when Saddam Hussein occupied Kuwait. American planes rushed troops to neighboring Saudi Arabia, guarded the Saudi oil fields from attack, and then went to work on the Iraqi army. Operations Desert Storm and Shield were about protecting oil by projecting power. "If Kuwait grew carrots, we wouldn't give a damn," was how one former defense official summed up the matter.[31]

Put another way, the automobility Americans enjoyed in the late twentieth century depended on their airmobility. No C-130s and aircraft carriers, no cheap gas and three-car families. That is why it is hard to compare the relative effects of cars and planes. They were linked through the supply of oil, and oil was what made America go. The jet hood ornaments and tail fins that decorated the classic gas guzzlers inadvertently symbolized the relationship, part of the larger national pattern of interdependent mechanized expansion through multiple domains of space and nocturnal time.

The relentless quest for Middle Eastern oil came at a political price, paid in the coin of mounting Arab suspicion and resentment. Editorialists vituperated Americans as pork-eating channel surfers greedy to consume Muslim resources. In 1998, a wealthy Saudi exile, angered by American bases in the land of Mecca and Medina, signed a *fatwa,* or judgment, calling for the killing of "Americans and their allies, civilians and military, . . . in any country in which it is possible."[32] Unlike the blowhards in the press, however, Osama bin Mohammad bin Laden had the will and the means to do something about it.

Strange what a difference it makes who rides the flames.

—JOHN CIARDI, *SAIPAN*

CHAPTER 12

A Storm of Planes

If flying transformed the way Americans lived and worked in the second half of the twentieth century, it brought an even more dramatic change to the way they fought. Though the nation's military planners had to absorb hard lessons along the way, aerospace advances enabled them to field history's most integrated and sophisticated fighting force. Comparing four conflicts—the most intense phase of the Vietnam War (1965–72), the Gulf War (1990–91), the Afghanistan campaign (2001–2002), and the Iraq War (2003)—shows how far and how fast their fortunes changed. It also reveals a paradox. Even as the Pentagon achieved unprecedented power in the air, the nation's commercial aviation industry, whose fate had long been intertwined with the military, found itself coping with unprecedented vulnerability.

Vietnam

From the standpoint of sheer destructive power, the United States possessed a formidable air weapon when Lyndon Johnson commenced his 1965 Vietnam buildup. B-52 attacks on jungle sanctuaries were terrifying, the noise and shock waves from the cascading explosions knocking out guerrillas as far as a kilometer away. Fighter-bombers struck at more specific targets. Tobias Wolff, a Special Forces lieutenant, was laying down artillery fire on

My Tho, a Delta town seized by the Viet Cong during the 1968 Tet offensive, when the jets showed up:

> Their run into My Tho took them right over our compound, sometimes low enough that we could see the rivets on their skin. Such American machines, so boss-looking, so technical, so loud. *Phantoms.* When they slowed overhead to lock into formation the roar of their engines made speech impossible. Down here I was in a deranged and malignant land, but when I raised my eyes to those planes I could see home. They dove screaming on the town, then pulled out and banked around and did it again. Their bombs sent tremors pulsing up through our legs. When they used up all their bombs they flew off to get more. Flames gleamed on the underside of the pall of smoke that overhung My Tho, and the smell of putrefaction soured the breeze, and still we served the guns, dropping rings of ruination around every frightened man with a radio transmitter.

All this firepower failed to turn the tide of the war. Perhaps nothing could have, given the absence of a coherent strategy to defeat a determined nationalist enemy. Still, air strikes proved a clumsy weapon, even when directed by forward air controllers in low-flying Cessna observation planes. Repeated attacks failed to stop the flow of men and *matériel* along the Ho Chi Minh Trail. By one count it took three hundred bombs to kill a single infiltrator. In populated areas bombs were as apt to kill civilians as they were combatants. Control and pacification of the people was, or should have been, the primary objective in a guerrilla war. Collateral casualties simplified the task of Viet Cong recruiters. "This is a political war and it calls for discrimination in killing," the adviser John Paul Vann warned. "The best weapon for killing would be a knife, but I'm afraid we can't do it that way. The worst is an airplane. The next worst is artillery. Barring a knife, the best is a rifle—you know who you're killing."[1]

The one theater in which airplanes might have been used to decisive effect was North Vietnam. Critics such as Benjamin Lambeth have charged that piecemeal application of U.S. air power during the "Rolling Thunder" campaign (1965–68) frittered away a powerful asset, that a decisive early attack could have disrupted the North's ability to support the war in the South. The motive for restraint was plain. Johnson and Defense Secretary Robert McNamara wanted to avoid a larger conflict with the Soviet Union or China, allies of North Vietnam. The Korean War had taught them that too much provocation could lead to a wider war, the Cuban Missile Crisis that restraint could achieve the desired diplomatic result. So they hand-picked the targets at their Tuesday lunch meetings and kept the Joint Chiefs of Staff on a short leash.

The North Vietnamese thus had time to build up their air defenses. They acquired so many Soviet surface-to-air missiles (SAMs), they sometimes fired them in salvoes. Frightened pilots got on their radios and called out the incoming missiles' locations. But if the pilots dived to avoid the SAMs, they flew straight into deadly flak. Navy pilot John McCain thought it was like running a "nearly impossible obstacle course of antiaircraft fire and flying telephone poles." The "Hanoi Hilton" began filling up with prisoners, McCain among them. Close to a thousand planes had been lost by the time Johnson called a halt to the bombing in 1968.[2]

Johnson's successor, Richard Nixon, decided to employ air power more ruthlessly. "The North Vietnamese bombing is a tragedy," he told his chief of staff, Bob Haldeman, "but it's even more immoral to send Americans abroad and not back them up with air power." The president, Haldeman noted in his diary, "got quite cranked up on this whole subject, and made the point that he will not go out of Vietnam whimpering." Instead, he went out with a bang. "Whatever happens to South Vietnam, we are going to *cream* North Vietnam," Nixon told his advisers on May 4, 1972. "For once, we've got to use the maximum power of this country . . . to win the war."[3]

The Linebacker I and II bombing operations (May-October and December 1972) aimed to destroy North Vietnam's logistical and air-defense capabilities and to force its leaders to come to terms at the stalled Paris peace talks. The climactic phase, commencing on December 18, pitted the largest fleet of bombers assembled since World War II against the world's densest array of antiaircraft artillery and missiles. SAM hits turned B-52s into giant flares, illuminating the Hanoi night sky with tens of thousands of gallons of burning fuel. An anxious North Vietnamese officer told Air Force Col. "Bud" Day, a long-time POW, that the bombing was over, that they had shot down all the B-52s. "Bullshit," Day said, laughing in his face. The B-52s were back the next night and for the next nine nights after that. Fighter-bombers kept up the assault during the daylight hours.[4]

What made the 1972 Linebacker raids effective, apart from their intensity and systematic targeting, was that American planes were beginning to make extensive use of laser-guided bombs. Small attack formations knocked out bridges and other targets that had withstood hundreds of Rolling Thunder sorties. Eighty percent of the laser-guided bombs scored direct hits. Accuracy reduced collateral casualties. For every ten tons of bombs dropped during the Linebacker II raids, on average less than one North Vietnamese civilian died.

(The same amount of explosives had killed more than four hundred civilians at Guernica in 1937, and five hundred civilians in Tokyo in March 1945.) Though the settlement ultimately failed to preserve South Vietnam's independence—war weariness and the Watergate scandal ruled out further U.S. military involvement after 1973—the Linebacker raids showed what sophisticated aircraft equipped with precision munitions could do. Rather like the *Luftwaffe's* deployment of jet fighters, it was a case of the right weapon emerging too late in a long, mismanaged war.[5]

Vietnam showed something else: the potential of the UAV. Despite some missions wasted scattering leaflets telling Communists to abandon their "foolish ways," pilotless vehicles completed 3,435 reconnaissance sorties between 1964 and 1975. Many of these were deep into North Vietnam. Prisoners in the Hanoi Hilton, some downed during their own "recce" missions, heard the drones overhead and took heart. The Pentagon took note. When the generals headed up to Capitol Hill, they carried briefing photos taken by pilotless planes.[6]

The Middle East and Central Asia

Over the next two decades the sophistication of the planes and the precision of the munitions kept improving. U.S.-Soviet rivalry spawned new weapons like radar-evading F-117 attack fighters and laser-guided Hellfire missiles. Saddam Hussein's 1990 invasion of Kuwait provided the opportunity for a combat demonstration. Desert Storm began with a precision strike, when Apache helicopters fired Hellfire missiles at Iraqi early warning radars. Coalition commanders quickly suppressed Iraq's air defenses with stealth aircraft attacks. That done, they went to work on transportation, communication, and electrical facilities. In World War II, bomber formations had to drop hundreds of bombs to ensure the destruction of a single target. In the Gulf War, one bomb from one plane often sufficed for either stationary or moving targets. An F-111, out of missiles, even managed to bomb an Iraqi helicopter in flight. The dream of "precision engagement from virtual sanctuary" had been achieved. B-52s still rained gravity bombs over broad areas, stunning Iraqi troops who neither heard nor saw their approach. But smart bombs and cruise missiles did three-quarters of the militarily significant damage. And UAV cameras guided "dumb" weapons, allowing naval gunfire to quickly range in.[7]

Wars produce indelible visual images. Nick Ut's photograph of Kim Phuc, the napalm-splashed girl running naked and terrified down the refugee-filled road, defined the misapplication of air power in the Vietnam War. The equivalent image for the Gulf War, video footage of a smart bomb zooming into its target, could not have been more different. More dramatic still was the war's opening. CNN's Peter Arnett disappeared in mid-sentence, cut off when an F-117 flattened the Baghdad telecommunications building with a laser-guided bomb. As the screen went blank, cheers rang out in the Pentagon.[8]

Thirty-eight days of air attacks sufficed to destroy the Iraqi army's command centers, cut its supply lines, and demoralize its troops. Psy-ops choppers blared Led Zeppelin tapes at bomb-frazzled conscripts. One group of Iraqis surrendered to a UAV. Coalition forces encountered little effective resistance when they launched their ground attacks, if "ground" describes an offensive that relied so heavily on satellites for communications, weather, navigation, and targeting information. "Pluggers" (portable lightweight GPS receivers) made the nearly completed Navstar global positioning system available for troops sweeping across the desert and for aircrews operating in close support. The Outer Space Treaty had prohibited weapons in space, but the Gulf War proved that everything else—the means of controlling, coordinating, and directing them—worked from orbit. Just as airplanes integrated the American economy, satellites integrated its military, permitting land, sea, and air forces to share unprecedented amounts of information in real time. It was, said Air Force Chief of Staff Merrill McPeak, history's "first space war."[9]

Though not its last. The most striking aspect of the campaign to overthrow the Taliban and destroy al-Qaeda bases was the United States' occupation of the sky above Afghanistan, with assets deployed at every altitude. Geostationary satellites, bombers, tankers, electronic warfare planes, camera- and missile-equipped drones, gunships, and helicopters lingered above the battlefield, in constant communication with troops trained to direct precision air strikes. Night-vision equipment, which magnified infrared and near-infrared light, let them operate around the clock. In the Gulf War, space and air assets had located and softened up the enemy before the big ground attack. In Afghanistan, ground forces, including air controllers riding horses, used pluggers and laser range finders to pinpoint the enemy for destruction from above. B-52s that had once carpet-bombed Vietnamese and Cambodian jungles delivered individual, satellite-guided bombs. "When they gave us the co-ordinates, we'd kill whatever they told us to," said "Wall Street," a B-52 pilot who flew nineteen missions over Afghanistan. His plane was one of fewer than two dozen bombers used in the winter 2001–2002 campaign. "You don't need so many bombers," explained Air Force Secretary James G. Roche, "because they carry so many bombs and each one is so accurate."[10]

The spring 2003 campaigns in northern and western Iraq resembled those in Afghanistan: special forces on the ground, UAV and radar surveillance planes in the air, attack aircraft on call 24-7, everybody linked through satellites to central command. Coalition forces tracked targets of opportunity, destroying them with precision weapons. Iraqi commanders faced a Hobson's choice. To maneuver was to be caught in the open, to stay put was to endure relentless attack. Iraqi soldiers defended themselves by running *out* of their bunkers, lying face down, and covering their heads as the jets roared in. One terrified conscript ran through the drill a dozen times a day. All he could think of was "death, nothing else." He wound up in a hospital with a piece of shrapnel in his head.[11]

In southern Iraq, aircraft and helicopters ranged ahead of mechanized columns, devastating Iraq's armored divisions. No Iraqi tank destroyed an American tank. Few had the chance to engage in battle. Iraq's planes never left the ground. The Coalition's never left the skies. (They had, in fact, been there months before the war began, destroying military communications networks under the guise of reprisals for Iraqi violations of the southern "no-flight" zone.) In the Gulf War, only a fifth of the Coalition planes could carry precision-guided munitions. Twelve years later they all could, often hitting targets through darkness, smoke, cloud cover, and sandstorms. At one point the airspace over Baghdad became so crowded that traffic controllers stacked up planes northeast of the city, where they waited their turns to attack. The city's lights stayed on throughout the bombardment, a testament to both the precision of the attack and the irrelevance of blackout. The bombs and cruise missiles kept coming. "We're just grinding it out," one general said of the air campaign.[12]

"Grinding it out" had once described infantry clashes. Iraq further blurred the distinctions between air and ground operations. Even artillery batteries used radar to fix sources of enemy fire. All branches of the military had quick access to tactical air power, if "tactical" meant anything when fighters, kept aloft by the world's largest aerial tanker fleet, carried weapons that could destroy a command center. Or centers. In the Gulf War, as one air force general put it, "the issue was always how many sorties it took to destroy a given target. In this war the issue is how many targets can be destroyed in a given sortie." A single bomber could, theoretically, "kill" up to twenty-four targets. The actual number of hits under battlefield conditions remains classified, and some of the hits, owing to faulty intelligence, destroyed the wrong buildings and their civilian occupants. But the overall precision was enough to make air power the foundation of a flexible "regime change" campaign designed to overthrow Saddam Hussein while minimizing damage to Iraq's infrastructure.[13]

Before the war—or more precisely, before two F-117s tried to decapitate his regime—Saddam Hussein had boasted that Iraq would retaliate "wherever there is sky, land or water." In fact, the Coalition controlled all three domains, not to say the night and the unseen, virtual dimension of electronic simulation. Aircrews pre-flew missions using Topscene, a computerized simulation of attack runs. Earlier, pilots who survived six missions over North Vietnam were less likely to be shot down because they had gained familiarity with the combat environment. Now, pilots could fly their first six missions over Iraq in their khakis, sitting before a console, absorbed in hyperrealistic detail. The navy equipped all its carriers with Topscene simulators and interchangeable hard drives. Each drive contained a 3-D model of one of the world's hot spots. Pop out Afghanistan, pop in Iraq.[14]

The events of 1991–2003 unleashed a flood of commentary by defense experts and military historians. The gist of it was that electronically integrated space-air-land-sea operations had given the United States a towering, mobile superfortress from which stealthy, opportunistic, and coordinated attacks could rain down on any opponent. "Netwar" (to pick the briefest of many suggested names) constituted the biggest revolution in military affairs since the atomic bomb. "This combination of U.S. air and ground power is truly unstoppable," said one analyst. "This is it—the Roman legions, the German panzers. Truly unstoppable." Less sanguine observers wondered whether the United States was actually behaving like Rome, tempted to imperial overreach by the formidable power at its disposal.[15]

Netwar had its skeptics. The 1991–2003 operations depleated already-isolated and ineptly led regimes fighting with hardware two decades out of date. "If our troops had good air cover and good technology," said one embittered Iraqi major, "I don't think the Americans would have dared to cross the border and fight us." Given the national distaste for heavy casualties in elective wars, he was probably right. America's "unstoppable" weapons and tactics remained unproven against a sophisticated foe. They were expensive, cruise missiles sometimes costing more than the targets they obliterated. They could not prevent the reprisals and bombings that roiled postwar Iraq, or the ambushes of occupying troops, or the controversy over the wisdom of the war itself. Like all military revolutions, Netwar provoked countermeasures. By 2000, the Chinese had reportedly ground-tested "parasitic" satellites that could latch onto larger satellites and, when activated, destroy them. Nuclear weapons offered another check. If threatened regimes could acquire a modest *force de frappe,* the United States would not risk an attack. The strategic logic of Netwar favored nuclear proliferation.[16]

Admitting all this, and admitting the danger of making historical judgments about recent events, two things still stand out. First, the same process that transformed commercial aviation, aeronautical advances combined with improved data flow, trannsformed air warfare by making it easier to get the right ordnance on the right target. But John Paul Vann's remark about Vietnam, that airplanes were the worst weapon because they were the least precise, no longer applied in many contexts. Planes could "plink" berm-protected tanks or zero in on individual bunkers. Once you "put a cursor over a target," said Air Force Chief of Staff John P. Jumper, "you can decide what you're going to do with it. You can kill it, you can save it as in a humanitarian operation, you can study it further."

Enjoying this sort of flexibility required a growing constellation of satellites to connect and coordinate real-time operations. When the 2003 Iraq War commenced, the U.S. military controlled roughly 100 of the world's 550 working satellites, not counting the 28 GPS satellites that directed its weapons and planes, most of which no longer carried human navigators. The second obvious lesson of 1991–2003 was that the nation's air forces had evolved into air and space forces, with emerging manned and unmanned camps comparable to those within NASA. Some dared speak of "space and air forces," reversing the priority.[17]

This suggests another way to think of the nation's post-Apollo space efforts. Despite the shuttle fiasco, the space frontier was a godsend to the Pentagon, which had the resources to redesign its weapons systems around data streams relayed from earth orbit. By 2003, wrote air force pilot-turned-historian Phillip Meilinger, the most basic fact about national security—one might say about the international system itself—was that the United States had become "the world's first and only air and space nation."[18]

Vulnerabilities

Americans, Meilinger thought, had come to take dominance of the sky for granted. They should not have. Even as the smoke cleared over Baghdad, their aerospace industry was suffering through a prolonged crisis. Airlines and their suppliers had been especially hard hit. For most of the twentieth century, their fortunes had moved in tandem with military aviation. Military research had sped the development of commercial aircraft, and commercial aircraft had sped military personnel and cargoes all over the world. Then, at century's end, their paths diverged. Military aviation entered an electronic golden age of precision and stealth, the airlines a turbulent time of discontent and instability. For all their expansion, they remained vulnerable, a point driven home by the recession and terror attacks that devastated the industry in 2001.

Even before September 11, however, the airlines were in trouble. The major carriers, Southwest excepted, had never resolved the problem of heavy fixed costs and thin profit margins. The history of airliner design was a history of pricey upgrades, in which each new generation of planes wound up costing four times more than the one it replaced. High labor costs added to the burden of equipment debt service. Wages and benefits ran 40 percent or more of total expenses. Unions had tremendous leverage. Ronald Reagan himself had offered the Professional Air Traffic Controllers an 11 percent raise before they struck, prompting en masse dismissals. (Usually interpreted as breaking a recalcitrant union, Reagan also meant to signal the Soviets that he would at all costs maintain access to controlled airspace.) The threat of strikes, slowdowns, and sickouts against the big commercial carriers yielded better cumulative results. By 2000, a United 747 captain earned more than most college presidents.[19]

High wages had not mattered much when the CAB regulated fares and limited competition. They mattered a lot after deregulation, because discount upstarts could siphon off business. Established carriers responded with computerized fare competition, cost-cutting, and the hub system. If the old airline maxim had been to "put bums on seats," the new one was keep them on *your* seats, using hubs to maximize load factors and minimize interline transfers. An airline like Continental would charge passengers low fares for any one of its spoke destinations, provided they were willing to fly through its Newark hub. "For years, you're sitting around Sleepy Hollow [Newark] eating your brown bag lunches," an air traffic controller remembered, "then one day you look up and, Jesus, you've got a hundred airplanes inbound and every one of them is low on fuel."[20]

Therein lay the rub. Designed to enhance the productivity of individual airlines, the hub system could not handle the rising volume. With 90 percent of passenger traffic connected through the nation's sixty busiest airports, with safety constraints on the number of takeoffs and landings, and with hubs scheduled as tightly as possible under optimistic weather assumptions, the industry had created a proving ground for chaos theory. When something happened at one of the busier airports—rain, equipment failure, or a heavy travel day—delays rippled through the system. Why clear a flight for takeoff if the destination airport already had more incoming planes than it could handle? "Flow control" meant that passengers sat in Orlando because of sleet in Atlanta. Fuller planes meant trouble accommodating cancellations and missed connections. The more saturated the system became, the less capacity it had to absorb spillover passengers.

Frustrations mounted. One day Eastern Captain Ray Davidson picked up his mic and told his passengers, "I'm fed up with it. I'm sick and tired of the delays, tired of the waiting. I'm hanging it up. You can have it. This flight will be my last." He taxied out of the Atlanta takeoff line, returned to the terminal, and walked away from his job. Equivalent forms of acting out, dubbed "air rage," spread among passengers. Everything had speeded up: faster food, wider bandwidth, one-touch dialing. Air travel had become the great, un-American exception. Accustomed to ample space, wide seats, and traveling when they pleased, coach passengers squeezed three abreast into stuffy, germy cabins. "The fat guy next to me had on a tank top, need I say more?" wrote one disgruntled customer. "Next time, Amtrak," wrote another.[21]

Others went by car. NASA research showed that, by the late 1990s, travelers could make trips of less than five hundred miles as quickly by auto as by plane. In 1999, a year of record delays and widely publicized snafus, including one in which Northwestern passengers endured more than eight hours trapped on a snowy Detroit runway, the situation took on the attributes of a crisis. Congress held hearings. Walter Brown's ghost hovered over the proceedings. Talk of reregulation, or at least of a "passenger bill of rights," was in the air.

The industry preferred the time-honored solution of using public money for air traffic control upgrades and more runways. But airport expansion and construction had run into growing local and environmental opposition. Though annual passenger volume rose more than 200 million between 1991 and 2000, just one new airport, Denver International, opened during the decade. Some critics, who thought bigger airports the problem rather than the solution, foresaw a less-is-more alternative. A new generation of "air taxis," five- and six-passenger planes with ultraefficient jet engines, simplified instrumentation, and GPS navigation systems, could shuttle passengers directly to their destinations, bypassing the crowded hubs. The air transport system had become like a giant marshaling yard in which, perversely, a few big trains used only a few tracks. More and smaller planes could take full advantage of the nation's 18,000 landing facilities, acting as a sort of "Airborne Internet" to get passengers to their destinations more quickly.[22]

The Small Aircraft Transportation System (SATS) had just emerged as a widely discussed alternative when the terror attacks of September 11, 2001, resolved the crowding crisis. Just as settlers retreated in the face of Indian uprisings (Lindbergh's own father and grandfather among them), anxious passengers quit their flights. "My flying fears and terrorism . . . it's too much," admitted one woman. "There's not a pill big enough that could make me handle both." Six weeks after the attack the airlines were carrying only seven passengers for every ten they had carried before. That at least broke the logjam: on-time arrivals improved as airlines canceled flights and parked idle airliners in the Mojave Desert. But that was of little consolation for nervous passengers who had to deal with serpentine lines at security checkpoints. Young men traveling light drew particular scrutiny. No one noticed the irony. In aviation's early-bird days, they had been just about the only ones who flew.[23]

The post-September 11 regime capped a three-decade process of mounting restrictions. During World War II, FBI regulations required flight attendants to inspect baggage, lock away cameras, cover windows while flying over military bases, and even check ash trays to make sure nothing had been left behind that might damage the plane. After the war the airlines went back to their casual ways. Pilots often left the cockpit curtain open so passengers could see what was going on. One Republican Convention delegate boarded his plane with a holstered gun. The system ran on trust and—reading between the lines—on assumptions about air travelers' social class. A Republican would not likely shoot anybody or hijack the plane.[24]

All this changed in the late 1960s and early 1970s. A rash of hijackings and terrorist attacks, including a bloody 1972 shootout at Tel Aviv's Lod Airport, revealed how vulnerable the air-transport system had become. Large jets made particularly tempting targets. All it took was a dime in a pay phone. One bomb threat cost Pan Am $58,000 when a 747 captain made an emergency landing and deployed his plane's evacuation chutes. "We just couldn't take a chance," he explained. "Nuts who make phone calls like that probably wouldn't know a bomb if they saw one, but on the other hand those guerrilla people are real professionals."[25]

The real professionals who turned Flight 103 into radar-screen debris trails wound up costing insurers $527 million and Pan Am between $400 and $450 million in lost revenues, hastening the once-mighty airline's decline into bankruptcy. The Lockerbie bombing accelerated airports' evolution into heavily policed spaces, with banks of metal detectors, armed guards, bomb-sniffing dogs, and all-baggage-is-subject-to-search announcements sounding over the heads of queued passengers. Airports had become "total institutions," complete with shopping.[26]

Tightened security prevented many hijackings. No longer did the navy order its submarine intelligence officers to travel by train, for fear that their commercial flights would wind up in Fidel Castro's Cuba. Metal detectors and spot inspections weeded out the amateurs who lost their nerve and ditched their weapons in airport trash cans. But they failed to stop determined terrorists who studied security weaknesses and who were willing to go down with their planes. Precisely because air transport was so vital to the American economy, it remained the priority target. When National Public

Radio's Bob Edwards calmly announced, on the morning of September 11, 2001, that the entire country had shut down, he conveyed the purpose of the attack as well as the fact of paralysis. If the airlines remained vulnerable, so did America.[27]

The political response was to pour billions into a federalized security system. Before September 11, the primary goal had been to keep weapons off planes. After September 11, it was to keep the terrorists themselves from boarding the planes or from planting explosives on them. The price, in addition to extensive airport redesign and a $4.8 billion budget for the Transportation Security Administration, was more delays. Random searches stretched out boarding time. A hurried idiot sprinting past a checkpoint could disrupt dozens of flights: concourse evacuations joined the weather as one of air travel's uncontrollables. Short trip passengers reached for their car keys. Bookings on commercial flights of less than 400 miles declined 22 percent in the year after September 11, a drop due as much to airport inconvenience as to apprehensions of new attacks.[28]

Commercial aviation's troubled history in the decades after 1970 illustrates the familiar paradox of success imposing its own limits. In overcoming air travel's two great obstacles, fares and fear, the airlines had created two new problems, crowded hubs and security bottlenecks, that offset the two great attractions of speed and convenience. The yin of hassle chased the yang of growth, catching up with it during the tumultuous years of 1999–2001. When the airlines' financial hole deepened after September 11, a rival communications technology, the Internet, made it even harder for them to crawl out. Consumers, business travelers included, had learned to shop for discount fares. United, the industry's highest-cost carrier, was losing more than $20 million a day when it entered Chapter 11 bankruptcy in December 2002. "The Web exposed unfair pricing structures that penalized business travelers," explained airline analyst Ed Greenslet. "Suddenly, there's no mystery. It's certainly good for the traveling public."[29]

Those who were still willing to fly.

Aviation's Short, Fast Century

The events of 2001 prompt a final reflection: when was America's first century of aviation? The quiz show answer, 1903–2003, fails to match the key events. Most people discounted the airplane as a practical possibility until 1908, when the Wrights put on a show in America and Europe. Only then did the prospect of controlled flight seize the mass imagination. September 11 symbolized the opposite condition, one of vulnerable maturity. Looking

The passengers aboard United Airlines Flight 93, imagined in Igor Kordey's powerful psychological rendering, foiled the attempt to crash their fuel-laden jet into a national landmark. Three other al-Qaeda teams succeeded, damaging the Pentagon, destroying the World Trade Center, and bringing to a head a festering crisis in the air transport industry. The attacks immediately imprinted themselves on the collective memory. One testament to aviation's importance is that so many of American history's indelible moments—Lindbergh's flight, Pearl Harbor, the lunar landing, the *Challenger* explosion, the night attacks on Baghdad, September 11, the *Columbia* break-up—have involved air- or spacecraft.

on from an apartment in Brooklyn Heights, watching the World Trade Center towers collapse into smoking ruins, it occurred to John Updike that the oddest feature of the blue sky above Manhattan was the absence of jet contrails. "American freedom of motion, one of our prides, had taken a hit." So had orthodox centenary chronology. Call aviation's first century in America a short one, running from the Wrights' triumph of 1908 to the catastrophe of 2001.[30]

Three things stand out about those years. The first, and most universally remarked, was the speed of change. Improvements in early trains and steamships were glacial compared to the first three decades of the airplane's development. "I sometimes feel those of us who grew up in aviation have lived much more than an average lifetime," Lindbergh said. "It seems almost as though we had the opportunity of living in the future and looking back on our lives, of judging our work through another generation's eyes. The whole world has never changed faster than at the present time, and during this change nothing has developed more rapidly than aviation." He spoke those words in 1936, the year of the DC-3's debut. And he spoke them in Berlin, a city that would, in the next dozen years, fall and then rise again on American wings.[31]

Though the fields are seldom compared, the fast maturation of American aviation bore a strong resemblance to that of American medicine. Medicine entered the last quarter of the nineteenth century as a marginal, divided, and suspect profession. Skeptics mocked doctors, calling them the only ones who buried their mistakes. Yet, by the mid-1930s medicine was a powerful, united, and prestigious profession. Aviation, an occupation in which the mistakes buried the practitioners, underwent the same transformation, and for the same reasons: scientific and technological advances within the field, philanthropic and political support from without. Medical institutions and airlines both prospered, maintaining high approval ratings until the last two decades of the century. Then consumers soured. Having come to rely upon modern medicine and air transport, they grew impatient when they encountered problems of access and impersonal service—even though many of these problems were simply the legacy of rapid growth.[32]

The second striking feature of aviation's development was the clash between adventure and commerce. Commerce won, and it did so in the early innings. All through the 1920s, air-transport apostles demonized the "gypsy fliers," whose crashes they cataloged in the sober pages of the *Aircraft Year Book*. Aviation had no future as a circus. Its natural progress was from spectacle to amusement ride to practical transport. Many barnstormers conceded as much, setting aside their goggles for commercial pilots' hats. They submitted to the new regulations, internalized the code. It was remarkable, really, that Lindbergh, an ex-wing walker who had braved the Atlantic, should feel guilty about a passenger who tossed out an unauthorized baseball. The sky, like the land frontier before it, followed the quintessentially modern trajectory of rationalization, profit, and disenchantment. Having subdued the earth's surface, having colonized the nighttime, capitalists and bureaucrats set to work ordering the sky, or such usable portions of it as they took to calling "airspace."

The sense of adventure lingered in a few frontier niches, such as flying high-performance aircraft. It also lived on, vicariously, in the Smithsonian Institution. The aviation displays in the Arts and Industries Building, moved in 1976 to a separate National Air and Space Museum, stressed the pioneering aspects of flight. The millions who flocked to the new facility—three times the volume originally anticipated, the museum sharing the fate of the deregulated airlines—wanted to see the Wright Flyer and the *Spirit of St. Louis* and the lunar command module, not another version of the packed commercial jets that had borne them hence. Aviation history, like Gold Rush art, was both wildly popular and nostalgically skewed. As early as the mid-1850s artists were painting California mining, not as the tedious, capital-intensive operation it had become, but as the more individualistic enterprise it had been in the forty-niners' heyday. Bearded prospectors with picks and pans held the viewer's interest better than stamp mills and hydraulic mining. The contents of the National Air and Space Museum showed a comparable bias toward aviation's pioneering and envelope-pushing aspects. It was, in fact, a frontier museum.[33]

One might also say it was an imperial museum. Visitors absorbed the third great lesson of aviation's short century, that national prestige had become tied to aerospace development. John Kennedy was right. The world watched and judged great powers by what they did in the skies. The exhibits memorialized, if implicitly, American aeronautical creativity and military might. One day in January 2002, studying the uplifted faces of Asian tourists, it dawned on me that I had never fully appreciated this political subtext, so apparent to fresh eyes. This was the *National* Air and Space Museum. Americans had invented the airplane. Western rivalries had turned it into a weapon. Great nations rose and fell by dint of air power. The United States had, in the end, achieved preeminence. A fortunate thing, too. The sleek ME-262 symbolized the contingency of aeronautical advantage, its black swastikas the consequences of defeat.

One of the peculiarities of the National Air and Space Museum is that no airplane can fly anywhere near it, due to its sensitive location on the Mall.

Leaving the museum that afternoon, walking up Capitol Hill, watching the National Guardsmen shiver in the cold, I was reminded of why that ban had been imposed. Nineteen determined men had recently taught the world another set of lessons. Rome's roads ran two ways. Technology could be turned against itself. Nothing could make a fundamentally insecure thing perfectly secure. Power had its limits. So did trust. No place on earth was safe from a storm of planes.

Acronyms and Abbreviations

AAF	Army Air Forces
AAIAA	Archives of the American Institute of Aeronautics and Astronautics, Library of Congress, Manuscript Division
AHC	American Heritage Center, University of Wyoming, Laramie
ATA	Air Transport Association Office of Economics
ATC	Air Transport Command
CAA	Civil Aeronautics Administration
CFCAA	Central Files of the Civil Aeronautics Administration, 1926–1943, RG 237, National Archives II, College Park, Maryland
CSC	Carl Solberg Collection, American Heritage Center, University of Wyoming, Laramie
FAA	Federal Aviation Agency
JWTA	J. Walter Thompson Company Archives, Special Collections Library, Duke University
LCMD	Library of Congress, Manuscript Division, Washington, D.C.
NA	National Archives, Washington, D. C.
NA II	National Archives II, College Park, Maryland
NACA	National Advisory Committee for Aeronautics
NACAGC	National Advisory Committee for Aeronautics, General Correspondence, RG 255, National Archives II, College Park, Maryland
NASA	National Aeronautics and Space Administration
NASAHO	National Aeronautics and Space Administration History Office, Washington, D.C.
NASMAD	National Air and Space Museum Archives Division, Smithsonian Institution, Garber Facility, Suitland, Maryland
NATS	Navy Air Transport Service
OMB	Office of Management and Budget
PAWAR	Pan American World Airways, Inc., Records, Otto G. Richter Library, University of Miami, Coral Gables, Florida

PODR	Post Office Department Records, Air Transportation Branch, Historical Files, 1911–1960, RG 28, National Archives, Washington, D.C.
RG	Record Group
UAV	Unmanned aerial vehicle

Notes

Chapter 1

1. "Last 'Pony' Plane Quits Flying Mail," *New York Times,* November 27, 1935. Hamilton: Ralph S. Barnaby, "Early Birds—40 Years Ago," *Philadelphia Inquirer Magazine,* June 11, 1950. Rickenbacker's flight: "Pioneer's Air Trail, Made in a Day in 1910, is Retraced in Hour" and "Aviation Progress is Hailed by Flier," *New York Times,* June 14, 1935.
2. Charles A. Lindbergh, ". . . We Must Measure Scientific Accomplishments by Their Effect on Man Himself," *Bee-Hive* 25 (February 1950): 12.
3. Frederick Jackson Turner, *The Frontier in American History* (1920; reprint, Tucson: University of Arizona Press, 1992), 259. For a concise, fair-minded introduction to Turner and his critics, see John Mack Faragher, *Rereading Frederick Jackson Turner* (New York: Henry Holt, 1994).
4. Howard E. McCurdy, *Space and the American Imagination* (Washington: Smithsonian Institution Press, 1997), chap. 6; Susan Landrum Mangus, "Conestoga Wagons to the Moon: The Frontier, the American Space Program, and National Identity" (Ph.D. diss., Ohio State University, 1999), quotation on p. 70; Robert Zubrin, "A New Martian Frontier: Recapturing the Soul of America," in *Frontiers of Space Exploration,* ed. Roger D. Launius (Westport, Ct.: Greenwood Press, 1998), 152–60.
5. Wernher von Braun remarks in *Congressional Record* 121 (July 25, 1975): E4130–31; Carl Sagan, *Pale Blue Dot: A Vision of the Human Future in Space* (New York: Random House, 1994), xii.
6. *Land of Their Choice: The Immigrants Write Home,* ed. Theodore Blegen (Minneapolis: University of Minnesota Press, 1955), 227.
7. Ibid., 227; Richard L. Hale, *The Log of a Forty-Niner,* ed. Carolyn Hale Russ (Boston: B. J. Brimmer, 1923), 120 ("Can he").
8. One-fifth: J. Ross Browne and James W. Taylor, *Reports Upon the Mineral Resources of the United States* (Washington, D.C.: Government Printing Office, 1867), 38. California insurance: David T. Courtwright, *Violent Land: Single Men and Social Disorder from the Frontier to the Inner City* (Cambridge, Mass.: Harvard University Press, 1996), 68. Chapters 3–9 offer additional examples and discuss differences among frontier types in greater detail.
9. Walter Nugent, "Frontiers and Empires in the Late Nineteenth Century," *Western Historical Quarterly* 20 (1989): 400.
10. *A Woman's Reminiscences of Six Years in Camp with Texas Rangers* (Austin: Von Boeckmann-Jones, 1928), 48.
11. "Air Collision Kills Six in California," *New York Times,* April 22, 1929; "Accident Details," accessed at http://www.planecrashinfo.com/1929/1929-4.htm, July 14, 2002.

12. Horace Brock, *Flying the Oceans: A Pilot's Story of Pan Am, 1935–1955* (Lunenburg, Vt.: Stinehour, 1979), 207; Bernie Lay, Jr., "The Airman," *Fortune* 23 (March 1941): 137.
13. Charles A. Lindbergh, *Autobiography of Values* (New York: Harcourt Brace Jovanovich, 1978), 32. Horace Brock, one of Lindbergh's contemporaries, remarked that Africa produced the opposite effect. Flying from Léopoldville to Johannesburg in the years after World War II, only lightning flashes and dim village campfires penetrated the total nighttime blackness. Brock, *Flying the Oceans,* 274.
14. Murray Melbin, "Night as Frontier," *American Sociological Review* 43 (1978): 3–22. It was subsequently expanded into a book, *Night as Frontier: Colonizing the World after Dark* (New York: Free Press, 1987). Lighting history, Paris: Wolfgang Schivelbusch, *Disenchanted Night: The Industrialization of Light in the Nineteenth Century,* trans. Angela Davies (Berkeley: University of California Press, 1988). Nighttime accidents: Courtwright, *Violent Land,* 222.
15. "Air Safety Record . . .," *New York Times,* March 28, 1935 (160 mph); Richard K. Smith, "The Weight Envelope: An Airplane's Fourth Dimension . . . Aviation's Bottom Line," *Aerospace Historian* 33 (Spring 1986): 30–44, quotation on 42; Bernard Lewis, *The Crisis of Islam: Holy War and Unholy Terror* (New York: Modern Library, 2003), 53.
16. R. E. G. Davies, *A History of the World's Airlines* (London: Oxford University Press, 1964), 116–18, 295–96.
17. "The Significance of the Frontier in American History," in Faragher, *Rereading Frederick Jackson Turner,* 81.
18. Gilbert S. Guinn, "A Different Frontier: Aviation, the Army Air Forces, and the Evolution of the Sunshine Belt," *Aerospace Historian* 29 (March 1982): 44.
19. Wesley Frank Craven and James Lea Cate, eds., *The Army Air Forces in World War II,* vol. 6 (Chicago: University of Chicago Press, 1955), 120–21; Janet R. Daly Bednarek, *America's Airports: Airfield Development, 1918–1947* (College Station: Texas A&M University Press, 2001), 164, 165, 178–80; H. McKinley Conway, *The Airport City and the Future Intermodal Transport System* (Atlanta: Conway Publications, 1977), 160.
20. William Edward Fischer Jr., *The Development of Military Night Aviation to 1919* (Maxwell Airport Base: Air University Press, 1998). Lighting details: folders E and F, box 6, Record Group (RG) 28-MS, National Archives II (NAII); Francis Vivian Drake, "Pegasus Express," 1932 *Atlantic Monthly* reprint, pp. 12, 17, box 2, Post Office Department Records, Air Transportation Branch, Historical Files, 1911–60, RG 28, National Archives (NA), Washington, D.C. (hereafter, PODR).
21. Robert V. Hine, *Josiah Royce: From Grass Valley to Harvard* (Norman: University of Oklahoma Press, 1992), 29; Courtwright, *Violent Land,* chap. 8; Gunther Peck, *Reinventing Free Labor: Padrones and Immigrant Workers in the North American West, 1880–1930* (Cambridge: Cambridge University Press, 2000), 80.
22. Mark Gottdiener, *Life in the Air: Surviving the New Culture of Air Travel* (Lanham, Md.: Rowman & Littlefield, 2001), 1, 84 (quotation); "World Airline Traffic Statistics–2000," *Air Traffic World* (on-line version) 38 (July 2001): 74. The five million

estimate, based on a global total of 1.82 billion commercial passengers for 2000, is conservative. It excludes commercial aircrews, private pilots, and military personnel. Hence the average number of people venturing aloft on a given day was undoubtedly higher.

23. "Biography of Captain E. Hamilton Lee" (typescript, 1949), box 2, PODR; Lee Smith interview, August 18, 1976, p. 9, box 18, Carl Solberg Collection, American Heritage Center, University of Wyoming, Laramie (hereafter Carl Solberg Collection, AHC).
24. Hailey quoted in Conway, *Airport City,* 176; William Langewiesche, *Inside the Sky: A Meditation on Flight* (New York: Pantheon, 1998), 112. Aimée Bratt, *Glamour and Turbulence: I Remember Pan Am, 1966–1991* (New York: Vantage, 1996), describes some of the less appealing aspects of life in the air.
25. Letters from Rabin, June 23, 1978; Pam Corkins, October 5, 1978; and Fodor, January 4, 1978, all to Carl Solberg, box 15, Carl Solberg Collection, AHC.
26. Gottdiener, *Life in the Air,* chap. 4; "On a Wing and a Hotel Room," *The Economist* 350 (January 9, 1999): 64.
27. Larissa MacFarquhar, "The Better Boss," *New Yorker* 78 (April 22 & 29, 2002), 120–21; Kirn, *Up in the Air* (New York: Doubleday, 2001), 7.

Chapter 2

1. Jefferson to Lee, April 27, 1822, box 52, Archives of the American Institute of Aeronautics and Astronautics, Library of Congress, Manuscript Division, Washington, D.C. (hereafter, AAIAA).
2. Arthur Mark Cummings, "The Uselessness of Flying-Machines," *North American Review* 152 (January 1891): 118.
3. "Balloon Wreck Kills Sixteen," *Richmond Times-Dispatch,* June 23, 1907; Mark Twain, *Collected Tales, Sketches, Speeches, and Essays, 1891–1910* (New York: Library of America, 1992), 941.
4. This account of ballooning draws on John Wise, *Through the Air: A Narrative of Forty Years' Experience as an Aëronaut* (Philadelphia: To-day Printing Company, 1873), "greatest voyage" on page 519; Jeremiah Milbank Jr., *The First Century of Flight in America* (Princeton: Princeton University Press, 1943); Roger Bilstein, *Flight in America: From the Wrights to the Astronauts,* revised ed. (Baltimore: Johns Hopkins University Press, 1994), 6–7; Courtney Gould Brooks, "American Aeronautics as Spectacle and Sport" (Ph.D. diss., Tulane University, 1969), chaps. 1–4; and Robeson S. Moise, "Balloons and Dirigibles," in *The American Aviation Experience,* ed. Tim Brady (Carbondale: Southern Illinois University Press, 2000), 311–23.
5. W. O. Saunders, "Then We Quit Laughing," *Collier's* 80 (September 17, 1927): 24 (quoting John T. Daniels).
6. *The Pioneers of Flight: A Documentary History,* ed. Phil Scott (Princeton: Princeton University Press, 1999), 131. Here, and below, my account draws upon Orville Wright, "How We Made the First Flight," *Flying* 2 (December 1913): 10–12, 35–36; Tom Crouch, *The Bishop's Boys: A Life of Wilbur and Orville Wright* (New York: W. W. Norton, 1989); and James Tobin, *To Conquer the Air: The Wright*

Brothers and the Great Race for Flight (New York: Free Press, 2003). Tobin notes that the actual flight time, fifty-nine seconds, was garbled in communication (193–94).

7. Letter of December 27, 1905, *The Papers of Wilbur and Orville Wright, including the Chanute-Wright Letters and Other Papers of Octave Chanute,* vol. 1: *1899–1905,* ed. Marvin W. McFarland (New York: McGraw Hill, 1953), 538.
8. Wilbur Wright to Octave Chanute, June 1, 1905, ibid., 495; Crouch, *Bishop's Boys,* 302, 304; Tobin, *To Conquer the Air,* 192, 226–27.
9. Charles Harvard Gibbs-Smith, *The Rebirth of European Aviation, 1902–1908: A Study of the Wright Brothers' Influence* (London: Her Majesty's Stationery Office, 1974), 288.
10. Wilbur Wright to Katharine Wright, September 13, 1908, in McFarland, *Papers,* vol. 2: *1906–1948,* 923.
11. Byron R. Newton, "Watching the Wright Brothers Fly," *Aeronautics* 2 (June 1908): 6.
12. Seth Shulman, *Unlocking the Sky: Glen Hammond Curtiss and the Race to Invent the Airplane* (New York: Harper-Collins, 2002); Roy Knabenshue, "How Flying Began in America" (Typescript, n.d.), box 58, AAIAA (litigation cost estimates); Glenn Curtiss, *The Curtiss Aviation Book* (1912), excerpted in Scott, *Pioneers,* chaps. 40, 41, 45; Crouch, *Bishop's Boys,* chaps. 29–33. Tobin, *To Conquer the Air,* is especially good on the family's pattern of righteous litigation. How much any of this ultimately mattered is another question. In "Blaming Wilbur and Orville: The Wright Patent Suits and the Growth of American Aeronautics," in *Atmospheric Flight in the Twentieth Century,* eds. Peter Galison and Alex Roland (Dordrecht: Kluwer, 2000), 287–300, Tom Crouch concludes that European research priorities, rather than the effects of prolonged litigation, explain the widening transatlantic aeronautical gap.
13. *Fifteenth Census of the United States, 1930,* vol. 5: *General Report on Occupations* (Washington, D.C.: Government Printing Office, 1933), 45n. 36; Wilbur Wright, "Flying as Sport—Its Possibilities," *Scientific American* 98 (February 29, 1908): 139; Orville Wright, "The Future of the Aeroplane," *Country Life in America* 15 (January 1909): 252–53; "Strong Wind Stops Flight," *Dayton Journal,* September 29, 1909 (Curtiss).
14. Henry H. Arnold, *Global Mission* (1949; reprint, Blue Ridge Summit, Pa.: TAB Books, 1989), 14 ("neck"); Crouch, *Bishop's Boys,* 429; Knabenshue to Orville Wright, February 25, 1912, box 14, Wilbur and Orville Wright Papers, Library of Congress, Manuscript Division, Washington, D.C. (hereafter, Wright Papers, LCMD). Sales agreements are in box 40.
15. All quotations and statistics are from the Hoxsey file of undated clippings, box 51, AAIAA. See also Knabenshue to Wilbur Wright, undated (probably January 1911), box 14, Wright Papers, LCMD; and Wilbur Wright to Hoxsey, September 19, 1910, McFarland, *Papers,* vol. 2: *1906–1948,* 998. Mortality figures: Henry Serrano Villard, *Contact! The Story of the Early Birds* (New York: Thomas Y. Crowell, 1968), 115–16, 242–43.
16. Hope Bouvette Thornberg, "Women in Aviation," in Brady, *American Aviation Experience,* 368–70; quotations from Mary Cadogan, *Women with Wings: Female*

Flyers in Fact and Fiction (Chicago: Academy Chicago Publishers, 1993), 33, 39, 49; Villard, *Contact!*, 144. The rules of the Early Bird Society (whence the designation) specified that American pilots had to have soloed before December 17, 1916, to be eligible for membership. European pilots had to have soloed before August 4, 1914.

17. Frank Marerro, *Lincoln Beachey: The Man Who Owned the Sky* (San Francisco: Scottwall Associates, 1997), 1, 29, 85; Hoxsey file, box 51, AAIAA; Tom Phillips, *The Postcard Century: 2000 Cards and Their Messages* (London: Thames and Hudson, 2000), 18.
18. Tom Wolfe, *The Right Stuff* (New York: Farrar, Straus, Giroux, 1979), 24.
19. Quotations from Anthony H. G. Fokker and Bruce Gould, *Flying Dutchman: The Life of Anthony Fokker* (New York: Henry Holt, 1931), chap. 7; and Knabenshue to Wright, January 19, 1914, Wright Papers, box 14, LCMD. Beachey: Marerro, *Lincoln Beachey*, rhyme on page 187; Sherwood Harris, *The First to Fly: Aviation's Pioneer Days* (New York: Simon and Schuster, 1970), 292; Villard, *Contact!*, 196–97; and Lester J. Maitland, "Knights of the Air," *World's Work* 57 (November 1928): 94–95 ("I will show").
20. Fokker and Gould, *Flying Dutchman*, chaps. 8, 13–22; Marc Dierikx, *Fokker: A Transatlantic Biography* (Washington, D.C.: Smithsonian Institution Press, 1997), chap. 2; Dominick A. Pisano, "The Crash that Killed Knute Rockne," *Air and Space Smithsonian* 6 (December 1991–January 1992): 88–93; "safest" from unpaginated Atlantic Aircraft ad, *Who's Who in American Aeronautics, 1925*, 2d ed. (New York: Gardner Publishing, 1925).
21. "Causes of Aviation Accidents," *Scientific American* 105 (July 22, 1911): 74; Crouch, *Bishop's Boys*, 434–35; Lee Kennett, *The First Air War, 1914–1918* (New York: Free Press, 1991), 114; Arnold, *Global Mission*, 15.
22. Robert Gandt, *Skygods: The Fall of Pan Am* (New York: William Morrow, 1995), 11; Douglas J. Ingells, *The Plane that Changed the World: A Biography of the DC-3* (Fairbrook, Calif.: Aero Publishers, 1966), 21; Harold Mansfield, *Vision: A Saga of the Sky* (New York: Duell, Sloan and Pearce, 1956), 5–7 (Boeing); John Tebbel, *The Life and Good Times of William Randolph Hearst* (New York: Dutton, 1952), 349; Claire Lee Chennault, with Robert Holtz, *Way of a Fighter: The Memoirs of Claire Lee Chennault* (New York: G.P. Putnam's Sons, 1949), 7; Curtis E. LeMay, with MacKinlay Kantor, *Mission with LeMay: My Story* (Garden City, N. Y.: Doubleday, 1965), 13–14, 23–24; A. Scott Berg, *Lindbergh* (New York: G. P. Putnam's Sons, 1998), 43; Joseph J. Corn, *The Winged Gospel: America's Romance with Aviation, 1900–1950* (New York: Oxford University Press, 1983), chap. 6. Stinson's license: Debra L. Winegarten, personal communication, March 10, 2002.
23. Editorial clippings in Hoxsey file, box 51, AAIAA; "Daring that Leads to Death," *Outlook* 109 (March 24, 1915): 661 ("morally"); Maitland, "Knights of the Air," 93 (Kearney).

Chapter 3

1. Nine million: Niall Ferguson, *The Pity of War* (New York: Basic Books, 1999), 295. Steam clouds, four miles up: "A Lifetime in Aviation: The Biography of Allan F. Bonnalie" (typescript, n.d.), pp. 55, 71, box 111, Bonnalie Collection, AHC.

2. This sketch of WWI aviation draws on Air Corps Tactical School, "Pursuit" (typescript, 1929), box 3, Arthur Raymond Brooks Papers, National Air and Space Museum Archives Division, Smithsonian Institution, Garber Facility, Suitland, Maryland (hereafter, NASMAD); Lee Kennett, *The First Air War, 1914–1918* (New York: Free Press, 1991), three-quarters figure on page 220; John Buckley, *Air Power in the Age of Total War* (Bloomington: Indiana University Press, 1999), chap. 3; Denis Winter, *The First of the Few: Fighter Pilots of the First World War* (Athens: University of Georgia Press, 1982); and John H. Morrow Jr., *The Great War in the Air: Military Aviation from 1909 to 1921* (Washington: Smithsonian Institution Press, 1993), percentages on p. 346.
3. Juliette A. Hennessy, *The United Sates Army Air Arm, April 1861 to April 1917* (1958; reprint, Washington, D.C.: Government Printing Office, 1986), 196–97; Louis R. Eltscher and Edward M. Young, *Curtiss-Wright: Greatness and Decline* (New York: Twayne, 1998), 19–24; Bilstein, *Flight in America,* 36.
4. *Sailor of the Air: The 1917–1919 Letters and Diary of USN CMM/A Irving Edward Sheely,* ed. Lawrence D. Sheely (Tuscaloosa: University of Alabama Press, 1993), 27 (quotation), 132. French fliers called the arena of ground combat *rue de merde*—shit street.
5. John M. Loeblein, *Memoirs of Kelly Field, 1917–1918* (Manhattan, Ks.: Aerospace Historian, 1974), 23; Alfred Goldberg, "The Air Service in the Great War," in *A History of the United States Air Force,* ed. Alfred Goldberg (New York: Arno Press, 1974), 19.
6. [Elliott White Springs and] John MacGavock Grider, *War Birds: Diary of an Unknown Aviator* (College Station: Texas A&M University Press, 1988), quotations on pages 38, 108, 109; Burke Davis, *War Bird: The Life and Times of Elliott White Springs* (Chapel Hill: University of North Carolina Press, 1987).
7. Cecil Lewis, *Sagittarius Rising* (New York: Harcourt, Brace, 1936), quotation from the unpaginated preface; Winter, *First of the Few,* 24; [Springs and] Grider, *War Birds,* 267; *The U.S. Air Service in World War I,* vol. 2: *Early Concepts of Military Aviation,* ed. Maurer Maurer (Washington, D.C.: Government Printing Office, 1978), 99 (Squier); Edward V. Rickenbacker, *Rickenbacker* (Englewood Cliffs, N.J., Prentice-Hall, 1967), 90.
8. Jeffrey L. Ethell, "Wings of the Great War," *Air and Space Smithsonian* 6 (October–November 1991): 60–69; Josiah P. Rowe Jr., *Letters from a World War I Aviator,* ed. Genevieve Bailey Rowe and Diana Rowe Doran (Boston: Sinclaire Press, 1986), 32; Kennett, *First Air War,* 117; Winter, *First of the Few,* 151; Rickenbacker, *Rickenbacker,* 117.
9. Winter, *First of the Few,* 148; Sheely, *Sailor of the Air,* 119; Brooks to Ruth N. Connery, July 27, 1918, Brooks Papers, NASMAD.
10. James J. Cooke, *The U.S. Air Service in the Great War, 1917–1919* (Westport, Conn.: Praeger, 1996), 14; Winter, *First of the Few,* 148, 152 (quotation), 191.
11. Bonnalie, "A Lifetime in Aviation," 64 (quotation), 78; Brooks to Ruth N. Connery, August 2, 1918, Brooks Papers, NASMAD; *An American Pilot in the Skies of France: The Diaries and Letters of Lt. Percival T. Gates, 1917–1918,* ed. David K. Vaughan (Dayton: Wright State University Press, 1992), 142, 144, 163; Kennett, *First Air War,* 164 (statistics).

12. *Thinking of Home: William Faulkner's Letters to His Mother and Father, 1918–1925*, ed. James G. Watson (New York: W. W. Norton, 1992), 63 (spelling corrected); Joseph Blotner, *Faulkner: A Biography* (New York: Random House, 1984 one-volume ed.), 63; Rowe and Doran, *Letters from a World War I Aviator,* x, 135; "Account of Operations, 99th Aero Observation Squadron" (Typescript, n.d.), p. 51, box 1, Lyle S. Powell Collection, AHC.
13. Vaughan, *An American Pilot,* 9–10 (40 percent), 75 (quotation).
14. Loeblein, *Memoirs,* 18; *Notes and Rules for Pilots and Crews* (n.p.: U.S. War Office, 1917), p. 3, box 8, Brooks Papers, NASMAD; Cooke, *U.S. Air Service,* 184–85 (Luke); Air Corps Tactical School, "Pursuit," 26; Winter, *First Air War,* 155–56 (quotation).
15. John Davies, *The Legend of Hobey Baker* (Boston: Little, Brown, 1966), xi (quotation), xix, 91–107.
16. Stephen Marshall, "Aeroplanes, Zeppelins, and the Construction of Three-Dimensional Sovereignty: Airspace and the International System, 1910–1919," unpublished 1999 paper used with permission of the author.
17. Ferguson, *Pity of War,* 157–58; "Blériot XI 'Domenjoz,'" accessed at http://www.nasm.si.edu/nasm/aero/aircraft/bleriotx.htm, July 8, 2003; Kennett, *First Air War,* 105 (Liberty engine); Mitchell, "America in the Air," *National Geographic* 39 (March 1921): 341.
18. Rickenbacker, "Is Aviation Starting to Repeat Auto History?" *Sales Management* 8 (June 13, 1925): 859; Laurence La Tourette Driggs, "The Future of Aviation," *Outlook* 121 (April 9, 1919): 608.
19. Edward Rickenbacker, typescript of speech given March 22, 1944, roll 19, Henry Arnold Papers, LCMD; Howard Mingos, *Birth of an Industry* (New York: W. B. Conkey, 1930), 10–95; John B. Rae, *Climb to Greatness: The American Aircraft Industry, 1920–1960* (Cambridge, Mass.: MIT Press, 1968), 2–3.
20. Hattie Meyers Junkin, "The Human Investment in WACO" (Typescript, 1929), p. 2, envelope 15, Junkin Papers, NASMAD. Weaver cofounded Weaver Aircraft Company (WACO) in 1921.
21. John F. Hayford to Joseph F. Ames, November 22, 1920, file 11-9, National Advisory Committee for Aeronautics, General Correspondence, RG 255, National Archives II, College Park, Maryland (hereafter, NACAGC). Some of the more outrageous barnstorming antics are preserved in boxes 2, 9, and 10 of the Roger Q. Williams Collection, AHC.
22. Carl Solberg, *Conquest of the Skies: A History of Commercial Aviation in America* (Boston: Little, Brown, 1979), 30 (million); Tex Johnston, with Charles Barton, *Tex Johnston: Jet-Age Test Pilot* (Washington, D.C.: Smithsonian Institution Press, 1991), 4–6, quotation on page 6. Don Dwiggins, *The Barnstormers: Flying Daredevils of the Roaring Twenties* (New York: Grosset and Dunlap, 1968), 130–31; Dwiggins claims, without evidence, that ten million or more flew in the 1920s.
23. A. Scott Berg, *Lindbergh* (New York: G. P. Putnam's Sons, 1998), 82; Charles A. Lindbergh, *The Spirit of St. Louis* (1953; reprint, St. Paul: Minnesota Historical Society, 1993), 431–32.
24. Dean C. Smith, *By the Seat of My Pants* (Boston: Little, Brown, 1961), 91–92; Henry

Woodhouse, "Prosperous Outlook for Aeronautics on the Sixteenth Anniversary of the First Flight," *Flying* 8 (January 1920): 977; *Fourteenth Census of the United States, 1920,* vol. 4: *Occupations* (Washington, D.C.: Government Printing Office, 1923), 42; Johnston and Barton, *Tex Johnston,* 6. The price decline was not uniform. Some sources, e.g., Basil Rowe, *Under My Wings* (Indianapolis: Bobbs-Merrill, 1956), 37–38, indicate that five dollar rides persisted into the mid-1920s. Prices varied, depending on the number of pilots working an area, previous exposure, and length of the promised ride. But all sources (including Rowe) agree that the easy pickings had disappeared by 1926. Note also that some passengers flew before World War I, e.g., taking short hops in seaplanes moored at oceanside resorts. The combination of high fares and few reliable planes limited prewar volume.

25. Richard White, *"It's Your Misfortune and None of My Own": A History of the American West* (Norman: University of Oklahoma Press, 1991), 191; *The Mining Frontier: Contemporary Accounts from the American West in the Nineteenth Century,* ed. Marvin Lewis (Norman: University of Oklahoma Press, 1967), xi–xiii; Browne and Taylor, *Reports Upon the Mineral Resources of the United States,* 20–21; Malcom J. Rohrbough, *Days of Gold: The California Gold Rush and the American Nation* (Berkeley: University of California Press, 1997), 267.
26. Lindbergh, *Spirit of St. Louis,* 57, 272, 276, 279–80 (seasonality); Lester J. Maitland, "Knights of the Air," *Outlook* 57 (December 1928): 203; Carroll V. Glines, *Roscoe Turner: Aviation's Master Showman* (Washington, D.C.: Smithsonian Institution Press, 1995), 49–50.
27. *The Journals of Alfred Doten, 1849–1903,* vol. 1, ed. Walter Van Tilburg Clark (Reno: University of Nevada Press, 1973), 52; *Overland to California with the Pioneer Line: The Gold Rush Diary of Bernard J. Reid,* ed. Mary McDougall Gordon (Stanford: Stanford University Press, 1983), 145.
28. Rowe, *Under My Wings,* 37–38; Glines, *Roscoe Turner,* 49; "W. H. Parker a 'History Book' on Aircraft Maintenance," *AM* [Maldron Air Base monthly newspaper], April 1953.
29. Rowe, *Under My Wings,* 37; Lindbergh, *Autobiography of Values,* 64, 121, 123 (quotations); Lindbergh, *Spirit of St. Louis,* 261–62, 266–68, 273, 277. The Ballard interview is in the documentary film *Lindbergh* (Boston: WGBH and Insignia Films, 1997). Ernest Hemingway worked a variation on the stereotype of the hypermasculine pilot. Jake Barnes, the hero of *The Sun Also Rises* (1926), suffered his famously emasculating wound over the Italian front. This piece of freakish bad luck altered his nature from flying stallion to grounded gelding.
30. Courtwright, *Violent Land,* 16.
31. Rowe, *Under My Wings,* 84; Dwiggins, *Barnstormers,* chap. 10; Dixon Merritt, "America in the Air," *Outlook* 147 (October 19, 1927): 208; Johnston and Barton, *Tex Johnston,* 11–29.
32. "Fairchild Summarizes 1929 Sales Problems in Aircraft Industry," *Sales Management* 18 (April 6, 1929): 40.
33. Johnston and Barton, *Tex Johnston,* 6 (quotation), 21; Tibbets, with Clair Stebbins and Harry Franken, *The Tibbets Story* (New York: Stein and Day, 1978), chap. 3;

Richard Hack, *Howard Hughes: The Private Diaries, Memos and Letters* (Beverly Hills: New Millennium, 2001), 42.

34. Donald Duke, "Are We Airworthy?" *Annals of the American Academy* 131 (May 1927): 151; Dwiggins, *Barnstormers*, 107 (Rodgers); *Aircraft Year Book, 1924* (New York: Aeronautical Chamber of Commerce of America, 1924), 104 and 109 (statistics), and chap. 9.
35. Dwiggins, *Barnstormers*, 88–89; Smith, *By the Seat of My Pants*, 92–96.
36. Brock, *Flying the Oceans*, 27–28.
37. Glines, *Roscoe Turner*, chap. 4; Donald L. Barlett and James R. Steele, *Empire: The Life and Madness of Howard Hughes* (New York: W. W. Norton, 1979), 68; Hack, *Howard Hughes*, 80.
38. Robert Wohl, "Republic of the Air," *Wilson Quarterly* 17 (Spring 1993): 115; Michael Wood, *America in the Movies* (New York: Columbia University Press, 1979), 42–43.
39. Examples of nightmares, complaints: Merton R. Lovett interview of Vito Cacciola, no. 35, March 24, 1939, Federal Writers' Project MSS, LCMD, accessed at http://lcweb2.loc.gov/mss/wpalho/09/0905/09052104.tif, May 23, 2003; Richard Martin, "Aviation's Apostle," *Flying and Popular Aviation* 27 (October 1940): 72 (quotation). Turner: David M. Wrobel, "Frontier," *Encyclopedia of the United States in the Nineteenth Century*, vol. 1 (New York: Charles Scribner's Sons, 2001), 521. See also Courtwright, *Violent Land*, 103–107.

Chapter 4

1. Smith, *By the Seat of My Pants*, 104.
2. E. Hamilton Lee interview, January 17, 1977, p. 3, box 18, Carl Solberg Collection, AHC. My account of early airmail operations draws on the official typescript histories in boxes 1–3, PODR; F. Robert van der Linden's comprehensive *Airlines and Air Mail: The Post Office and the Birth of the Commercial Aviation Industry* (Lexington: University Press of Kentucky, 2002), chap. 1; and Donald Dale Jackson's popular but still valuable *Flying the Mail* (Alexandria, Va.: Time-Life, 1982), chaps. 1–3.
3. H. McKinley Conway, *The Airport City and the Future Intermodal Transport System* (Atlanta: Conway Publications, 1977), 31–34.
4. Smith, *By the Seat of My Pants*, part II; Jackson, *Flying the Mail*, 92–93 (Hill); Juan T. Trippe, "Building the Airways of America," May 2, 1940, address to the U.S. Chamber of Commerce, p. 2, box 120, AAIAA ("hatful"); Lindbergh, *Spirit of St. Louis*, 65.
5. Dean Smith interview, January 22, 1977, p. 3, box 18, Carl Solberg Collection, AHC.
6. Smith, *By the Seat of My Pants*, 136; J. R. Hildebrand, "Man's Amazing Progress in Conquering the Air," *National Geographic* 46 (July 1924): 108 ("gone west"). Mortality: Jackson, *Flying the Mail*, 6; Donald Dale Jackson, "Slim Lewis Slept Here," *Air and Space Smithsonian* 6 (October–November 1991): 43; and Solberg, *Conquest of the Skies*, 22.
7. Smith, *By the Seat of My Pants*, 139–46, quotation on pages 139–40. The typescript is in box 8 of the Dean C. Smith Collection, AHC, with examples from chaps. 22–26. My comments on Smith's aesthetic sensibilities follow those of Jack Rogers, personal communication.

8. "Air Mail Statistics" (typescript, n. d.), box 2, PODR (forced landings); Lindbergh, *Spirit of St. Louis,* 7; Jackson, *Flying the Mail,* 70–94, 85 (fatality statistics).
9. Smith, *By the Seat of My Pants,* 115–16, 159–61; Lindbergh, *Spirit of St. Louis,* 325–26; "Ask Capitol Dome Beacon," *New York Times,* February 27, 1929.
10. Smith, *By the Seat of My Pants,* 154, 172. Airway details from box 2, PODR; and Jackson, *Flying the Mail.*
11. Lester D. Seymour, "Insuring Safety on Airlines," *Scientific American* 141 (December 1929): 506 (teeth); "Reduced Rates for Long Distance Telephoning," *American City* 35 (November 1926): 745; Roger Bilstein, "Technology and Commerce: Aviation in the Conduct of American Business, 1918–1929," *Technology and Culture* 10 (1969): 400, 402 (ad copy); Hildebrand, "Man's Amazing Progress," 109 ($100,000); "Finds Air Travel Growing More Safe," *New York Times,* January 24, 1926.
12. Van der Linden, *Airlines and Air Mail,* 8.
13. "Air Mail Statistics" (typescript, n. d.), box 2, PODR; Lipsner, *The Airmail: Jennies to Jets* (New York: Wilcox & Follett, 1951), 210; Francis Vivian Drake, "Pegasus Express," 1932 *Atlantic Monthly* reprint, p. 17, box 2, PODR.
14. *Statutes at Large,* vol. 43, part 1 (Washington, D.C.: Government Printing Office, 1925), 805–806; "A Brief History of the Contract Air Mail Service from 1925 to 1933" (typescript, n.d.), box 2, PODR; Lindbergh, *Spirit of St. Louis,* 9–10, 10 (quotation); Bilstein, "Technology and Commerce," 402, 403n. 39.
15. Edwin H. Shanks, "When the Sales Department Begins Using Airplanes," *Sales Management* 11 (September 18, 1926): 417; William Stout, "Flying Sales Executives," *Sales Management* 12 (April 2, 1927): 615.
16. G. Lloyd Wilson and Leslie A. Bryan, *Air Transportation* (New York: Prentice-Hall, 1949), 265, 267 (5,800).
17. Albert A. LeShane Jr., "Florida Airways," *Journal of the American Aviation Historical Society* 22 (1977): 123–35; Rickenbacker, *Rickenbacker,* 176; Brooks to E[ddie] R[ickenbacker], April 24, 1926, and Brooks to Ted Haight, May 7, 1926 ("cracker cities"), Brooks Papers, NASMAD. So much for the company's prospectus, which promised that only total abstainers had been hired as pilots and mechanics.
18. Clifford A. Tinker, "Is Fear Keeping Us Back?" *Collier's* 75 (January 31, 1925): 42.
19. Nick A. Komons, *Bonfires to Beacons: Federal Civil Aviation Policy under the Air Commerce Act, 1926–1938* (Washington, D.C.: Government Printing Office, 1978), chaps. 3–4; and Thomas Worth Walterman, "Airpower and Private Enterprise: Federal Industrial Relations in the Aeronautics Field, 1918–1926" (Ph.D. diss, Washington University, 1970). My account of the early airlines also draws on R. E. G. Davies, *Airlines of the United States* (London: Putnam, 1972), chaps. 2–3; and van der Linden, *Airlines and Air Mail,* chaps. 2–4.
20. *Statutes at Large,* vol. 44, part 2 (Washington, D.C.: Government Printing Office, 1927), 568–76. One reason for the belated legislative declaration of sovereignty was that the United States Senate had never ratified the 1919 Aerial Convention, which was part of the Versailles Treaty. David Butler, personal communication, June 20, 2002.

21. "A Brief History of the Contract Air Mail Service from 1925 to 1933" (typescript, n. d.), box 2, PODR; T. A. Heppenheimer, *Turbulent Skies: The History of Commercial Aviation* (New York: John Wiley, 1995), chap. 1.
22. Lindbergh, *Spirit of St. Louis,* 13–14, 60–61.

Chapter 5

1. *Congressional Record* 123 (May 23, 1977): H 4809; Charles Lindbergh, *The Wartime Journals of Charles A. Lindbergh* (New York: Harcourt Brace Jovanovich, 1970), 320.
2. Charles A. Lindbergh, *Lindbergh Looks Back: A Boyhood Reminiscence* (St. Paul: Minnesota Historical Society Press, 2002); "Speech at the IAS Honors Night Dinner" (typescript, 1954), p. 7, Lindbergh biographical file 001307, National Aeronautics and Space Administration History Office, Washington, D.C. (hereafter, NASAHO). The following account of Lindbergh's early career and epic flight draws primarily upon *Spirit of St. Louis,* the fullest of his several autobiographical writings, and A. Scott Berg, *Lindbergh* (New York: G. P. Putnam's Sons, 1998), the most complete biographical account. For economy's sake I have paraphrased some long passages from Lindbergh's *Spirit of St. Louis.* The notes provide pages for direct quotations and key details.
3. Lindbergh, *Spirit of St. Louis,* 247–50, 261, 266; Mark Twain, *Life on the Mississippi,* in *Mississippi Writings* (New York: Library of America, 1982), 283–85, 284 (quotation).
4. Wolfgang Langewiesche, "The Lindbergh Story, a Pilot's Mind in Action," *Air Line Pilot* 23 (February 1954): 12.
5. Lindbergh, *Spirit of St. Louis,* 266; Berg, *Lindbergh,* 56, 90; Rowe, *Under My Wings,* 35 ("hung-over").
6. Lindbergh, *Spirit of St. Louis,* 251, 268, 407–409.
7. Fitzhugh Green's afterword to Lindbergh, "*We*" (New York: Grosset and Dunlap, 1927), 275.
8. Berg, *Lindbergh,* 84; Lindbergh, *Spirit of St. Louis,* 11.
9. Reeve Lindbergh, *Under a Wing: A Memoir* (New York: Simon and Schuster, 1998), 26–37; Lindbergh, *Spirit of St. Louis,* 23–24.
10. Lindbergh, *Spirit of St. Louis,* 31 ("some flight"); Wright, "Airship Safe: Air Motoring No More Dangerous than Land Motoring," Cairo, Ill., *Bulletin,* March 25, 1909.
11. Lindbergh, *Spirit of St. Louis,* 83, 87, 191, 203, 227.
12. [Harm Jon van der Linde,] "How We Built Slim's 60-Day Wonder," *Air and Space Smithsonian* 2 (April–May 1987): 92–95 (quotations); Donald Hall, "Technical Preparation of the Airplane 'Spirit of St. Louis,'" National Advisory Committee for Aeronautics (hereafter, NACA) Technical Note No. 257 (typescript, 1937), p. 5, file 001313, NASAHO; Lindbergh, *Spirit of St. Louis,* 128; Dominick A. Pisano and F. Robert van der Linden, *Charles Lindbergh and the Spirit of St. Louis* (New York: Harry N. Abrams, 2002), 52 (spinner).
13. Bob Buck, *North Star over My Shoulder* (New York: Simon & Schuster, 2002), 42.
14. Lindbergh, *Spirit of St. Louis,* 299, 340–41, 389, 424, 466–67.

15. Ibid. 88, 362 (instability). For examples of close calls, see also pages 216, 268, 284, 308, 412, 473.
16. Ibid., 495, 501, 548; Berg, *Lindbergh,* 131, 135. "There is one thing I long to know," King George V asked Lindbergh when they met in England. "How did you pee?" (Reporters often asked the same question.) Lindbergh, blushing, explained that he had used an aluminum container and that he had dropped it over the outskirts of Paris: "I was not going to be caught with that thing on me at Le Bourget!" Lloyd Shearer, "Charles Lindbergh Flew the Atlantic 50 Years Ago," *Washington Post,* March 13, 1977, *Parade* section, 7.
17. Lauren D. Lyman, "How Lindbergh Wrote a Book," *Bee-Hive* 29 (Summer 1954): 20 (ten drafts); Charles Lindbergh biographical file 001316, NASAHO; Claude Witze, "Lindbergh's Journalistic Flight," *Air Force Magazine* 60 (May 1977): 40, 45; Laurence Goldstein, "Lindbergh in 1927: The Response of Poets to the Poem of Fact," in *Prospects: An Annual of American Cultural Studies,* vol. 5, ed. Jack Salzman (New York: Burt Franklin, 1980), 294, 303; Thomas V. DiBacco, "A Hero's Welcome for Flier," *Washington Times,* May 20, 1987; "Why the World Makes Lindbergh Its Hero," *Literary Digest* 93 (June 25, 1927): 5; Berg, *Lindbergh,* 170; "Lindbergh's Unhappy Lot," *Minneapolis Daily Star,* August 29, 1927; "'Lindbergh for President,'" *New York Times,* January 13, 1928.
18. Lindbergh to Daniel Guggenheim, August 20 and September 18, 1927, box 2, Harry Frank Guggenheim Papers, Library of Congress, Mauscript Division, Washington, D.C.; Charles Lindbergh, *Autobiography of Values,* 310 (quotation), 312.
19. R. E. G. Davies, *Charles Lindbergh: An Airman, His Aircraft, and His Great Flights* (McLean, Va.: Paladwr Press, 1997), 10 (117 flights); "Alumnus Recalls Lindbergh's Landing," Randolph Macon College *Bulletin* 48 (May 1977): 3.
20. John M. Ward, "The Meaning of Lindbergh's Flight," *American Quarterly* 10 (Spring 1958): 3–16; Alden Whitman, "The Price of Fame," *New York Times Magazine,* May 19, 1977, 14–15 (Merton); F. Scott Fitzgerald, "Echoes of the Jazz Age," in *The Crack-Up,* ed. Edmund Wilson (New York: New Directions, 1945), 20.
21. Berg, *Lindbergh,* 78; Smith, *By the Seat of My Pants,* 232.
22. Back-cover cigarette ads, *Time,* November 25, 1935, *Life,* August 14, 1939; Elgen M. Long and Marie K. Long, *Amelia Earhart: The Mystery Solved* (New York: Simon and Schuster, 1999), 47, 49; Berg, *Lindbergh,* 162–63, 168.
23. Witze, "Lindbergh's Journalistic Flight," 44; Harold A. Holbrook, "Why Not Fly?" *Outlook* 146 (June 29, 1927): 287; "A Brief History of the Air Mail Service" (typescript, 1940), p. 27, box 3, PODR; *Aircraft Year Book, 1928,* 47, 49; "Aircraft," *Standard Trade and Securities Service* 51 (February 15, 1929), p. U-2; "Survey Shows Airplane Plants All Running at Capacity," *Sales Management* 13 (July 23, 1927): 134; Berg, *Lindbergh,* 171; "10,472,024 Miles Flown on Nation's Airways," *New York Times,* March 11, 1929; G. Ray Boggs to Roscoe Turner, June 4, 1929, box 85, Roscoe Turner Papers, AHC ("Yellow").
24. Berg, *Lindbergh,* chap. 7; Richard P. Hallion, "Philanthropy and Flight: Guggenheim Support of Aeronautics, 1925–1930," *Aerospace Historian* 28 (Spring 1981): 13.
25. Davies, *Charles Lindbergh,* 28–29; Douglas J. Ingells, *The Plane that Changed the World: A Biography of the DC-3* (Fallbrook, Calif.: Aero Publishers, 1966), 35;

Lindbergh to G. E. Woods Humphery, December 1, 1937, Charles Lindbergh biographical file, NASAHO; Brock, *Flying the Oceans,* 230.

26. Lindbergh's foreword to Michael Collins, *Carrying the Fire: An Astronaut's Journeys* (New York: Farrar, Straus and Giroux, 1974), xii; Berg, *Lindbergh,* 210–14; "Lindbergh Backs Rocket Travel," *Aero Field* 4 (July 1937): 165 ("freedom").
27. Alden Whitman, "The Return of Charles Lindbergh," *New York Times Magazine,* May 23, 1971, 59; Russell W. Fridley, "A Life Marked by Continued Growth," *Minneapolis Tribune,* May 15, 1977 (Volkswagen); obituary in *New York Times,* August 27, 1974.
28. Lindbergh, *Spirit of St. Louis,* 469; Melvin Altshuler, "Lindbergh Cites Threat to Survival," *Washington Post,* December 12, 1949; "Speech at the IAS Honors Night Dinner" (typescript, 1954), 7–8 (quotation), file 001307, NASAHO; Lindbergh, "Is Civilization Progress?" *Reader's Digest* 85 (July 1964): 68; "A Letter from Lindbergh," *Life* 67 (July 4, 1969): 60A.
29. Lindbergh, *Wartime Journals,* xv; and "Challenge," *Congressional Record* 106 (May 19, 1960): 9887.
30. Whitman, "Return of Charles Lindbergh," 49 (snowmobiles); Lindbergh's 1974 foreword to John Nance, *The Gentle Tasaday: A Stone Age People in the Philippine Rain Forest* (reprint, Boston: David R. Godine, 1988), x.
31. Leonard Mosley, *Lindbergh: A Biography* (Garden City: New York: Doubleday, 1976), 354–55; Marilyn Bender and Selig Altschul, *The Chosen Instrument* (New York: Simon and Schuster, 1982), 459–61.
32. Peggy Noonan, *When Character Was King: A Story of Ronald Reagan* (New York: Viking, 2001), 30; Lindbergh to Guggenheim, March 16, 1960, Harry Frank Guggenheim Papers, LCMD; Leonard S. Reich, "From the Spirit of St. Louis to the SST: Charles Lindbergh, Technology, and Environment," *Technology and Culture* 36 (1995): 373–74; Lindbergh, "Is Civilization Progress?" 69 ("birds"); Juan Trippe, "Charles A. Lindbergh and World Travel," talk before Wings Club, May 20, 1977, p. 5, box 48, Pan American World Airways, Inc., Records, Otto G. Richter Library, University of Miami, Coral Gables, Florida (hereafter, PAWAR), "facts".
33. Schlesinger, "Lindbergh: Hero and Victim," *Washinton Post Book World* 4 (September 27, 1970): 3; Reeve Lindbergh, *Under a Wing,* 15, 96 (deafness); *New York Times,* July 27, 1972 (op ed); Berg, *Lindbergh,* 560 (funeral). Lindbergh's racial views also began shifting during World War II, a conflict whose annihilatory racism he found appalling. Cf. "Aviation, Geography, and Race," *Reader's Digest* 35 (November 1939): 64–67, and Lindbergh, *Wartime Journals,* 853–54, 997–98.

Chapter 6

1. Harold Holbrook, "Why Not Fly?" *Outlook* 146 (June 29, 1927): 286 ("bogy"); "Is it Safe to Fly? Some Say No," *Holiday* 46 (July 1969): 53.
2. Laurence Gonzales, "Airline Safety: A Special Report," *Playboy* (June 1980), excerpt in box 402, PAWAR (faces); Joe Brennan to Carl Solberg, April 16, 1977, box 14, Carl Solberg Collection, AHC (Rockne); Rickenbacker, *Rickenbacker,* 237.
3. *New York Times,* April 1, 1931; P. P. Willis, *Your Future is in the Air: The Story of How*

American Airlines Made People Air-Travel Conscious (New York: Prentice-Hall, 1940), 74–75; Charles D. Bright, "Aviation Literature—A Changing Art," *Aerospace Historian* 31 (March 1984): 68–69; Harry F. Guggenheim, *The Seven Skies* (New York: G. P. Putnam's Sons, 1930), 102 (Rogers).

4. George H. Gallup, *The Gallup Poll,* vol. 1, *1935–1948* (New York: Random House, 1972), 156; Holmes letter and related clippings kindly furnished by Sheril Whitehouse; "Nationwide Public Attitude Survey—June 1942—Among Boys of Enlistment Age, Parents and Girls," microfilm reel 338, J. Walter Thompson Company Archives, Special Collections Library, Duke University (hereafter, JWTA).
5. "Pan American World Airways: Survey to Determine Airline Preferences in Nine Cities" (typescript, 1945), 33, box 465, PAWAR; Ross A. McFarland, *Human Factors in Air Transportation* (New York: McGraw-Hill, 1953), 22.
6. Solberg, *Conquest of the Skies,* 109, 221; Vance Packard, *The Hidden Persuaders* (New York: David McKay, 1957), 65–66.
7. Roger Bilstein, "Technology and Commerce," 405; Buck, *North Star,* 78.
8. Eugene Vidal, "Love of Flying," in *Anthology: Selected Essays from Thirty Years of The New York Review of Books,* ed. Robert B. Silvers and Barbara Epstein (New York: New York Review of Books, 2001), 275.
9. F. Robert van der Linden, *Airlines and Air Mail: The Post Office and the Birth of the Commercial Aviation Industry* (Lexington: University Press of Kentucky, 2002); Rickenbacker, *Rickenbacker,* 188; W. David Lewis, "Edward V. Rickenbacker's Reaction to Civil Aviation in the 1930s: A Hidden Dimension," in *Reconsidering a Century of Flight,* ed. Roger D. Launius and Janet R. Daly Bednarek (Chapel Hill: University of North Carolina Press, 2003), 124; Komons, *Bonfires to Beacons,* 261 ("butchery"); Henry Ladd Smith, *Airways: The History of Commercial Aviation in the United States* (New York: Alfred A. Knopf, 1942), 255. The 1930 and 1934 legislation is in *Statutes at Large,* vol. 46, part 1, 259–60; and vol. 48, part 1, 933–39.
10. Janet R. Daly Bednarek, *America's Airports: Airfield Development, 1918–1947* (College Station: Texas A&M University Press, 2001), chaps. 4, 6; "Nation's Air Havens Show Gain to 2,656," *New York Times,* January 5, 1941; Rickenbacker, *Rickenbacker,* 189; van der Linden, *Airlines and Air Mail,* 290. The Civil Aeronautics Administration legislation is in *Statutes at Large,* vol. 52, 973–1030. The four New Deal agencies were the FERA, CWA, WPA, and NYA.
11. John B. Rae, *Climb to Greatness: The American Aircraft Industry, 1920–1960* (Cambridge, Mass.: MIT Press, 1968), 98, 103, 114–15, 124; Aircraft Industries Association of America, "Aircraft Manufacturing in the United States," in *The History of the American Aircraft Industry: An Anthology,* ed. G. R. Simonson (Cambridge, Mass.: MIT Press, 1968), 163; "Text of Roosevelt Bond Drive Talk," *New York Times,* June 13, 1944 ("crazy"); "Half a Million Workers," *Fortune* (March 1941): 96.
12. Bednarek, *America's Airports,* 116–17, 155–56; Wilson and Bryan, *Air Transportation,* 567; Dominick A. Pisano, *To Fill the Skies with Pilots: The Civilian Pilot Training Program, 1939–1946* (Washington, D.C.: Smithsonian Institution Press, 2001), 127.
13. Gilbert Grosvenor, "Flying," *National Geographic* 63 (May 1933): 587; *Aircraft Year Book, 1933,* 58.

14. "Progress in Aircraft Performance" (typescript, 1930), p. 1, box 41, NACAGC (doubled range).
15. Wilson and Bryan, *Air Transportation*, 576 (budget); Heppenheimer, *Turbulent Skies*, chaps. 2–3; Ruth Schwartz Cowan, *A Social History of American Technology* (New York: Oxford University Press, 1997), chap. 11.
16. Glines, *Roscoe Turner*, 205 (quotation), and chaps. 7–8; Ingells, *The Plane that Changed the World*, 75.
17. Ingells, *The Plane that Changed the World*, 72, 93; Davies, *Airlines of the United States*, 80–93, 608; Ernest K. Gann, *Ernest K. Gann's Flying Circus* (New York: Macmillan, 1974), 213–14 (speed, seating); Gottdiener, *Life in the Air*, chap. 26 ("bi-coastalism").
18. *Aircraft Year Book, 1930*, chap. 4; Gann, *Ernest K. Gann's Flying Circus*, 75 (quotation), and chap. 10; Lindbergh, *Wartime Journals*, 706–707, italics in original.
19. Rowe, *Under My Wings*, 123; Brock, *Flying the Oceans*, 36–37 (jumped out); Solberg, *Conquest of the Skies*, 129–31; Buck, *North Star*, 133.
20. Roger Bilstein, *Flight in America*, 99; "Defends Safety in Flying," *New York Times*, September 26, 1936; Trippe, "Building the Airways of America," offprint of May 2, 1940, address before the U.S. Chamber of Commerce, p. 10, box 120, AAIAA.
21. The data from which these statistics are derived are in Wilson and Bryan, *Air Transportation*, 178, 265, 268, 274, 280, 443. The average block speeds (based on terminal to terminal travel times) are in B. A. McDonald and J. L. Drew, *Air Transportation in the Immediate Post-War Period* (Buffalo: Curtiss-Wright Corporation, 1944), 36. (I used 1932 data to estimate the average speeds and load factors, for which 1930 data were unavailable.) Third fewer: United States Department of Commerce, Bureau of the Census, *Historical Statistics of the United States*, part 2 (Washington, D.C.: Government Printing Office, 1975), 769.
22. August Loeb, "More Trips by Air," *New York Times*, June 16, 1940 (fares); H. J. E. Reid to G. W. Lewis, March 19, 1934, box 254, NACAGC (spelling corrected); Helen E. McLaughlin, *Walking on Air: An Informal History of Inflight Service of Seven U.S. Airlines* (Glendale, Calif.: Aviation Book Co., 1986), 55, 159.
23. Buck, *North Star*, 110.
24. Stinson Aircraft correspondence with G. W. Lewis regarding oxygen deprivation, February 12, 1935, box 254, NACAGC.
25. Merrill Lynch, Pierce, Fenner and Beane, Inc., *Airlines 1945* (New York: Merrill Lynch, Pierce, Fenner and Beane, 1945), 2.
26. Davies, *Airlines of the United States*, 205–206, 291, 326; Robert W. Rummel, *Howard Hughes and TWA* (Washington, D.C.: Smithsonian Institution Press, 1991) chap. 4; Peter Harry Brown and Pat H. Broeske, *Howard Hughes: The Untold Story* (New York: Dutton, 1996), 183; "Airliner Crosses Country in 7 Hours, Setting a Record," *New York Times*, April 18, 1944; and Johnson interview, January 18, 1977, p. 4, box 18, Carl Solberg Collection, AHC. TWA promised fifty-seven seats, but I am following the fifty-four given in Davies, *Airlines of the United States*, 659.
27. John B. Lansing, *The Travel Market, 1964–1965* (Ann Arbor: University of Michigan Press, 1965), 15; Buck, *North Star*, 152 (quotation).
28. Buck, *North Star*, 76; Solberg, *Conquest of the Skies*, 109; "Wives to Ride Free on Three Airlines," *New York Times*, January 28, 1938.

29. "Movie Entertains Air Travelers Flying from St. Paul to Chicago," *New York Times*, February 18, 1929; McLaughlin, *Walking on Air*, 7–8, 18, 166 et passim; Solberg, *Conquest of the Skies*, 215.
30. Henry LaCossitt, "The Woman's Touch," in *Airways of America*, ed. Poyntz Tyler (New York: H. W. Wilson, 1958), 47–50; joint Russell Bowen-Gay Smith interview, January 13, 1977, p. 7, box 19, Carl Solberg Collection, AHC (girdle).
31. Courtwright, *Violent Land*, 133–36; Abby Mansur letter of May 28, 1853, in *Let Them Speak for Themselves: Women in the American West, 1849–1900*, ed. Christiane Fischer (Hamden, Conn.: Archon, 1977), 52 (quotation, spelling altered).
32. LaCossitt, "Woman's Touch," 49; undated American Airlines press release, p. 4, and Marilyn Moeller Wilson interview, June 20, 1976, p. 3, both in box 29, Carl Solberg Collection, AHC; Keith Lovegrove, *Airline: Identity, Design, and Culture* (London: Laurence King, 2000), 32.
33. Charles Goodrum and Helen Dalrymple, *Advertising in America: The First 200 Years* (New York: Harry N. Abrams, 1990), 117–23; Michael Maxtone-Graham, "The Air Campaign," *Air and Space Smithsonian* 7 (April–May 1992): 62–66.
34. Stanley E. Knauss, "Coaxing Folks to Fly," *Sales Management* 21 (January 1930): 67–68, 87; "Gives Ad Theme for Air Travel," *New York Times*, September 27, 1937 ("Tell them"); Alice Rogers Hager, "More Women Take to Air," *New York Times*, July 11, 1937 ("tempting").
35. "Woman,"*New York Times*, August 3, 1926; Guggenheim, *Seven Skies*, 10–11; Roger Bilstein, "Travel by Air: The American Context," *Archiv fur Sozialgeschichte* 33 (1993): 279–80.
36. Anne Millbrooke, "Humorist in Flight," *Air Power History* 41 (Fall 1993): 42–51; Solberg, *Conquest of the Skies*, 222; McLaughlin, *Walking on Air*, 78 ("My Day").
37. John M. Ward, "The Meaning of Lindbergh's Flight," *American Quarterly* 10 (Spring 1958): 9 (quoting Theodore Roosevelt Jr.); Patricia Nelson Limerick, *The Legacy of Conquest: The Unbroken Past of the American West* (New York: Norton, 1987), 84; Richard White, *"It's Your Misfortune and None of My Own": A History of the American West* (Norman: University of Oklahoma Press, 1991), 57.
38. Addresses and speeches folder, box 11, Eugene L. Vidal Collection, AHC, quotations from typescript addresses of August 15, 1934, p. 2 ("romance"), and April 16, 1934, p. 1; Joseph J. Corn, *The Winged Gospel: America's Romance with Aviation, 1900–1950* (New York: Oxford University Press, 1983), 98–104; Susan Butler, *East to the Dawn: The Life of Amelia Earhart* (Reading, Mass.: Addison-Wesley, 1997), 294–95 (lovers).

Chapter 7

1. "Air Currents," *New York Times*, May 4, 1941; Lindbergh, "Speech at the IAS Honors Night Dinner" (typescript, 1954), 4, Lindbergh biographical file 001307, NASAHO; William H. Hessler, "America's Merchant Marine of the Air: A Vital National Asset," *United States Naval Institute Proceedings* 85 (May 1959): 48–63.
2. Donald M. Pattillo, *A History in the Making: 80 Turbulent Years in the American General Aviation Industry* (New York: McGraw-Hill, 1998), 43 (staticstics), and

chap. 3; Office of War Information, *American Air Transport* (Washington, D.C.: Government Printing Office, 1943), 6; Donald R. Whitnah, *Safer Airways: Federal Control of Aviation, 1926–1966* (Ames: Iowa State University Press, 1966), 179–80, 186; John M. Wilson, "The Shape of Things to Come: The Military Impact of World War II on Civil Aviation," *Aerospace Historian* 28 (December 1981): 266.

3. Office of War Information, *American Air Transport,* 5; Wesley Frank Craven and James Lea Cate, eds., *The Army Air Forces in World War II,* vol. 7 (Chicago: University of Chicago Press, 1958), 21; "Priorities for Air Transportation," January 15, 1942, file 132.3, Central Files of the Civil Aeronautics Administration, 1926–43, RG 237, NAII; Solberg, *Conquest of the Skies,* 277–75; Lloyd M. Wilson interview, February 27, 1977, p. 3, box 18, Carl Solberg Collection, AHC (missionaries); Thomas M. Coffey, *Iron Eagle: The Turbulent Life of General Curtis LeMay* (New York: Crown, 1986), 175. Excess "airmail" was also diverted to trains, a sore point with those who had paid the extra postage.
4. H. H. Arnold, "Mobilizing for War," in *Airways of America,* ed. Poyntz Tyler (New York: H. W. Wilson, 1958), 126–27; *Aircraft Year Book, 1943–1945,* chaps. 8, 6, and 4, respectively; Office of War Information, *American Air Transport,* 1 (quarter); National Airlines, *Annual Report, 1945,* box 50, PAWAR; Lindbergh, *Wartime Journal,* 925; Merrill Lynch, Pierce, Fenner and Beane, *Airlines 1945,* 20.
5. Office of War Information, *American Air Transport,* 3 (biological cargos); Brock, *Flying the Oceans,* 184–85; Buck, *North Star,* 285; and interviews with Mr. and Mrs. Al Mitchell, February 24, 1978, p. 1 (American), and E. O. "Oz" Cocke, January 17, 1977, p. 5 (TWA), both box 18, Carl Solberg Collection, AHC.
6. Air Transport Command operations: Oliver La Farge, *The Eagle in the Egg* (reprint, New York: Arno Press, 1972), esp. chap. 11; Craven and Cate, *Army Air Forces in World War II,* vol. 7, esp. chap. 1; Noël Riley Fitch, *Appetite for Life: The Biography of Julia Child* (New York: Doubleday, 1997), 106; and interviews with C. R. Smith, May 4, 1977, p. 12, box 18, and Sam Irwin, December 30, 1977, p. 3, box 19 (seventy hours) both in Carl Solberg Collection, AHC.
7. Grover Loening, "Airplanes for Peace," *Atlantic Monthly* 172 (November 1943): 44.
8. Personal Diary of Weldon E. Rhoades, vol. 1, June 18, 1942, box 1, Rhoades Collection, AHC; Olivier Razac, *Barbed Wire: A Political History,* trans. Jonathan Kneight (New York: New Press, 2002); Gudrun Schwarz, *Die nationalsozialistischen Lager* (Frankfurt: Campus Verlag, 1990), 221–22 (ten thousand). This figure includes facilities of all types, from small labor camps to death mills like Treblinka.
9. Stephen E. Ambrose, *The Wild Blue: The Men and Boys Who Flew the B-24s Over Germany* (New York: Simon and Schuster, 2001), 151 (Heller); Chuck Yeager, *Yeager: An Autobiography* (New York: Bantam, 1985), 68; Edward Diemente, personal communication, November 20, 2000.
10. Solberg, *Conquest of the Skies,* 173–74; Mark K. Wells, *Courage and Air Warfare: The Allied Aircrew Experience in the Second World War* (London: Frank Cass, 1995), 8 ("frank"), 63, 174; "Naval Aviation Cadet Survey, August 1942" (typescript, 1942), 5, 14, and attached August 31, 1942, memo, microfilm reel 338, JWTA; Ambrose, *Wild Blue,* 232–33; Yeager, *Yeager: An Autobiography,* 69; Robert Morgan,

with Ron Powers, *The Man Who Flew the Memphis Belle: Memoir of a World War II Bomber Pilot* (New York: Dutton, 2001), "underwear" on page 98.

11. Solberg, *Conquest of the Skies*, 275 (percentages); McLaughlin, *Walking on Air*, 60 (quotation). Prewar passenger demographics varied by season and route. Cross-country flights, for example, had heavier male majorities than international flights. *Aircraft Year Book, 1931*, 226.
12. *Sixteenth Census of the United States, 1940*, vol. 3: *The Labor Force*, part 1: *United States Summary* (Washington, D.C.: Government Printing Office, 1943), 75; Barbara Craig, "The Day Bob Fogg Flew under the Bridge with His Friend Eleanor Roosevelt," *Yankee* 37 (November 1973): 175 (quotation); Blanche Wiesen Cook, *Eleanor Roosevelt*, vol. 1: *1884–1933* (New York: Viking, 1992), 363–64. Eleanor flew "with excitement and pleasure" on at least one another occasion, when Tom Boyd let her take the controls of his Stinson. Boyd interview of February 7 and 8, 1979, p. 1, box 19, Carl Solberg Collection, AHC.
13. Craven and Cate, *Army Air Forces in World War II*, 6:528, 530, 535; Solberg, *Conquest of the Skies*, 215; Robert Daley, *An American Saga: Juan Trippe and His Pan American Empire* (New York: Random House, 1980), 469 ("male preserve"); "Eddie Rickenbacker Looks Ahead," *Fortune* 33 (March 1941): 119 ("more work"); "Women—Ground Jobs, 1941–60," box 259, PAWAR; Whitnah, *Safer Skyways*, 178. Pan Am's Lloyd Wilson thought the change was also prompted by stewardesses' popularity on other airlines. After the war, Pan Am hired as many as seven hundred a year, each with an average career length, including training, of twenty-four months. Interview of February 27, 1977, pp. 3–4, box 18, Carl Solberg Collection, AHC.
14. Craven and Cate, *Army Air Forces in World War II*, 6:523–34; "Negro Aviators," *Negro Statistical Bulletin*, no. 3 (typescript, September 1940), p. 1, file 060A, CFCAA, 1926–43, RG 237, NAII; Stanley Sandler, *Segregated Skies: All-Black Combat Squadrons of WWII* (Washington, D.C.: Smithsonian Institution Press, 1992); and Lawrence P. Scott and William M. Womack Sr., *Double V: The Civil Rights Struggle of the Tuskegee Airmen* (East Lansing: Michigan State University Press, 1994), 217, 226. There were twenty-one licensed black pilots in 1936, including only five with limited commercial or transport licenses.
15. Craven and Cate, *Army Air Forces in World War II*, 6:xxv, 423; "Total Combat Airplanes on Hand in Overseas Theaters," roll 268, Henry Arnold Papers, LCMD.
16. "Our Aircraft Industry is Expanding Rapidly," *New York Times*, February 11, 1940; Aircraft Industries Association of America, "Aircraft Manufacturing in the United States," in *The History of the American Aircraft Industry: An Anthology*, ed. G. R. Simonson (Cambridge, Mass.: MIT Press, 1968), 163; Constance Bowman and Clara Marie Allen, *Slacks and Calluses: Our Summer in a Bomber Factory* (reprint, Washington, D.C.: Smithsonian Institution Press, 1999), 101 (more money); Wayne Biddle, *Barons of the Sky* (New York: Simon and Schuster, 1991), 271; Craven and Cate, *Army Air Forces in World War II*, 6:501–505; Solberg, *Conquest of the Skies*, 291; Paul C. Holinger, *Violent Deaths in the United States: An Epidemiologic Study of Suicide, Homicide, and Accidents* (New York: Guilford, 1987), 208.

17. *Forty Years, 1903–1943* (Dearborn: Ford Motor Co., 1943); Robert Lacey, *Ford: The Men and Machine* (Boston: Little, Brown, 1986), 292–93 (Sorensen).
18. Tami Davis Biddle, *Rhetoric and Reality in Air Warfare: The Evolution of British and American Ideas About Strategic Bombing* (Princeton: Princeton University Press, 2002), esp. chap. 5; James Dugan and Carroll Stewart, *Ploesti: The Great Ground-Air Battle of 1 August 1943*, rev. ed. (Washington, D.C.: Brassey's, 2002), 22; "Life History of the Average 8th AF Heavy Bomber," roll 268, Henry Arnold Papers, LCMD; Gerald Astor, *The Mighty Eighth: The Air War in Europe as Told by the Men Who Fought It* (New York: Donald I. Fine, 1997), 420 (casualties); Ambrose, *Wild Blue*, 110, 181. The typical bomber actually took off on 20.8 missions, but 6.2 of these were aborted. It was also battle-damaged 6.5 times.
19. Wells, *Courage and Air Warfare*, 66 (Ryan).
20. Morgan, with Powers, *Memphis Belle*, 245–46.
21. Robin Neillands, *The Bomber War: The Allied Air Offensive Against Nazi Germany* (Woodstock, N.Y.: Overlook Press, 2001), 224–26, 256, 294; Buckley, *Air Power in the Age of Total War*, chap. 6; Astor, *Mighty Eighth*, chap. 22; Gill Robb Wilson, "This is It!" and "Aircraft Plant in Paris Metro," *New York Herald Tribune*, March 15, 1944, and September 15, 1944; Barrett Tillman, "Age and the Fighter Ace," *Aerospace Historian* 27 (June 1981): 112; "P-47 Operations," roll 268, Henry Arnold Papers, LCMD; Richard Overy, *Interrogations: The Nazi Elite in Allied Hands, 1945* (New York: Viking, 2001), 147–48, 281 (quotation), 282, 298, 303.
22. Buckley, *Air Power in the Age of Total War*, chap. 7; Henry H. Arnold, *Global Mission* (1949; reprint, Blue Ridge Summit, Pa.: TAB Books, 1989), 382 (Kenney).
23. Morgan, with Powers, *Memphis Belle*, 318 (120 hours); E. Bartlett Kerr, *Flames Over Tokyo: The U.S. Army Air Forces' Incendiary Campaign Against Japan, 1944–1945* (New York: Donald I. Fine, 1991); Personal Diary of Weldon E. Rhoades, vol. 3, August 30, 1945, box 1, Rhoades Collection, AHC (tin); Richard Overy, *Why the Allies Won* (New York: Norton, 1995), 132 (absentees).
24. Bet memoranda for July 16 and 19 (typed August 4), 1945, roll 268, Henry Arnold Papers, LCMD; Arnold, *Global Mission*, 598; Richard Rhodes, *Dark Sun: The Making of the Hydrogen Bomb* (New York: Simon and Schuster, 1995), 227 (LeMay).
25. Joseph Stalin, *On the Great Patriotic War of the Soviet Union* (London: Hutchinson, 1943), 19; Henry Arnold, "If War Comes Again," *New York Times Magazine*, Nov. 18, 1945, 5, 38, 39; Edward Nellor, "Arnold Foresees Atom Bombs Radar-aimed from Space Ships," *New York Sun*, November 12, 1945; Arnold, "U.S. Air Power, Limited," *American Legion Magazine* 43 (August 1947): 12–13, 28–30; Dwight D. Eisenhower, *Messages and Papers of the Presidents: Dwight D. Eisenhower, 1960–1961* (Washington, D.C.: Government Printing Office, 1961), 1038.
26. Arnold, *Global Mission*, 599–600 (quotation); "Disposition of Drugs . . . ," file 0450-7A, box 18, Records of the Drug Enforcement Administration, RG 170-74-4, NAII; Solberg, *Conquest of the Skies*, 314.
27. Karen S. Miller, *The Voice of Business: Hill and Knowlton and Postwar Public Relations* (Chapel Hill: University of North Carolina Press, 1999), chap. 2; joint interview of Haakon Gulbransen and R. J. Celestre, January 24, 1977, p. 7 (prostitutes), and interview of Hal Hibbard, January 19, 1977, p. 7, both box 18, Carl Solberg

Collection, AHC; "Aircraft Manufacturing in the United States," in Simonson, *History of the American Aircraft Industry,* 167 ($9 billion).

28. Hessler, "America's Merchant Marine of the Air, 48–63; Beverley M. Bowie, "MATS: America's Long Arm of the Air," *National Geographic* 111 (March 1957): 283–317.
29. Bednarek, *Americas Airports,* 164–65; Roscoe Turner, Senate testimony, June 1, 1945, box 120, AAIAA (three million); Ludwig Lederer interview, March 14, 1977, p. 1, box 18, Carl Solberg Collection, AHC ("normal").
30. C. R. Smith interview, May 4, 1977, pp. 5–6, box 18, Carl Solberg Collection, AHC.
31. Priester to Juan Trippe, March 1, 1943, "PAA Airplanes," box 54, PAWAR; Willis Lipscomb interview, box 19, November 19, 1976, p. 9, Carl Solberg Collection, AHC. In these interviews Carl Solberg often asked whether Lindbergh's Paris flight and jet airliners had been the decisive events—one might say the historical bookends—of commercial aviation's development. What struck me, as I reread them a quarter century later, was that World War II, with its airport building, pilot training, aeronautical advances, attitudinal changes, and overseas experience, deserved at least equal weight.
32. Buck, *North Star,* 30 (quotation), 198; "All Mother Earth's," accessed at http://scriptorium.lib.duke.edu/dynaweb/adaccess/transportation/airlines1946/%40Generic_BookTextView/714, July 13, 2002.
33. McFarland, *Human Factors,* 17, 27; Solberg, *Conquest of the Skies,* 328–30 (nonskeds).
34. Harry C. Stonecipher, "Airplane 101: A Primer on Aviation," http://www.boeing.com/news/speeches/1997/971015.html; McFarland, *Human Factors,* 677 (airsickness).
35. "What's Wrong with the Airlines," *Fortune* 34 (August 1946): 73–78, 190–202, 199 (quotation).
36. Blackburn to Carl Solberg, "M'aidez" [i.e., May 1], 1978, box 14, Carl Solberg Collection, AHC; Kirk, "March 1958 NYC System Public Relations Meeting: Ground Handling of Jets," p. 25, box 37, PAWAR.
37. Clayton Knight and K. S. Knight, *Plane Crash: The Mysteries of Major Air Disasters and How They Were Solved* (New York: Greenberg, 1958), 79, 81.
38. Safety and load-factor data: American Transport Association Office of Economics home page, http://www.airlines.org/econ/d.aspx?nid=1026. Airplane prices: Heppenheimer, *Turbulent Skies,* 115; Buck, *North Star,* 266; Davies, *Airlines of the United States,* 334.
39. "Today's Most Talked About Travel Bargain! Air Coach," accessed at http://scriptorium.lib.duke.edu/adaccess/T/T11/T1155-72dpi.jpeg, July 16, 2002; joint interview with Russell Bowen and Gay Smith, Jan. 13, 1977, box 19, Carl Solberg Collection, AHC ("cattle"); McFarland, *Human Factors,* 18.
40. Solberg, *Conquest of the Skies,* 345 ("ordinary"), 346 ("first"), and chap. 27; Juan Trippe, "Air Travel for Everybody," *Hartford Courant,* August 7, 1951; *The Jet Clipper* (1958), 2, 5 ("first overseas"), and "The Study of the Effects of the New Jet Planes" (typescript, March 28, 1956), 1 (westbound), both box 37, PAWAR; "Who Said It's a Man's World" (typescript, June 12, 1959), box 465, PAWAR. The 22 per-

cent figure is based on a random sample of the passenger ledger entries for 1932–34 (n = 1,982), box 49, PAWAR.

41. John B. Lansing and Ernest Lilienstein, *The Travel Market, 1955* (Ann Arbor: Survey Research Center, Institute for Social Research, University of Michigan, 1957), 28–29, 36–38; William A. Jordan, *Airline Regulation in America: Effects and Imperfections* (Baltimore: Johns Hopkins Press, 1970), 64–65, 75 (domestic coach); "Pan American World Airways Advertising Plan for 1957," in 1956 minutes folder, box 22, Review Board Records, JWTA; Virgil D. Reed, "Basic Trends in Population Marking Continued Growth," *Commercial and Financial Chronicle,* November 1, 1956; "Public Relations Meeting, 1958," typescript notes, box 285, PAWAR (newspapers).

Chapter 8

1. William E. MacDaniel, "Free Fall Culture," *Space World* V-8-260 (August 1985): 12.
2. Terri G. Jordan and Matti Kaups, *The American Backwoods Frontier* (Baltimore: Johns Hopkins University Press, 1989). Terry Jordan's subsequent book, *North American Cattle-Ranching Frontiers: Origins, Diffusion, and Differentiation* (Albuquerque: University of New Mexico Press, 1993), explores cultural blending in frontier pastoral zones.
3. Tom Crouch, *The Bishop's Boys: A Life of Wilbur and Orville Wright* (New York: W. W. Norton, 1989), 172 (quote), and chaps. 11–13.
4. "Roger Kahn in Plane Picks Bags from Roof," *New York Times,* April 22, 1931.
5. Henry Ford, "Never Has Been Airplane Engine [*sic*]," in *Aces of the Air,* ed. Joseph Lewis French (Springfield, Mass.: McLoughlin Bros., 1930), 266–67.
6. Francis Vivian Drake, "Pegasus Express," 1932 *Atlantic Monthly* reprint, p. 18, box 2, PODR; Johnston with Barton, *Tex Johnston,* 187; Corley McDarment, "Martyrs of the Air Conquest," *Popular Mechanics* 55 (January 1931), 52; "Aeronautical Rules of the Air and Aviation Sayings," accessed at http://www.betrimtoo.com/airrules.htm, July 23, 2002; Lindbergh, *Spirit of St. Louis,* 263; Buck, *North Star,* 33, 45, 69, 111, 140, 154; Rowe, *Under My Wings,* 151; James Gleick, *Faster: The Acceleration of Just About Everything* (New York: Pantheon, 1999), 25–26 (Wright).
7. Frederick Graham, "Winged Hostess," *New York Times Magazine,* January 7, 1940, 15. Some historians, notably Robert Wohl, have used the concept of a "culture of aviation" to describe the high cultural response of artists and intellectuals to powered flight in the early twentieth century. I am using the term in a different, "low" sense to describe the evolving collective wisdom for safe and comfortable flying.
8. Bender and Altschul, *The Chosen Instrument,* 156; Langewiesche, *Inside the Sky,* 84–87; Heppenheimer, *Turbulent Skies,* 122–23; Lindbergh, *Wartime Journals,* 716.
9. McLaughlin, *Walking on Air,* 109; "Contact," *New York Times,* July 11, 1937.
10. Jack Stark, *Air Hostess* (Boston: Bellman, 1946), 14–15; Thomas W. Ennis, "Edwin A. Link, 77, Invented Instrument Flight Simulator," *New York Times,* September 9, 1981.
11. Buck, *North Star,* 45, 158 (quotation).
12. Johnston and Barton, *Tex Johnston,* 45 (P-39); "Excerpt from Lewis Report 53–11" (typescript, 1953), box 9, Harry Frank Guggenheim Papers, LCMD (B-29 flaps); Ricardo Alonso-Zaldivar and Eric Malnic, "Rudder Shifts Can Spell Doom, Pilots Warned," *Los Angeles Times,* February 9, 2002.

13. Johnston and Barton, *Tex Johnston,* 20; Buck, *North Star,* 250 (hurt feelings); Gerald Astor, *The Mighty Eighth: The Air War in Europe as Told by the Men Who Fought It* (New York: Donald I. Fine, 1997), 180–81; Neillands, *The Bomber War,* 168–69.
14. David F. Noble, *Forces of Production: A Social History of Industrial Automation* (New York: Alfred A. Knopf, 1984), esp. chap. 10; "ALPA Extended Disability Coverage," *The Airline Pilot* 23 (February 1954), 16; Buck, *North Star,* 38; J. G. Constantino interview, August 3, 1997, p. 1, box 18, Carl Solberg Collection, AHC (scarf).
15. Little, "The Passing of the Pioneer Days," in *Aces of the Air,* ed. French, 169, 171–72.
16. Buck, *North Star,* 101; M. O. "Mo" Bowen interview, January 15, 1977, pp. 8–9, box 19, Carl Solberg Collection, AHC; Smith, *Pilot's Progress* (typescript, n.d.), p. 306, box 8, Dean C. Smith Collection, AHC.
17. Solberg, *Conquest of the Skies,* chap. 25; Buck, *North Star,* 95; Heppenheimer, *Turbulent Skies,* chap. 7.
18. Brock, *Flying the Oceans,* 216 (quotation), 218.
19. MacKinlay Kantor, "A Girl Named Frankie," *Reader's Digest* 88 (May 1966): 86–90.
20. "Routine Stuff," accessed at http://scriptorium.lib.duke.edu/adaccess/T/T23/T2317–72dpi.jpeg, July 26, 2002.
21. Handwritten notes, November 23, 1959, box 22, Review Board Records, JWTA (Northeast Airlines); "This is the Story of News and How You Can Make It Work for You" (undated brochure, 1955?), "Public Relations Dept. History," box 285, PAWAR.
22. Wolfe, *The Right Stuff,* chap. 3; Vance Packard, *The Hidden Persuaders* (New York: David McKay, 1957), 64–66.
23. Walter Bullock interview, August 12, 1976, p. 5, and joint interview with Haakon Gulbransen and R. J. Celestre, January 24, 1977, p. 7, both box 18, Carl Solberg Collection, AHC; Ed Modes, ed., *The ALPA Story* (n.p.: Air Line Pilots Association, 1954), 5 (quotation); Personal Diary of Weldon E. Rhoades, vol. 3, July 7, 1945, box 1, Rhoades Collection, AHC (abstinence).
24. Hank Henry, "Air Travel Has Really Taken Off," accessed at http://www.mailtribune.com/primet/archive/1999/42799p2.htm, July 27, 2002; W. G. Weisbecker, "First Flight Enjoyed," *New York Times,* July 28, 1938.
25. "Airliner Crash at Philadelphia Fatal to Seven," *Florida Times-Union,* January 15, 1951; Bernard De Voto, "Transcontinental Flight," *Harper's* 205 (July 1952): 48; Lindbergh correspondence, box 6, Harry Frank Guggenheim Papers, LCMD.
26. "Pan American-LAD" (typescript, April 1951), p. 8, box 2, Shirley F. Woodell Papers, JWTA (KLM); Solberg, *Conquest of the Skies,* 378–79; interviews with Gordon Parkinson, January 6, 1977, p. 13; R. C. Scruggs, November 18, 1976, p. 3; Ludwig Lederer, March 14, 1977, p. 3; Don Maggarell, March 30, 1977, p. 8; and Lloyd M. Wilson, February 27, 1977, p. 4, all box 18, Carl Solberg Collection, AHC; joint interview of Russell Bowen and Gay Smith, January 13, 1977, pp. 2–3, box 19, Carl Solberg Collection, AHC.
27. Clippings and press releases in "Movies—Inflight Entertainment, 1945–1967," box 42, PAWAR. Daniel Lee Rust, "Flying across America: The Evolving Transcontinental Airline Passenger Experience, 1927–1960" (Ph.D. diss., University of Idaho,

2003), which I read after completing my manuscript, reaches the same conclusion, that changes in speed, pressurization, fenestration, and service denatured passengers' experience of flight.

28. Gann, *Ernest K. Gann's Flying Circus,* 20, 150; Weldon Rhoades, January 9, 1977, p. 2, corroborated by Stuart Tipton, October 26, 1976, p. 1, both interviews box 18, Carl Solberg Collection, AHC; Willis, *Your Future is in the Air,* 34 (Maxwell), italics in original.
29. Jack Rennert, foreword to Henry Serrano Villard and Willis M. Allen Jr., *Looping the Loop: Posters of Flight* (San Diego: Kales Press, 2000), 24.
30. James L. Fleming interview, January 9, 1977, p. 4, box 18, Carl Solberg Collection, AHC; "Jet Service Girdles the Globe," *New York Times,* February 28, 1960, and "Overbooking Jet Planes," *New York Times,* May 23, 1960 (Gabor letter).
31. Clive Irving, *Wide-Body: The Triumph of the 747* (New York: William Morrow, 1998); Gandt, *Skygods,* 71 (quotation).
32. Juan Trippe, "Charles A. Lindbergh and World Travel," Wings Club lecture of May 20, 1977, p. 21, box 48, PAWAR ($525 million, 90 percent); Hugh Parker, "Pan Am Television: A Special Problem," 1962 minutes, box 23, Review Board Records, JWTA (load factors).
33. "The 1962 Campaign—Creative Plan and Proposition" (typescript, 1961), box 23, Review Board Records, JWTA.
34. November 11, 1964, Panagra summary, box 22, Review Board Records, JWTA. Complaints, e.g., letters of October 5, 1943 ("hell"), June 5 and 21, 1946, June 22, 1946, and March 3, 1951, box 2, Shirley F. Woodell Papers, JWTA; and Brock, *Flying the Oceans,* 61–68, 149–63.
35. Rosalie Schwartz, *Pleasure Island: Tourism and Temptation in Cuba* (Lincoln: University of Nebraska Press, 1997), 111, 202–203.
36. Panagra minutes, July 16, 1958 ("squalor," "smart"); Panagra minutes, June 29, 1959 (Young); Panagra summaries, 1961–66; and Pan Am account phone memorandum, May 10, 1957 ("arouse"), all box 22, Review Board Records, JWTA.
37. Schwartz, *Pleasure Island,* 108; Tom Lane memo, July 24, 1972, IHC account, box 16, Review Board Records, JWTA (quotation); "Pan Am Loves Children" (1966), "PAA-Advertising Brochures," box 52, PAWAR.
38. Pan Am minutes, November 18, 1958, and June 1972 confidential account summary, both box 23, Review Board Records, JWTA; IHC summaries, 1963–74, box 16, Review Board Records, JWTA; typescript notes on Roger Lewis presentation, "Public Relations Meeting, 1958," box 285, PAWAR; Bender and Altschul, *The Chosen Instrument,* 485–86; William Robbins, "Hotel-Construction Boom Opens New Beachhead in Bahamas," *New York Times,* March 16, 1969.
39. News summary, September 1973, "Pubrel Notes from Headquarters, 1973–1975," box 285, PAWAR.
40. Louis Turner and John Ash, *The Golden Hordes: International Tourism and the Pleasure Periphery* (New York: St. Martin's Press, 1976); Patricia Goldstone, *Making the World Safe for Tourism* (New Haven: Yale University Press, 2001), 9 ("cocoon"), 45; Anthony Sampson, *Empires of the Sky: The Politics, Contests and Cartels of World Airlines* (New York: Random House, 1984), 111, 114, 225.

41. Interview with Samuel H. Miller, May 29, 1978, p. 4, box 18, Carl Solberg Collection, AHC.

Chapter 9

1. "TWA Symposium on Air Travel in 1985" (typescript, 1955), box 45, Wernher von Braun Papers, LCMD; Francis Spufford, "Love that Bird," *London Review of Books* 24 (June 6, 2002): 29 (Batmobile). R. E. G. Davies discusses the limitations of SSTs and helicopters in *Fallacies and Fantasies of Air Transport History* (McLean, Va.: Paladwr Press, 1994).
2. Robert M. Kane and Allan D. Vose, *Air Transportation* (Dubuque: William C. Brown, 1967), 95–96; George Gallup Jr., *The Gallup Poll: Public Opinion 1987* (Wilmington, Del.: Scholarly Resources, 1988), 230.
3. Based on Air Transportation Association, Office of Economics, yield data (hereafter, ATA), http://www.airlines.org/econ/d.aspx?nid=1026.
4. Interviews with C. R. Smith, May 4, 1977, p. 7, and Walter Bullock, August 12, 1976, p. 4, both box 18, Carl Solberg Collection, AHC; *The Birth of NASA: The Diary of T. Keith Glennan,* ed. J. D. Hunley (Washington, D.C.: NASA History Office, 1993), 148.
5. For engine development, see Irving, *Wide-Body,* chap. 5; and Heppenheimer, *Turbulent Skies,* 300 (billion), and chaps. 8, 11.
6. Hallion, "A Short History of Aircraft Survivability," paper presented at the Aircraft Survivability 2000 Symposium, Monterey, Calif., November 15, 2000, p. 11; R. Dixon Speas interview, June 3, 1978, pp. 3–4, Box 18, Carl Solberg Collection, AHC (flight paths); Heppenheimer, *Turbulent Skies,* chaps. 10–11.
7. James E. Tomayko, *Computers Take Flight: A History of NASA's Pioneering Digital Fly-By-Wire Project* (Washington, D.C.: NASA, 2000); Langewiesche, *Inside the Sky* 97–98.
8. Barbara Sturken Peterson and James Glab, *Rapid Descent: Deregulation and the Shakeout in the Airlines* (New York: Simon & Schuster, 1994), 61–62, 117, 169–70 (quotation); Harry C. Stonecipher, "Airplane 101: A Primer on Aviation," accessed at http://www.boeing.com/news/speeches/1997/971015.html, February 23, 2004 (tree lot).
9. Peterson and Glab, *Rapid Descent,* 68 ("three people"), 75 ("insane"); Ivor P. Morgan, "Toward Deregulation," in *Airline Deregulation: The Early Experience,* eds. John R. Meyer et al. (Boston: Auburn House, 1981), 41–52.
10. Charles P. Alexander et al., "Super Savings in the Skies," *Time* 127 (January 13, 1986), 40, 41 (Kahn quote); Peterson and Glab, *Rapid Descent,* 105 (Buffalo). The legislation is in *Statutes at Large,* vol. 92, part 2 (Washington, D.C.: Government Printing Office, 1980), 1705–54.
11. Thomas Petzinger Jr., *Hard Landing: The Epic Contest for Power and Profits that Plunged the Airlines into Chaos* (New York: Times Books, 1995), ix ("rotten"), xx–xxi ("zero-sum"), 137, 149–50, 199, 207, 311; Peterson and Glab, *Rapid Descent,* 121 (hubs), 248 (Lorenzo), 252 (olives); David Leonhardt with Micheline Maynard, "Troubled Airlines Face Reality," *New York Times,* August 18, 2002 ("justification"). Cost and passenger data: ATA, http://www.airlines.org/econ/d.aspx?nid=1026.

Transcript: *U.S. v. American Airlines, Inc., and Robert L. Crandall,* No. 83–1831, U.S. Court of Appeals for the Fifth Circuit, October 15, 1984, with expletives restored.

12. Lane E. Wallace, *Flights of Discovery: 50 Years at the NASA Dryden Flight Research Center* (Washington, D.C.: NASAHO, 1996), 93 (winglets).
13. Income and education data: U.S. Bureau of the Census, accessed at http://www.census.gov/hhes/income/histinc/rdi01.html, and http://www.census.gov/apsd/cqc/cqc13.pdf, August 19, 2002; John B. Lansing and Ernest Lilienstein, *The Travel Market, 1955* (Ann Arbor: Survey Research Center, Institute for Social Research, University of Michigan, 1957), 36.
14. *Air Travel Survey, 1984* (Washington, D.C.: Air Transport Association, 1984); and *Air Travel Survey, 1998* (Washington, D.C.: Air Transport Association, 1998).
15. Dwight M. Blood and John B. Lansing, *The Changing Travel Market* (Ann Arbor: University of Michigan Press, 1964), 102; Kevin Phillips, *The Politics of Rich and Poor: Wealth and the American Electorate in the Reagan Aftermath* (New York: Random House, 1990), 202–207; Barbara Kantrowitz, "The Youngest Jet-Setters," *Newsweek* 109 (June 29, 1987): 52–53.
16. Petzinger, *Hard Landing,* 33 ("coop"); Paul Critchlow, "Cut-Rate Air Fares Lure Young," *Philadelphia Inquirer,* July 31, 1972; C. R. Smith interview, May 4, 1977, p. 11, box 18, Carl Solberg Collection, AHC; Robert Lindsey, "Airlines and Agents Aim to Foil Youth Fare Ban," *New York Times,* May 13, 1974; Alexander, "Super Savings," 40.
17. Blood and Lansing, *Changing Travel Market,* 103; C. Vann Woodward, *The Strange Career of Jim Crow,* 2d rev. ed. (New York: Oxford University Press, 1966), 117; Trudy Baker and Rachel Jones, *Coffee, Tea, or Me? The Uninhibited Memoirs of Two Airline Stewardesses* (New York: Bartholomew House, 1967), 151 (Ellington).
18. Gill Robb Wilson, "Private Planes Most Numerous in West," *New York Herald Tribune,* November 5, 1948; White, *"It's Your Misfortune and None of My Own,"* 184; Raphael Pumpelly, *Across America and Asia* (New York: Leypoldt and Holt, 1870), 4; Smith, *By the Seat of My Pants,* 12.
19. *Air Travel Survey, 1998,* secs. 1, 5. Percent female: Port Authority of New York and New Jersey, *Profile of Departing Passengers, 1997–1998,* accessed at the Air Transport Association Library, Washington, D.C.
20. John Updike, *Bech at Bay* (New York: Knopf, 1998), 223; Buck, *North Star,* 94 (limos); Brock, *Flying the Oceans,* 97, 305 ("depressed"); Rhoades, Personal Diary, vol. 1, December 13, 1943; Eric Margolis, "Remembering the Days of Civilized Air Travel," accessed at http://www.flare.net/users/e9ee52a/letterpanam.htm, September 2, 2002 (torture); radio address transcript (typescript, December 30, 1934), p. 1, box 11, Eugene Vidal Collection, AHC. I fly a good deal, and the last time I saw airsickness on a jet was in 1978.
21. Robert Dallek, *An Unfinished Life: John F. Kennedy, 1917–1963* (Boston: Little, Brown, 2003) 59; Claudette Bradish, "A Tough Job Just Got Tougher," *Newsweek* 138 (November 19, 2001): 16; Bratt, *Glamour and Turbulence,* 88; Tom Kuntz, "High Crimes and Misdemeanors: The Flight Logs of Uncivil Aviation," *New York Times,* December 8, 1996 ("make love"); Kahn interview, accessed at http://www.pbs.org/fmc/interviews/kahn/htm, September 2, 2002.

22. Sarah Lyall, "Travel Advisory: British Abroad, Staggering About," *New York Times,* September 4, 2003; "Finding Discount Flights Within Europe," *Marketplace Morning Report,* transcript of May 1, 2002, Minnesota Public Radio; Hudson, *Air Travel: A Social History* (Totowa, N.J.: Rowman and Littlefield, 1972), 119. Video conferencing over the Internet, which will improve as bandwidth and computer speed increases, threatens airlines in another way, by reducing the necessity of business travel.
23. Francis Spufford, "Love that Bird," *London Review of Books* 24 (June 6, 2002): 28; "Concorde Special Fares," British Airways press release, July 16, 2002, accessed at http://biz.yahoo.com/prnews/020716/nytu017_1.html, September 2, 2002; Don Phillips, "With One Crash, Concorde Ranks Last in Safety," *Washington Post,* July 30, 2000; Alan Cowell, "British and French to Halt Concorde Flights," *New York Times,* April 10, 2003.
24. Tom D. Crouch, "General Aviation: The Search for a Market, 1910–1976," in *Two Hundred Years of Flight in America: A Bicentennial Survey,* ed. Eugene M. Emme (San Diego: Univelt, 1977), 127; James P. Woolsey, "Good Business," *Air Transport World* 33 (November 1996): 107; Henry Ehrlich, "Hugh Hefner's Jet Black Bunny in the Sky," *Look* 34 (June 2, 1970): 62–65.
25. George A. Wies, "Altitude for the Airplane Sales Curve," *Sales Management* 21 (January 4, 1930): 29 (prospects); Joseph J. Corn, *The Winged Gospel: America's Romance with Aviation, 1900–1950* (New York: Oxford University Press, 1983), chap. 5; Pattillo, *A History in the Making,* 50 and 57 (sales statistics), and chaps. 4–8.
26. F. Clifton Berry, "Wiping Out Jet Fighters," *Air Power History* 36 (Spring 1989): 40; Wolfe, *The Right Stuff,* 24; A. Scott Crossfield, with Clay Blair Jr., *Always Another Dawn: The Story of a Rocket Test Pilot* (Cleveland: World Publishing, 1960), 231 (skin).
27. Jean Zimmerman, *Tailspin: Women at War in the Wake of Tailhook* (New York: Doubleday, 1995), 6–7, 23, 24 (quotation), 213.
28. Anne Marie Squeo, "Pilots Fume at Duty on Unmanned Craft," accessed at http://www.careerjournal.com/salaries/industries/defense/20020509-squeo.html, July 25, 2002; and Matthew Brzezinksi, "The Unmanned Army," *New York Times Magazine,* April 20, 2003, 38–42, 80. Unpiloted aerial vehicles have also assumed some general-aviation chores, such as seeding rice paddies by air. Noah Shachtman, "Flying Solo, in the Extreme," *New York Times,* November 14, 2002.
29. Richard P. Hallion, *Test Pilots: The Frontiersmen of Flight,* revised ed. (Washington, D.C.: Smithsonian Institution Press, 1988), ix, xvii, 294–96; personal communication with Dave English, April 18, 2003 (Faull).
30. Robert Sherrod, "The Astronauts" (typescript, 1975), file 012835, Robert Sherrod Apollo Collection, NASAHO, Robert Voas on pages 3–4. Carol Auster points out that, unlike the land and night frontiers, government control of the space program weeded out the individualists and social misfits. What counted in space were "skills and conformity." See Carol Auster, "Specification of Melbin's Frontier Hypothesis: An Application to Outer Space Exploration," *Social Inquiry* 57 (1987): 106.
31. Robert Voas interview, January 12, 1970, file 013290; undated Aldrin questionnaire, file 013282, both Robert Sherrod Apollo Collection, NASAHO.

32. Susan Landrum Mangus, "Conestoga Wagons to the Moon: The Frontier, the American Space Program, and National Identity" (Ph.D. diss., Ohio State University, 1999), Carter on page 175; Robert Zubrin, *Entering Space: Creating a Spacefaring Civilization* (New York: Tarcher/Putnam, 1999), chap. 1.

Chapter 10

1. Roger D. Launius, *NASA: A History of the U.S. Space Program* (Malabar, Fl.: Krieger, 1994), 68–69; *Columbia* Accident Investigation Board, *Report,* vol. 1 (2003), 102, accessed at http://boss.streamos.com/download/caib/report/web/chapters/chapter5.pdf, September 9, 2003 (4 percent); Michael Cabbage, "NASA Continues Quest to Define Its Mission," *Florida Times-Union,* March 24, 2002 (one million); Walter C. Williams interview, June 29, 1968, file 013290, Robert Sherrod Apollo Collection, NASAHO (LBJ).
2. Jim G. Lucas, "Citizens Insist on Helping to Pay for Space Program," *Washington Daily News,* September 27, 1961; boxes 14–39, Wernher von Braun Papers, LCMD; Bill Maxwell, "Spirits Soaring with the Shuttle," *Washington Times,* November 7, 1998 (Cronkite).
3. *Frontiers of Space Exploration,* ed. Roger D. Launius (Westport, Conn.: Greenwood, 1998), 138–39 (Nixon); Wernher von Braun, *Space Frontier* (New York: Holt, Rinehart and Winston, 1971 rev. ed.), 94; Don Kirkman, "Von Braun Hopes to Fly in Space Shuttle," *Houston Post,* April 4, 1972; Robert Sherrod's typescript notes on Thomas Paine interview, November 5, 1968, file 013288, Robert Sherrod Apollo Collection, NASAHO.
4. Chris Kraft, *Flight: My Life in Mission Control* (New York: Dutton, 2001), 340.
5. Howard E. McCurdy, *Space and the American Imagination* (Washington: Smithsonian Institution Press, 1997), provides an excellent account of the imaginative "pre-construction" of space exploration.
6. McDougall, . . . *The Heavens and the Earth: A Political History of the Space Age* (Baltimore: Johns Hopkins University Press, 1985), 7; "U.S. Delays Gave Russia Lead," *El Paso Times,* November 10, 1957 (von Braun).
7. Michael J. Neufeld, *The Rocket and the Reich: Peenemünde and the Coming of the Ballistic Missile Era* (New York: Free Press, 1995), 218–20; Roger D. Launius and Howard E. McCurdy, *Imagining Space: Achievements, Predictions, Possibilities, 1950–2050* (San Francisco: Chronicle Books, 2001), 91.
8. *Exploring the Unknown: Selected Documents in the History of the U.S. Civil Space Program,* vol. 1, ed. John M. Logsdon et al. (Washington, D.C.: NASA, 1995), 333–34, 378. Eisenhower refused to allow the interview to be taped; this is Eugene Emme's reconstruction of April 1, 1969, file 013286, Robert Sherrod Apollo Collection, NASAHO.
9. "Orderly Formula," *Time* 70 (October 28, 1957): 19.
10. Allen J. Matusow, *The Unraveling of America: A History of Liberalism in the 1960s* (New York: Harper and Row, 1984), 18, 30.
11. John M. Logsdon, *The Decision to Go to the Moon: Project Apollo and the National Interest* (Cambridge, Mass.: MIT Press, 1970); Logsdon, *Exploring the Unknown,* vol. 1, chap. 3, quotations on pages 428, 444, and 453; Rudy Abramson, "Von Braun's

Rocket Team Fades Away," *Cincinnati Enquirer,* February 18, 1977 (erupted). Kennedy's deadline, together with the NASA managers' insistence on a high degree of reliability, both drove up Apollo's finals costs. See also Launius, *NASA,* 72.

12. Jules Crittenden, "Tape Shows JFK Clashed with NASA over Apollo," *Boston Herald,* August 23, 2001.
13. Robert Zimmerman, *Genesis: The Story of Apollo 8: The First Manned Flight to Another World* (New York: Four Walls Eight Windows, 1998), 206.
14. Simon Bourgin interview, September 2, 1969, file 013285, Robert Sherrod Apollo Collection, NASAHO; William Leavitt, "Apollo-11: Meaning Beyond the Moment," *Air Force and Space Digest* 52 (August 1969), 55; Hubert Humphrey interview, May 11, 1971, file 013287, Robert Sherrod Apollo Collection, NASAHO.
15. Englebert Kirchner, "Sorry, Virginia, There is No Space Program," *Innovation,* no. 20 (April 1971), unpaginated offprint, file 013086, Robert Sherrod Apollo Collection, NASAHO (boom town); Howard McCurdy interview of Christopher Kraft, file 006721, NASAHO, 37–38 (twenty-six years); Logsdon, *Exploring the Unknown,* vol. 1, 494–95; Launius, *NASA,* 51–52.
16. Zubrin, *Entering Space,* 12–14.
17. Julian Scheer interview, September 11, 1969, Robert Sherrod Apollo Collection, NASAHO ("Hebrews"); Lindbergh to Harry Guggenheim, April 26, 1966, box 3, Harry Frank Guggenheim Papers, LCMD. Vietnam runs like a bright red line through numerous interviews in the Robert Sherrod Apollo Collection, NASAHO, e.g., Rocco Petrone, July 29, 1974, file 013288.
18. Raymond Heard, *Montreal Star* draft story (typescript, 1972), file 013282, Robert Sherrod Apollo Collection, NASAHO.
19. R. Buckminster Fuller, "Vertical is to Live—Horizontal is to Die," 39 *American Scholar* (Winter 1969–70): 28.
20. John Logsdon's interviews of James Fletcher, September 21, 1977, and of John Ehrlichman, May 27, 1982, both file 007915, NASAHO; Allen J. Matusow, *Nixon's Economy: Booms, Busts, Dollars, and Votes* (Lawrence: University Press of Kansas, 1998), 35.
21. George Low memo of conversation with Johnny Foster, December 2, 1971 ("taxi"), John Logdson interviews of Don Rice, November 13, 1974 ("absurd"), and Ehrlichman interview, May 27, 1982, all in file 007915, NASAHO; Logsdon, *Exploring the Unknown,* vol. 1, 386–88, 547 (Weinberger).
22. George Low to Walter Mondale, September 28, 1970, file 013052, Robert Sherrod Apollo Collection, NASAHO; George Low memo of meeting with Nixon and Ehrlichman, January 12, 1972, file 007915, NASAHO.
23. T. A. Heppenheimer, *The Space Shuttle Decision: NASA's Search for a Reusable Space Vehicle* (Washington, D.C.: NASAHO, 1999), 306 (de Gaulle), 435 (shuttle problems), and chaps. 2, 4–9.
24. Robert Truax, "Shuttles—What Price Elegance?" *Astronautics and Aeronautics* 8 (June 1970): 22–23; "From Canyon to Cosmos," *Air and Space Smithsonian* 5 (October–November 1990): 102 (quotation).
25. Robert Truax, "The Future of Earth-to-Orbit Propulsion," *Aerospace America* 37 (January 1999): 34–41; Robert Truax biographical file 002368, NASAHO.

26. "Future of the U.S. Space Program," *Science* 251 (1991): 357 (procedures); Launius, *Frontiers of Space Exploration*, 144–46 (compartment). For shuttle development, see *Exploring the Unknown: Selected Documents in the History of the U.S. Civil Space Program*, vol. 4, ed. John M. Logsdon et al. (Washington, D.C.: NASA, 1999), 445 ("visible instrument"), and chap. 2; T. A. Heppenheimer, *History of the Space Shuttle*, vol. 2, *Development of the Shuttle, 1972–1981*, (Washington, D.C.: Smithsonian Institution Press, 2002); and Dennis R. Jenkins, "Broken in Midstride: Space Shuttle as a Launch Vehicle," in *To Reach the High Frontier: A History of U.S. Launch Vehicles*, ed. Roger Launius and Dennis Jenkins (Lexington: University Press of Kentucky, 2002), 386 (1.3 tiles).
27. Jenkins, "Broken in Midstride," 366 (cross-range); author's notes on Sean O'Keefe presentation at NASA Headquarters, January 4, 2002 ("dead"); Truax, "Future of Earth-to-Orbit Propulsion," 36.
28. James Glanz, "Scientists Question the Value of Shuttle Flights," *New York Times*, February 24, 2003. For a review of the history of resuable launcher experiments, see Andrew J. Butrica, "The Quest for Reusability," in Launius and Jenkins, *To Reach the High Frontier*, 443–69. Budget: *Columbia* Accident Investigation Board, *Report*, vol. 1 (2003), 103.
29. "President Bush Delivers Remarks on U.S. Space Policy," January 14, 2004, accessed at http://www.nasa.gov/pdf/54868main_bush_trans.pdf, February 14, 2004; William J. Broad, "History Offers Reasons to Be Cautious on Bush's Space Plan," *New York Times*, January 15, 2004.
30. *Exploring the Unknown*, vol. 4, chaps. 2 and 3, especially 181, 186, 383, 407, 412, 414–15, 422; NASA photograph S19-104-049, November 14, 1984, Johnson Space Center ("for sale").
31. William E. Burrows, *This New Ocean: The Story of the First Space Age* (New York: Random House, 1998), 616–17; Daniel S. Goldin, "Slash Costs to Open the Space Frontier," *Aviation Week & Space Technology* 144 (February 26, 1996), 74; Zubrin, *Entering Space*, 24–25 (attitude), 32–34.
32. Summary of January 16, 1947, speech, box 46, Wernher von Braun Papers, LCMD; "Moon Flight Waiting List," box 42, PAWAR; "Artists, in Survey, Say They Hear Space Call," *New York Times*, March 4, 1984; Kathy Sawyer, "Yeager, a Panel Absentee, is 'In Touch Every Day,'" *Washington Post*, March 22, 1986; "100 Million Americans Want to Ride the Space Shuttle!" (n.d.), and NASA newsletter, June 3, 1985, pp. 4–5, both in file 008072, NASAHO.
33. "X Prize," file 015133, NASAHO; Tom Clancy from Gannett wire story of May 21, 1998; "Incredible Adventures," accessed at http://www.incredible-adventures.com/edgeofspace.html, October 6, 2002.
34. "Shuttle Passengers," files 008702 through 008078, NASAHO, and Alan Ludwig, telephone interview, January 4, 2002. Apollo 15: James J. Gehrig interview, January 9, 1973, file 013286, Robert Sherrod Apollo Collection, NASAHO; Kraft, *Flight*, 343–45.
35. John Gibbons to Daniel Goldin, March 23, 1995, file 017978, NASAHO.
36. Burrows, *This New Ocean*, chap. 16; Timothy Ferris, "NASA's Mission to Nowhere," *New York Times*, November 29, 1998; and Timothy Ferris, "A Space Station? Big Deal!" *New York Times Magazine*, November 28, 1999, 124.

37. "Is NASA Among the Truly Needy?" *New York Times,* March 6, 1995.
38. "Apollo Geologist Quitting in March," *Washington Post,* October 9, 1969.
39. Launius, *NASA,* 101–104; Thomas Gold, "Don't Send People into Space Unnecessarily," *New York Times,* September 28, 1987.
40. Timothy Ferris, "Interstellar Spaceflight: Can We Travel to Other Stars?" *Scientific American Presents* 10 (Spring 1999): 88–91.
41. Robert Gilruth interview, November 16, 1972, file 013286; and Hubert Humphrey interview, May 11, 1971, file 013287, both Robert Sherrod Apollo Collection, NASAHO; Kraft, *Flight,* 354.
42. Howard McCurdy, *Space and the American Imagination,* 48; Launius, *NASA,* 120–23; Monica Munro, "UAV 'Pilot' Receives Air Metal," *Air Force News,* accessed at http://www2.acc.af.mil/accnews/nov/970229.html, March 13, 2003; Air Force Personnel Center messages of August 25, 1998, and February 4, 2003; and USAF Selection Board Secretariat, "Selection Board Procedures Operating Instruction" (typescript, 2001), n.p., items kindly provided by Capt. Christopher Parrish.
43. Howard McCurdy, *Faster, Better, Cheaper: Low-Cost Innovation in the U.S. Space Program* (Baltimore: Johns Hopkins University Press, 2001), chap. 9; Launius and McCurdy, *Imagining Space,* 85.

Chapter 11

1. Las Cruces speech (typescript, January 10, 1950), box 46, Wernher von Braun Papers, LCMD; Sarah L. Gall and Joseph T. Pramberger, *NASA Spinoffs: 30 Year Commemorative Edition* (n.p.: NASA Technology Transfer Division, 1992).
2. "Our Space Program," *Indianapolis Star,* February 16, 1999, (seven dollars); "NASA's Green Monster," *New York Times,* April 11, 1990.
3. Will Rogers, "Flying and Eating My Way East," *Saturday Evening Post* 200 (January 21, 1928): 110. Island communities: Robert H. Wiebe, *The Search for Order, 1877–1920* (New York: Hill and Wang, 1967).
4. *Aircraft Year Book, 1928,* 96; Petzinger, *Hard Landing,* 8 (Tulsa).
5. Grosvenor, "Flying," 585–630, 587 (United).
6. Rickenbacker, *Rickenbacker,* 163–64; Brock, *Flying the Oceans,* 121; "Freight by Air," *Fortune* 33 (May 1946): 134–39, 164–70; Richard Malkin, *Boxcars in the Sky* (New York: Import Publications, 1951), 72; Neal Ascherson, "In the Pit of History," *New York Review of Books* 48 (June 21, 2001), 26; *Statistics of Students Abroad, 1962–1968* (Paris: UNESCO, 1972), 19; *Statistics of Students Abroad, 1974–1978* (Paris: UNESCO, 1982), 17; William Seawell, "Ecumenicism and the Air Transport Industry" (typescript, March 14, 1978), p. 3, box 464, PAWAR.
7. William Fielding Ogburn et al., *The Social Effects of Aviation* (Boston: Houghton Mifflin, 1946), 414; "Is It Safe to Fly? Some Say No," *Holiday* 46 (July 1969): 53 (Jensen); Coach John Madden, accessed at http://www.mcicoach.com/madden/coachmadden.html, October 26, 2002.
8. Adam Goodheart, "The Skyscraper and the Airplane," *American Scholar* 71 (Winter 2002): 18; Andy Warhol, *From A to B and Back Again: The Philosophy of Andy Warhol* (London: Picador, 1976), 145–46.
9. Juan Trippe, "Building the Airways of America," May 2, 1940, address to the U.S.

Chamber of Commerce, p. 6 (quotation, spelling of "aids" corrected); and "One America," (typescript, 1947), p. 2, both box 120, AAIAA; Solberg, *Conquest of the Skies,* chap. 18.

10. Solberg, *Conquest of the Skies,* 412; "Passport Statistics," accessed at http://travel.state.gov/passport_statistics, November 9, 2002. The phrase "non-colonial imperial expansion" is William Appleman Williams's.
11. "A Brief History of the Air Mail Service" (typescript, 1940), p. 17, box 3, PODR; "Alaska Looks Ahead," offprint from *New Horizons* (November 1940), p. 14, box 286, PAWAR; Anthony Sampson, *Empires of the Sky: The Politics, Contests and Cartels of World Airlines* (New York: Random House, 1984), 14; Roger W. Pearson, "Where is Alaska?" accessed at http://www.institutenorth.org/where_is_alaska.htm, October 28, 2002.
12. Glines, *Roscoe Turner,* 109 (alimony); Irving, *Wide-Body,* 235.
13. "Aviation Economic Impact: Facts and Figures of the U.S. Scheduled Airlines," ATA, http://www.airlines.org/public/industry/display1.asp?nid=1175; Gottdiener, *Life in the Air,* 23–25.
14. DRI•WEFA, Inc., "The National Economic Impact of Civil Aviation;" and Air Transport Action Group, "The Economic Benefits of Air Transport," 2000 ed., both found on ATA home page, http://www.airlines.org/econ/d.aspx?nid=1026. Nancy Robinson, "One Language Crucial for Air Traffic Control," *Abilene Reporter-News,* June 27, 1999. "Civil aviation" includes commercial passenger and cargo service, general aviation, and related manufacturing, service, and support industries.
15. "The Domestic Air Transport Industry" (n.p.: Calvin Bullock Investment Management Division, June 6, 1947), 2; Najeeb Halaby, "Mass Transportation and Civilization" (typescript, January 30, 1966), 7 (spelling corrected), box 462, PAWAR.
16. Heppenheimer, *Turbulent Skies,* 191–95.
17. Dwiggins, *Barnstormers,* 104; Roger E. Bilstein, *Flight Patterns: Trends of Aeronautical Development in the United States, 1918–1929* (Athens: University of Georgia Press, 1983), 67 (Howard); Rowe, *Under My Wings,* 61; Brock, *Flying the Oceans,* 47–48.
18. *Aircraft Year Book, 1924,* 107; David T. Courtwright, *Forces of Habit: Drugs and the Making of the Modern World* (Cambridge, Mass.: Harvard University Press, 2001), 38; "Aircraft and Drug Smuggling" (typescript, 1985), n.p., "Smuggling" file, Drug Enforcement Administration Library, Arlington, Virginia; Nigel Moll, "Smugglers' Blues: Pilots in Jail Tell All," *Flying* 113 (January 1986): 83.
19. Ira C. Feldman, "Acute Shortage of Heroin in the District #2 Area of New York City," July 26, 1966, file 0480-203, no. 5, box 10, RG 170, NAII; "Customs Service, Airlines Adopt Guidelines to Fight International Drug Trafficking," *Narcotics Control Digest* 15 (August 7, 1985): 1 (percentages); tactics from the DEA Library "Smuggling" file, cited above.
20. Clifford A. Tinker, "Is Fear Keeping Us Back?" *Collier's* 75 (January 31, 1925): 17; Harold Harris interview, February 19, 1977, p. 2, box 18, Carl Solberg Collection, AHC; Edmund Russell, *War and Nature: Fighting Humans and Insects with*

Chemicals from World War I to Silent Spring (New York: Cambridge University Press, 2001), 135 (Iwo Jima); Solberg, *Conquest of the Skies,* 78.

21. Russell, *War and Nature*; Wilson and Bryan, *Air Transportation,* 424–27; Douglas H. Robinson, *The Dangerous Sky: A History of Aviation Medicine* (Seattle: University of Washington Press, 1973), 269–70; Seth Mydans, "Researchers Raise Estimate on Defoliant Use in Vietnam War," *New York Times,* April 17, 2003; and Seth Mydans, "Vietnam Finds an Old Foe Has a New Allure," *New York Times,* April 30, 2000.
22. Harry Rijnen, "Offsetting Environmental Damage by Planes," *New York Times,* February 18, 2003; John Fauber, "Tragedy Allows More Work on Theory About Jet Contrails," *Milwaukee Journal Sentinel,* May 27, 2002.
23. Forest Service memorandum to Nevada Airlines, August 3, 1929, box 85, Roscoe Turner Papers, AHC; "Tricks that Smugglers Use—and How They Get Caught," *U.S. News and World Report* 82 (March 14, 1977): 52; Steven Ambrus, "Animal Subtraction," *Los Angeles Times,* July 25, 1995; Marcia Mattson, "Moving in on Florida," *Florida Times-Union,* June 29, 2003; Abby Goodnough, "Forget the Gators: Exotic Pets Run Wild in Florida," *New York Times,* February 29, 2004.
24. "Noise Pollution," accessed at http://home.att.net/~nofedex/noise.html, November 3, 2002, typifies the controversy over nighttime operations. L.A.: Wellwood Beall interview, January 22, 1977, p. 1, box 19, Carl Solberg Collection, AHC.
25. Clyde Ormond, *Hunting Our Biggest Game* (Harrisburg, Pa.: Stackpole, 1956), 192–95; and *Complete Book of Hunting,* 2d ed. (New York: Harper & Row, 1972), 189–92, 210.
26. Page Shamburger, *Tracks Across the Sky: The Story of the Pioneers of the U.S. Air Mail* (Philadelphia: J. B. Lippincott, 1964), 130; Morgan B. Sherwood, *Big Game in Alaska: A History of Wildlife and People* (New Haven: Yale University Press, 1981), 75–76; "Airplane Hunters Prosecuted," *New York Times,* May 25, 1929; Jonathan Fisher, "When Birds and Airplanes Collide," *Washington Post,* March 26, 1978; "Big Plane Hits Condor," *New York Times,* December 15, 1929; "Civilian Flier Attacked in Plane by a Bald Eagle," *New York Times,* August 6, 1942.
27. Tinker, "Fear," 16 (thirty fold).
28. "Fighting Mosquitoes with Airplanes," *Literary Digest* 85 (April 4, 1925): 29; "5 Stowaway Mosquitoes," *New York Times,* April 23, 1939; Randy Shilts, *And The Band Played On: Politics, People, and the AIDS Epidemic* (New York: St. Martin's Press, 1987), 78–79, 147, 248; Gwen Robinson, "AIDS Infection of Prostitutes Threatens Thai Tourist Trade," *San Francisco Chronicle,* July 26, 1989; Madeline Drexler, *Secret Agents: The Menace of Emerging Infections* (Washington, D.C.: Joseph Henry Press, 2002).
29. The phrase is Kenneth Jackson's, from his book, *The Crabgrass Frontier: The Suburbanization of the United States* (New York: Oxford University Press, 1985).
30. Gordon P. Merriam, "Draft Memorandum to President Truman," *Foreign Relations of the United States, 1945,* vol. 8: *The Near East and Africa* (Washington, D.C.: Government Printing Office, 1969), 45; Carl Solberg, *Oil Power* (New York: Mason/Charter, 1976), 176–89, 182 (quote).
31. Svante Karlsson, *Oil and the World Order: American Foreign Oil Policy* (Totowa,

N.J.: Barnes & Noble Books, 1986), 229, 256–59; Lizette Alvarez, "U.S. Considered Using Force during Oil Embargo, Documents Show," *New York Times,* January 1, 2004; Rick Atkinson et al., "For U.S., Task is Now to Sustain Fragile Unity," *Washington Post,* August 20, 1990 ("carrots").

32. Paraphrasing an *Al-Riyadh* editorial of March 21, 2003, in "Middle East Press Coverage of the War in Iraq," *World Press Review Online,* accessed at http://www.worldpress.org/Americas/1020.cfm, July 7, 2003; "Saudi Arabia [*sic*] Text of Fatwa Urging Jihad against Americans," February 23, 1998, accessed at http://www.emergency.com/bladen98.htm, July 7, 2003.

Chapter 12

1. Truong Nhu Tang with David Chanoff and Doan Van Toai, *A Vietcong Memoir* (New York: Harcourt Brace Jovanovich, 1985), 167; Tobias Wolff, *In Pharaoh's Army: Memories of the Lost War* (New York: Vintage Books, 1994), 138; Christopher Robbins, *The Ravens: The Men Who Flew in America's Secret War in Laos* (New York: Pocket Books, 1989), 352; Neil Sheehan, *A Bright Shining Lie: John Paul Vann and America in Vietnam* (New York: Random House, 1988), 317.
2. Benjamin Lambeth, *The Transformation of American Air Power* (Ithaca: Cornell University Press, 2000), chap. 2; Robert S. McNamara, with Brian VanDeMark, *In Retrospect: The Tragedy and Lessons of Vietnam* (New York: Times Books, 1995), 109; John McCain, with Mark Salter, *Faith of My Fathers* (New York: Random House, 1999), 187–88, 188 ("obstacle course").
3. H. R. Haldeman, *The Haldeman Diaries: Inside the White House* (New York: G. P. Putnam's, 1994), 295; Nixon White House Tapes, conversation 334-44, May 4, 1972 (Executive Office Building), Nixon Presidential Material Staff, NAII.
4. McCain, with Salter, *Faith of My Fathers,* 337–39, 339 ("bullshit").
5. Richard P. Hallion, *Storm Over Iraq: Air Power and the Gulf War* (Washington, D.C.: Smithsonian Institution Press, 1992), 21; W. Hays Parks, "Linebacker and the Law of War," *Air University Review* 34 (January–February 1983): 21.
6. Richard M. Clark, *Uninhabited Combat Aerial Vehicles* (Maxwell AF Base: Air University Press, 2000), 14–17; Edgar Ulsamer, "The Robot Airplane is Here to Stay," *Air Force Magazine* 56 (October 1973): 25.
7. Malcolm W. Browne, "Invention that Shaped the Gulf War: The Laser-Guided Bomb," *New York Times,* February 26, 1991 (helicopter); Richard P. Hallion, "A Short History of Aircraft Survivability," paper presented at the Aircraft Survivability 2000 Symposium, Monterey, Calif., November 15, 2000, 13 ("virtual," quoting Fred Frostic); Tim Robinson, "Robot Wars," *Aerospace International* 28 (July 2001): 12–13 (naval). See also Stephen L. McFarland, *America's Pursuit of Precision Bombing, 1910–1945* (Washington, D.C.: Smithsonian Institution Press, 1995), esp. chaps. 10–11; Lambeth, *Transformation,* 160 (three-quarters), and chaps. 1, 4, 5, 7.
8. Hallion, *Storm,* 170.
9. Anthony Swofford, *Jarhead: A Marine's Chronicle of the Gulf War and Other Battles* (New York: Scribner, 2003), 199–200, 213 (psy-ops); Clark, *Uninhabited Combat Aerial Vehicles,* 35 (surrendered); Lambeth, *Transformation,* 237 (McPeak).

10. Eric Schmitt and James Dao, "Use of Pinpoint Air Power Comes of Age in New War," *New York Times,* December 24, 2001; "'Buff' at 50," *USA Today,* April 24, 2002 ("kill"); and "1's and 0's Replacing Bullets in U.S. Arsenal," *Washington Post,* February 2, 2002 (Roche).
11. Thom Shanker and Eric Schmitt, "A Campaign Invisible Except for the Results," *New York Times,* April 6, 2003; David Rohde, "On Pain of Death, Iraqi Soldier Kept at It," *New York Times,* April 3, 2003; Juan O. Tamayo et al., "U.S. Troops Push Deeper into Baghdad from All Directions," Knight Ridder/Tribune news wire, April 9, 2003.
12. John H. Cushman Jr. and Thom Shanker, "War in Iraq Provides Model of New Way of Doing Battle," *New York Times,* April 10, 2003; Michael R. Gordon, "American Forces Adapted to Friend and Foe," *New York Times,* April 10, 2003; Michael R. Gordon, "U.S. Air Raids in '02 Prepared for War in Iraq," *New York Times,* July 20, 2003; Bradley Graham, "U.S. Air Attacks Turn More Aggressive," *Washington Post,* April 2, 2003 ("grinding").
13. Anthony H. Cordesman, *The Iraq War: Strategy, Tactics, and Military Lessons* (Westport, Conn.: Praeger, 2003), 257 ("sorties"), 273, 278.
14. "Key Developments Concerning Iraq," *New York Times,* March 15, 2003 (Saddam); Eric Schmitt and Bernard Weinraub, "Battle for Baghdad Like War Plan," *New York Times,* April 3, 2003; David McGuire, "Military Brings 3-D Advantage to War Preparation," *Washington Post,* March 17, 2003.
15. Daniel Goure, quoted in Nicholas Lemann, "Order of Battle," *New Yorker* 78 (November 18, 2002): 45. Netwar: Nina Bernstein, "The Strategists Fight a War about the War," *New York Times,* April 6, 2003.
16. David Mulholland, "Luck or Good Judgment?" *Jane's Defence Weekly,* April 15, 2003; "Officer Tells Story of Retreat," *Florida Times-Union,* April 19, 2003; Cheng Ho, "China Eyes Anti-Satellite System," *SpaceDaily,* January 8, 2000; Gregg Easterbrook, "American Power Moves Beyond the Mere Super," *New York Times,* April 27, 2003.
17. Lambeth, *Transformation,* 210.
18. John P. Jumper, "Space as a Means Not as an End in Itself," *SpaceNews,* July 15, 2003; Phillip Meilinger, "The Air and Space Nation is in Peril," *Air & Space Power Journal* 12 (Spring 2003), accessed at http://www.airpower.maxwell.af.mil/airchronicles/apj/apj03/spr03/vorspr03.html, April 19, 2003.
19. Peter Brooks, "The Coming of Jet Transportation," *Aerospace Historian* 28 (Winter 1981): 228; Petzinger, *Hard Landing,* 154 (40 percent); Gottdiener, *Life in the Air,* chap. 34; Noonan, *When Character Was King,* 222–27; Adam Bryant, "The Cruel New Math," *Newsweek* 138 (November 26, 2001): 60.
20. Langewiesche, *Inside the Sky,* 180.
21. Peterson and Glab, *Rapid Descent,* 215 (Davidson); Anonymous and Andrew R. Thomas, *Air Rage: Crisis in the Skies* (Amherst, N.Y.: Prometheus Books, 2001), 35 (complaints), and chap. 2.
22. Gottdiener, *Life in the Air,* chap. 35; James Fallows, *Free Flight: From Airline Hell to a New Age of Travel* (New York: Public Affairs, 2001), 7 (NASA studies). Presum-

ably, raised speed limits as well as growing airport delays played a role in NASA's surprising findings.

23. Lindbergh, *Spirit of St. Louis,* 219–20; Bonnie Harris, "Forget Therapy; They're Not Flying Anymore," *Los Angeles Times,* November 16, 2001; Bryant, "New Math," 58.
24. McLaughlin, *Walking on Air,* 144, 161–62.
25. "Case History of a Bomb Hoax," *AMM/AA* offprint (November 1970): 36, box 52, PAWAR.
26. Sarah Goddard, "Lessons from Lockerbie," *Business Insurance* 32 (December 21, 1998): 1; Peterson and Glab, *Rapid Descent,* 255. Shortly after I wrote this chapter, a criminologist colleague chanced to remark that he had just finished a book on private prisons. "So have I," I replied.
27. Sherry Sontag and Christopher Drew, *Blind Man's Bluff: The Untold Story of American Submarine Espionage* (New York: Public Affairs, 1998), 50–51; Malcolm Gladwell, "Safety in the Skies," *New Yorker* 77 (October 1, 2001): 50–53.
28. "Responses to ASR's Survey on Aviation Security Post-September 11," *Airport Security Report* 9 (September 11, 2002): 1–4; Ricardo Alonso-Zaldivar, "Airport Unveils Faster, Safer Passenger Check," *Los Angeles Times,* April 5, 2002; "More People Taking Road Trips," *Associated Press Online,* October 21, 2002.
29. Keith L. Alexander, "United Seeks Bankruptcy Protection," *Washington Post,* December 10, 2002; Christopher Calnan, "Retire? Never," *Florida Times-Union,* November 9, 2002 (Greenslet).
30. John Updike, "Tuesday and After," *New Yorker* 77 (September 24, 2001): 28.
31. "Lindbergh in Reich Warns on Air War," *New York Times,* July 24, 1936.
32. Paul Starr, *The Social Transformation of American Medicine* (New York: Basic Books, 1982).
33. Janice T. Driesbach et al., *Art of the Gold Rush* (Oakland: Oakland Museum of California, 1998), 4, 100–115.

Suggestions for Further Reading

Those who wish to learn more about American aviation history might begin with one of three standard surveys, Carl Solberg's *Conquest of the Skies: A History of Commercial Aviation in America* (Boston: Little, Brown, 1979); Roger Bilstein's *Flight in America: From the Wrights to the Astronauts,* revised ed. (Baltimore: Johns Hopkins University Press, 1994); and T. A. Heppenheimer's *Turbulent Skies: The History of Commercial Aviation* (New York: John Wiley, 1995). Though dated, Solberg's book is well written and draws on extensive interviews and correspondence with aviation pioneers. Bilstein is especially good on commercial developments, Heppenheimer on aeronautical advances. R .E. G. Davies's *Airlines of the United States since 1914* (London: Putnam, 1972), and *A History of the World's Airlines* (London: Oxford University Press, 1964) are encyclopedic works of painstaking scholarship, useful things to have at one's elbow. Among the many aviation memoirs, I recommend three for starters: Lindbergh's *The Spirit of St. Louis* (1953; reprint, St. Paul: Minnesota Historical Society, 1993); Dean Smith's *By the Seat of My Pants* (Boston: Little, Brown, 1961); and Horace Brock's underrated *Flying the Oceans: A Pilot's Story of Pan Am, 1935–1955* (Lunenburg, Vt.: Stinehour, 1979). Tough guy, good writer: powerful combination.

Those who wish to study published primary sources have many choices. I found myself most often consulting Marvin McFarland's *The Papers of Wilbur and Orville Wright, including the Chanute-Wright Letters and Other Papers of Octave Chanute,* 2 vols. (New York: McGraw Hill, 1953); Phil Scott's *The Pioneers of Flight: A Documentary History* (Princeton: Princeton University Press, 1999); Charles Lindbergh's *The Wartime Journals of Charles A. Lindbergh* (New York: Harcourt Brace Jovanovich, 1970); and the series edited by John Logsdon and others, *Exploring the Unknown: Selected Documents in the History of the U.S. Civil Space Program,* 5 vols. (Washington, D.C.: NASA, 1995–2001). The bulk of the primary sources, however, remain in archives. Several of these are located in the Washington, D.C. area: the National Archives I and II, the National Air and Space Museum Archives Division, the Air Transport Association Library, and the Library of Congress. The NASA History Office, also in Washington, D.C., maintains extensive subject files on aviation as well as space flight. They proved a rich vein, as did the Pan American World Airways, Inc., records at the University of Miami's Richter Library. The University of Wyoming's American Heritage Center houses several aviation collections, including Carl Solberg's correspondence and interview notes.

Those who are curious about "type-II" frontiers may wish to read Murray Melbin's *Night as Frontier: Colonizing the World after Dark* (New York: Free Press, 1987), and my own *Violent Land: Single Men and Social Disorder from the Frontier to the Inner City* (Cambridge, Mass.: Harvard University Press, 1996). The present work extends many of the arguments of these two books. In fact, I had first intended to develop the aviation-frontier thesis in *Violent Land*, only to discover that the subject demanded more than the chapter I had envisioned. In for a penny, in for a pound: next to unemployment, it is the historian's leading occupational hazard.

Illustration Credits

Charles Hamilton	Library of Congress, Prints and Photographs Division, USZ62-35560; Ralph S. Barnaby, "Early Birds—40 Years Ago," *Philadelphia Inquirer Magazine*, June 11, 1950; and Sherwood Harris, *The First to Fly: Aviation's Pioneer Days* (New York: Simon and Schuster, 1970), 177–78.
Pilots' Card Game	National Archives II, no. 417658, box 1694, RG 80-G.
Algiers Air Raid	National Archives II, no. 182245, box 42, RG 111-SC.
Balloon with Cannon	*Boston Globe*, June 7, 1903; "War Balloons for the United States Army," *Scientific American* 96 (March 9, 1907): 213.
New Year's Card	Library of Congress, Manuscript Division, box 176, Archives of the American Institute of Aeronautics and Astronautics.
Glenn Curtiss	Library of Congress, Prints and Photographs Division, USZ62-114755; Glenn Curtiss, "The June Bug," *The Pioneers of Flight: A Documentary History*, ed. Phil Scott (Princeton: Princeton University Press, 1999), 158–59; and *Papers of Wilbur and Orville Wright, including the Chanute-Wright Letters and Other Papers of Octave Chanute*, vol. 2: *1906–1948*, ed. Marvin W. McFarland (New York: McGraw Hill, 1953), 907.
Harriet Quimby's Body	Boston Public Library, Print Department, Photo Collection. Photograph by Leslie Jones. Used with permission.

Mori Turi Salutamus	American Heritage Center, box 6, Allan F. Bonnalie Collection.
Louis Paulhan	Library of Congress, Prints and Photographs Division, USZ61-1752.
Eye Examination	National Archives II, no. 8234-A, box 62, RG 111-SC; James J. Cooke, *The U.S. Air Service in the Great War, 1917–1919* (Westport, Conn.: Praeger, 1996), 14; and "Colored Men as Aviators," *Cleveland Advocate*, December 15, 1917.
Three Women Stitching	National Archives II, no. 619, box 5, RG 111-SC; John M. Loeblein, *Memoirs of Kelly Field, 1917–1918* (Manhattan, Ks.: Aerospace Historian, 1974), 35–36.
W. E. Callander	From author's family collection, with thanks to Edith Yager.
King of All Dare Devils	American Heritage Center, "Stunt Flying" folder, box 10, Robert Q. Wilson Collection.
Reuben Fleet	National Archives II, no. 10626, RG 111-SC; Donald Dale Jackson, *Flying the Mail* (Alexandria, Va.: Time-Life, 1982), 24–30.
Jack Knight	National Air and Space Museum, Archives Division, Nathaniel L. Dewell Collection, Neg. SI 75-7023. Used with permission.
Post Office Map	National Archives II, based on map in folder A, box 2, RG 28-MS.
Spirit of St. Louis	Painting by William J. Reynolds, used with permission. From a copy in the National Aeronautics and Space Administration History Office, file 001304; Charles A. Lindbergh, *The Spirit of St. Louis,* (1953; reprint, St. Paul: Minnesota Historical Society, 1993), 395.

Lindbergh in Mexico	National Aeronautics and Space Administration History Office, File 001304; Charles A. Lindbergh, *The Wartime Journals of Charles A. Lindbergh* (New York: Harcourt Brace Jovanovich, 1970), 828; Charles A. Lindbergh, *Autobiography of Values* (New York: Harcourt Brace Jovanovich, 1978), 119–20.
TAT Trimotor	Library of Congress, Prints and Photographs Division, LC-USZ62-83653; quotation from D. W. Tomlinson interview, January 28, 1977, box 18, Carl Solberg Collection, American Heritage Center.
DC-2.	Library of Congress, Prints and Photographs Division, LC-H813-1358-003.
Pan Am Plane Diagram	Library of Congress, Manuscript Division; J. T. Trippe, "Ocean Air Transport," 1941 lecture offprint, p. 13, box 120, Archives of the American Institute of Aeronautics and Astronautics.
Map of Aerial Danger Areas	National Archives II, "Special Notice to Airmen," March 7, 1942, file 015.00, Central Files of the Civil Aeronautics Administration, 1926–1943, RG 237.
Burning A-20 Havoc	*Courtesy* Elise Perkins. Photo by Samuel Crook, Ninth Air Force.
Damaged B-17	American Heritage Center, "Scenes of Service Personnel," box 11, Gill Robb Wilson Collection.
P-51 with Drop Tanks	Library of Congress, Prints and Photographs Division, LC-USZ62-93690.
Carrier Crewmen	National Archives II, no. 417615, box 1694, RG 80-G.

B-47	American Heritage Center, box 6, Gill Robb Wilson Collection; Clive Irving, *Wide-Body: The Triumph of the 747* (New York: William Morrow, 1998), chap. 5.
One-engine Constellation	National Archives II, box 5, RG 28-MS.
Woman with Pan Am Logo.	Special Collections Library, Duke University, Henry Syverson Papers, J. Walter Thompson Company Archives. Used with permission of the artist.
Pan Am Captain	Special Collections Library, Duke University, Henry Syverson Papers, J. Walter Thompson Company Archives, Henry Syverson Papers. Used with permission of the artist.
747 Exterior and Interior	Library of Congress, Prints and Photographs Division, Look Magazine Photograph Collection, L9-70-5504 no. 8 (exterior) and L9-70-5504 no. 19 (interior); Clive Irving, *Wide-Body: The Triumph of the 747* (New York: William Morrow, 1998), 370–71.
"Fly Me" Advertisement	Otto G. Richter Library, University of Miami, box 192, Pan American World Airways, Inc., Records.
Vega Christening	American Heritage Center, two photographs, both labeled B-D228b, folder 7, box 112, Roscoe Turner Collection.
Robert Q. Lewis	Otto G. Richter Library, University of Miami, box 192, Pan American World Airways, Inc., Records.
X-15	National Air and Space Administration History Office, image 62-X15-13; Dennis R. Jenkins, *Hypersonics Before the Shuttle: A Concise History of the X-15 Research Plane*

	(Washington, D.C.: National Aeronautics and Space Administration History Office, 2000), 61, 65, 119.
JFK at Rice	National Aeronautics and Space Administration History Office, image 69-HC-1245; "Address at Rice University on the Nation's Space Effort," http://www.cs.umb.edu/jfklibrary/j091262.htm.
Apollo 17	National Aeronautics and Space Administration History Office, image 72C-5901.
Von Braun-Nixon Santa	National Aeronautics and Space Administration History Office, Wernher von Braun file 002472; and Wernher von Braun interview (quoting uncorrected transcript), August 25, 1970, file 013290, Robert Sherrod Apollo Collection.
Reconfigured Shuttle	National Air and Space Administration History Office: *The Space Shuttle Passenger Project: A Design Study* (Santa Clara, Calif.: Space Age Review Foundation, 1983), 4; and Leonard David, "Passenger-Carrying Space Shuttle?" *Future Life* no. 10 (May 1979), both file 008072.
Muhammad Ali	Otto G. Richter Library, University of Miami, box 192, Pan American World Airways, Inc., Records; David Remnick, *King of the World: Muhammad Ali and the Rise of an American Hero* (New York: Random House, 1998), 102.
Bear Hunter	National Archives II, box 4, RG 28-MS.
Flight 93	Library of Congress, Prints and Photographs Division. Igor Kordey, "Pennsylvania Plane," used with the artist's permission.

Index

DATE DUE
